P9-EDT-820

Gothic
Architecture
in France,
England,
and Italy

Volume Two

HACKER ART BOOKS, INC. NEW YORK, 1975

GOTHIC

SIR
THOMAS
GRAHAM
JACKSON

ARCHITECTURE
in France, England,
and Italy

Volume Two

First Published 1915
Reprinted by permission of Cambridge University Press.

Reissued 1975 by
Hacker Art Books, Inc.
New York.

Library of Congress Catalogue Card Number 77-158333
ISBN 0-87817-106-1

Printed in the United States of America.

NA
440
.J3
1975
v. 2
c. 1

37,322

GOTHIC ARCHITECTURE
IN
FRANCE, ENGLAND, AND ITALY

by

SIR THOMAS GRAHAM JACKSON, Bart., R.A., F.S.A.

Hon. D.C.L. Oxford, Hon. LL.D. Cambridge
Hon. Fellow of Wadham College, Oxford
Associé de l'Académie Royale
de Belgique

Nec minimum meruere decus vestigia Graeca
Ausi deserere et celebrare domestica facta.
HOR. *Ars Poetica.*

Cambridge:

at the University Press

1915

CAMROSE LUTHERAN COLLEGE
LIBRARY

CONTENTS OF VOLUME II

ERRATA

Page 50, line 16. *For* freizes *read* friezes.
Page 52, line 6. *For* freize *read* frieze.
Page 129, line 25. *For* built *read* begun.

CHAPTER XVII

THE GOTHIC WINDOW

THE traceried window plays so large a part in Gothic architecture that it stands sponsor to each successive period, which is named " lancet, geometrical, curvilinear, flamboyant, or perpendicular," according to the character of the stone framing in which the glass is set.

Tracery was not a sudden invention: like the vault Evolution itself it was developed logically, and we can trace its of tracery growth step by step from the older fenestration of the Romanesque period.   In the basilican church of the 5th and 6th centuries the window was a plain round-arched opening in the wall of aisle or clerestory.   With the articulation of the building, when cross-vaulting came in to replace the wooden roof or the barrel-vault, the windows had to conform to the bay, and if there were more than one in a bay it was natural to group them in pairs, or to arrange them symmetrically over one another.   In this way they first began to figure as an element in the design; for in the older buildings they were regarded as mere holes in the wall to admit light, and seldom treated architecturally.

From being cut square through the wall the next The step was to splay them on the inside so as to diffuse interior splay the light more widely in the building.   Having got so far the builders began to decorate them; they recessed them on the outside within an outer order, which they carried on little shafts and capitals in the jambs (Fig. 103) and then proceeded after a time to put similar colonnettes to the jambs inside. The disposition of the windows in the elevation became an important part of the design.

Win-chesterIn the transept at WINCHESTER[1] (Fig. 104) they are orderly disposed in three tiers between the

Fig. 103.

flat pilaster buttresses and gradated in importance as they rise storey by storey. At the east end of the Church of the Hospital of S. Cross they are similarly arranged, but the middle tier has four lights, coupled Canter-buryin pairs[2]. In Conrad's transept at Canterbury a similar arrangement to that at Winchester is interrupted by the Norwich and Peter-boroughrose window. The transepts at Norwich and Peterborough have large Norman windows regularly arranged between flat buttresses, but here there are three bays in the width instead of two[3].

In all these cases the windows are independent and at a distance, with nothing to say to one another. Approach-ment of windowsGradually however they were drawn together, and the idea was conceived of combining them into an artistic composition. This began on the inside, and for a time the windows remained apart on the outside as before. It was easier now to bring them together than it had been before the wide Romanesque light had given way Bottesfordto the narrow Early English lancet. At BOTTESFORD in

[1] The traceries in all but the lower storey are of course later insertions of the 15th century.

[2] Illustrated in Parker's *Rickman*, 1848, p. 47.

[3] Illustrated in Mr Bond's *Gothic Architecture in England*, p. 31.

Lincolnshire (Fig. 105), where the narrow lancet windows Bottesford
are pulled out to an enormous length, they are so widely
splayed inwards that the jambs nearly meet ; only a very
narrow space separates the shafts, and we get something

WINCHESTER CATHEDRAL
NORTH TRANSEPT

SCALE 10 10 20 30 40 FEET

Fig. 104.

like a studied composition. In the east end of Cheriton Cheriton
in Kent the lights are less closely combined, but they
are united by a string-course at the springing, and with
the vesica above they form a consistent design in which

1—2

Bottesford

Fig. 105.

all the parts are related.   At the east end of WESTWELL Westwell
in the same county (Plate LXXXI) the fusion is at last
complete on the inside of the wall, and the arches of the
triple lancet lights spring from a common shaft and
capital in the jamb.   There is a group of three lancets,

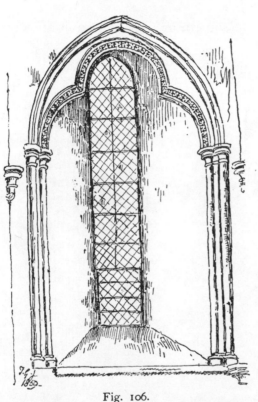

Fig. 106.

similarly combined on the inside, in the apse of Eynes- Eynesford
ford Church.   The enrichment of the inner arches was
carried to a much greater length before any alteration
was made to the window on the outside.   At Bredon Bredon
the inner arches are trefoiled and carried gracefully on
detached shafts.   At HYTHE they are treated with still Hythe

greater importance (Fig. 106).   In the vestibule to the
Deanery at Winchester the lights play a very secondary
part in a fine interior architectural composition.   Thus
far no approach has been made to the traceried window ;
the lights still remain widely separated by intervals of
solid wall.

There is something like a two-light window in the

Win-
chester
Deanery

Tower
windows

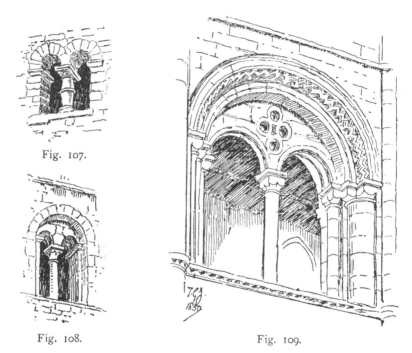

Fig. 107.

Fig. 108.

Fig. 109.

early campaniles of Italy, and the Romanesque towers of
France and England.   That of S. MICHAEL'S at OXFORD
has round-headed lights in pairs, divided by baluster
shafts (Fig. 107).   In the upper stage of the Saxon
tower of CLAPHAM near Bedford is a Norman window
of two lights divided by a colonnette under an including
arch (Fig. 108), and similar examples are common both

Plate LXXXI

Chancel of
Westwell Ch. Kent
July. 8. 1868 -

T. G. J. WESTWELL CHURCH

here and in France.   The Romanesque triforiums at Triforium
double
openings
PETERBOROUGH (Fig. 109) and Ely, in the churches of
Auvergne, at Mont St Michel, and many other places
in Normandy, have columns dividing them into two or
more lights, often under an including arch; and it has
been thought that from these came the idea of the
window-mullion.   I do not believe this is the case:
nothing is less suited than a column to receive either
glazing or the shutter that preceded glazing.   I doubt
whether any suggestion for reducing the pier between
the window lights into a mullion could have come in
this way; though I think this subdivision of the belfry
windows by a column led the way to the same thing
in the triforium.

At Bourne in Lincolnshire the two lancets are Bourne
brought so near that the jamb shafts on the outside
of the wall are only a few inches apart, and at last at
OAKHAM CASTLE we find the outside arches of the two Oakham
Castle
lights actually springing from the same capital, the shaft
of which forms the front of a veritable mullion (Plate
LXIV, vol. I. p. 198).   The lights were now brought so
close together that they could be grouped on the inside
under a single arch as in the east window at OCKHAM Ockham
Church
(Fig. 110).   This made it no longer necessary, nor
indeed possible, that the face within this arch should
be of the full thickness of the wall; it was therefore
recessed, and the lights are divided by stout upright
piers of wrought ashlar that are really mullions, in front
of which a detached shaft of Purbeck marble carries an
order over each light.   At Godalming is a group of Godal-
ming
three lancets with detached marble colonnettes carrying
the inner arch.

It is in this *recessing* of the window plane that the

secret of Gothic tracery lies.   As long as the lights were
pierced through the whole substance of the wall their

OCKHAM CHURCH

EAST WINDOW ·

REMAINS OF
OLD NORMAN TRIPLET

SCALE OF FEET

Fig. 110.

inner splay forced them apart like those at Bottesford
(Fig. 105 *sup.*). But now they were only pierced
through a thin wall, not built up like the Romanesque

pier but made of ashlar, which could be wrought and
shaped at pleasure.   At EAST DEREHAM (Fig. 111) the
window plane is recessed on both sides, within an outer
and inner enclosing order, and the division between the
lights is now perfectly developed as a mullion, though
a somewhat clumsy one, instead of the compound pier
and detached shaft at Ockham.

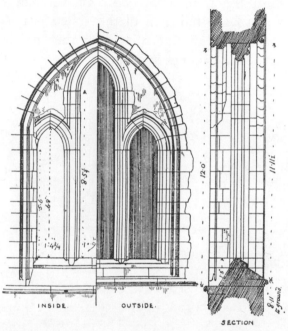

Fig. 111.

In all these cases there remains between the head
of the lights and the enclosing arch a piece of blank wall
as at Dereham, and the next step was to get rid of that.
The awkwardness of this plain shield had been felt
long before, and remedies had been attempted in the
Romanesque triforium where the same problem presented itself.   At Ely, Durham, and Christchurch Priory

the space is left plain, but a good beginning was made in
the nave of Peterborough, where the shield has a group
of piercings or sinkings (Fig. 109).   At S. Germer
in France an enriched circle is introduced (Fig. 112).
At Rochester the shield is not pierced but decorated
with diapers.   At Cerisy-la-Forêt there is a circular
moulding between the heads of the lights but it is not
pierced.   In the transitional work of William of Sens
at CANTERBURY the filling-in of the shield is not carried
up to the crown of the including arch, but finished on a
level line leaving an open segment above it (Fig. 78,

Fig. 112.

Fig. 113.

vol. I. p. 192).   At Lisieux there are piercings something
like those at Peterborough, and there are others in the
triforium of the choir at the Abbaye aux Hommes in
Caen, and that of the choir at Vézelay.

It was natural to follow suit in the windows, and to
pierce the plain shield between the head of the lights
and the including arch.   At GRAVILLE near Havre the
east end has a pair of two-light windows each under
an including arch, and the shield is pierced with a circle
(Fig. 113).   The belfry window at WEST WALTON in
Norfolk affords a still better example of this plate-tracery,

Plate LXXXII

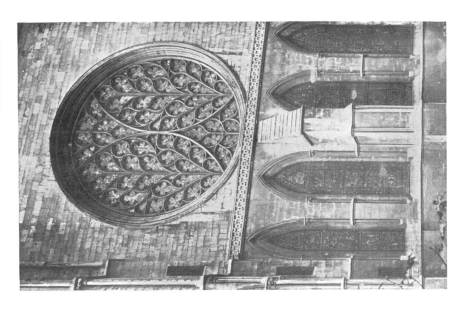

S. Transept—The Bishop's Eye

LINCOLN CATHEDRAL

N. Transept—The Dean's Eye

as it is called (Fig. 114). There are others in the windows of the granary of the Hospital of S. Jean at ANGERS (*v.* Fig. 70, vol. I. p. 164). At ILCHESTER the piercings assume a greater importance and are moulded and foliated (Fig. 115), but they are still mere piercings of the shield independent of the lights. A good instance

Plate
tracery

Angers.
Ilchester

Fig. 114.   Fig. 115.

of plate tracery is given by the window from S. Mary's Church, HAVERFORDWEST, shown in Fig. 116. Here and in the nave clerestory at Soissons the circle is cusped, but it remains still a detached figure. The grandest examples of plate-tracery are perhaps the circular window at LINCOLN, known as the Dean's Eye (Plate LXXXII), and the clerestory at CHARTRES, where an immense circle

Haver-
fordwest
Soissons

Lincoln
and
Chartres

surmounting the lights is filled with a thin plate of stone pierced with quatrefoils large and small, and cusped round the central opening (Fig. 40, vol. I. p. 100).

Removal
of blank
shield   The next step was to get rid altogether of what was left of the plain shield between the various openings. Additional piercings, even had there been room for them, would still have left very awkward relics of the plain

Tours and
Le Mans shield.   At Tours and Le Mans the blank stonework

Fig. 116.   Fig. 117.

was simply cut out squarely through the wall, on lines concentric with the curves of the lights and the circle[1]. S. Malo The same thing was done in the triforium at S. Malo, where however the blank stone is only partially removed, and the openings are cut square through the thickness of the shield (Fig. 117).   This still stops short of the invention of bar-tracery.

[1] Illustrated in Sir G. G. Scott's *Gleanings*, Plate III.

It is easy however to see how when this step had
been reached and the field had been cut out on lines
concentric with those of the piercings, giving them an
outline both at back and front, the idea was suddenly
conceived that the moulding on the inner edge of each
opening ought to be repeated on the outer edge; and
as the detail of this moulding, or chamfer as the case

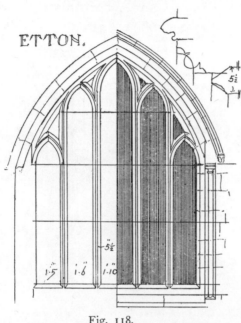

Fig. 118.

might be, was given in the jamb and mullion, the repetition of this on the back of the arched head of the light
gave the same section as that of the mullion. An early
example of this is afforded by the window at ETTON
(Fig. 118). If the same section is applied to a circle
in the shield it is obvious that the inside or sight-line
of the circle should meet at a tangent the outside sight-
line of the head of the light. Consequently at that

tangent point the stonework comes again to the section
of the mullion. The mullion thus becomes the module
which gives the detail of the tracery bar. On the left
of Fig. 119 is shown the method of setting out perfectly
developed tracery. From centre A a curve is drawn
with the radius AD, D being on the central line of the
mullion. A corresponding curve is drawn from centre
B. From the same centres curves are drawn from the
two edges of the mullion. The three parallel lines thus

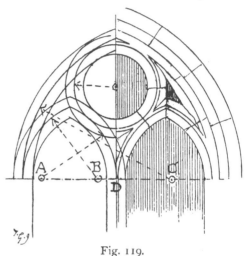

Fig. 119.

given are the central and two sight-lines of the tracery.
Then the central and two sight-lines of the circle are
drawn, each of which must be tangential to one of the
first three curves. The window arch again has its own
central and sight-lines drawn from the centre C, which
are tangential to those of the circle and the head of the
light. For greater ease in explanation we have begun
with the tracery, but in practice of course we reverse the
order of procedure and begin with the arch and fit the
tracery into it afterwards.

Having got our central and sight-lines it is easy to set out the fillet of the tracery on each side of the central line and to draw the window as on the right half of Fig. 119.   As the central lines of the tracery bar in circle, light, and arch meet at a tangent, of course the fillet of the tracery bar at those tangential points will coalesce and come to the same width as in the mullion, just as the tracery bar itself comes to the normal width of the mullion at those points.   On this principle all traceries, however elaborate, have to be set out for the mason.

The window had now become a new thing.   In place of the solid shield through which circles or other figures were cut to admit light, it now consisted of a framework of stone bars to which the glass was fitted.   In other words it has passed from plate-tracery to bar-tracery. Novel principle of bar-tracery

The mullion may now be conceived as running up and ramifying throughout the window-head as a tracery bar, always when not ramified returning to the normal section, enclosing the various figures of the openings, which are in fact the voids left by the bar, whereas in plate-tracery it was the openings that were first formed, and the stone-work that was left round them was the accidental remainder.

This is the great change that Ruskin deplores as the beginning of the decline of Gothic architecture. Ruskin on bar-tracery Hitherto he says the architect had thought only of the form of the penetrations, not of the stone between them. But now his eye, which had till then been watching only the star-like openings, was suddenly caught by the tracery. " It literally had not been seen before. It flashed out in an instant as an independent form. It became a feature of the work. The architect took it under his care ; thought it over and arranged and

Ruskin
on bar-
tracery

distributed it as we see[1]." For about 50 years, he continues, a pause followed, during which equal attention was given to both elements ; but the perfection thus reached was the turning-point of Gothic ; henceforth all was decay and weakness. He goes on to speak of tracery reduced to the slenderness of threads and seeming to rival their flexibility,—twisted and woven like a net,—and treated in any way but one expressive of the nature and weight of the material.

Ruskin's
view only
partially
justified

No doubt as time went on, and masons became more skilful, there was a tendency, especially towards the end of the Gothic period, to abuse their dexterity. Ruskin goes on to decry the clever trickery of interpenetrating

Gothic
a style of
progress

mouldings. But Gothic architecture, as I said before, never stood still ; it was always moving onwards to conquer fresh difficulties and solve fresh problems. It was impossible that the Gothic window could have remained in the stage of plate-tracery ; nor need we regret the change, or see in it nothing but a sign of decline. Admirable as is the stern grandeur of Chartres,

Beauty of
later work

and of Canterbury choir, we cannot afford to give up the lovely sweeping curves and delicate traceries of the Lady Chapel at Ely, or the choir screen at Southwell, or the windows at Selby, Sleaford, and Carlisle, nor the splendid luxuriance of French Flamboyant, or our own Perpendicular, without which art would have been sadly the poorer.

Date of
bar-tracery

There is not much difference in date between England and France in the appearance of bar-tracery, though the French seem entitled to priority. It is found, perhaps for the first time, in the apsidal chapels at Reims. Viollet-le-Duc says they were built about 1215. But

[1] *Seven Lamps of Architecture*, ch. II. Lamp of Truth.

it seems hardly possible that the building which was Early French and English tracery founded in 1212 should have reached that height in three years ; and the change in the plan of the chapels from round to polygonal, made in order to provide a flat plane for the traceried window, implies a change of design, and perhaps a later date.   Sir Gilbert Scott says there is perfect bar tracery in the east end of Netley which dates from 1240, and there was some in S. Paul's which must have been older, for the church was dedicated in that year[1], but there are signs that the window at Netley is an insertion, and the evidence is not complete for those at S. Paul's.   Similar windows with perfect bar-tracery occur at Notre-Dame, Paris, which date from 1235 to 1240, and at Amiens, of which the nave was occupied in 1236.

These windows at Reims are shown in Fig. 45 (vol. 1. Tracery at Reims p. 112), where it will be seen that the roll moulding forming the face of the tracery bar in the circle coalesces regularly with that in the head of the lights, but not with that in the arch.   It is in fact not bonded to it but worked on separate stones.   Viollet-le-Duc sees in this a careful provision for its safety, in case the arch above, which takes the weight of the wall, should settle ; but as the circle is bonded to the head of the lights, and the window arch rests upon it, I doubt the explanation.   It seems more like an imperfect understanding of the new system.   At Amiens, which is a little later, in some cases the circle is managed like these at Reims, but in others it ramifies with the arch moulding as well as with those of the lights[2].

---

[1] Sir G. G. Scott in *Gleanings*, p. 21.

[2] Professor Willis observes that both systems occur in the same four-light window at Amiens.   *Wilars de Honecort*, p. 222.—Ed. Willis.

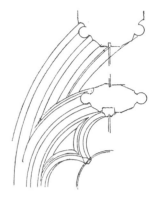

Fig. 120.

The cusping here is independent of the circle, cut in thin stone, and inserted in a groove of the circle ; and an iron ring sunk in the points of the cusps holds them in their place (Fig. 120). This is called soffit cusping, and was the earliest form that cusping took. Wilars de Honecort gives a number of sections of masonry in the new chapels at Reims, among which is a segment of soffit cusping detached[1].

Though bar-tracery seems to have become common in Northern France by 1230 to 1235 it did not immediately supersede plate-tracery. Sir Gilbert Scott observes that " Pierre de Montereau, the architect to the Ste Chapelle, in which the perfected tracery prevails, is said to have built also the refectory of S. Martin des Champs in which it does not appear at all[2] " (Fig. 121).

The windows of Henry III's apsidal chapels at Westminster Abbey, which was begun in 1245, resemble those at Reims, with six foils set square way ; in the transept aisle they are set with a foil at the top, and in the clerestory the cusped circle has five lobes of soffit cusping instead of six, which is perhaps an improvement —odd numbers generally lending themselves better to design than even. The cusping throughout in window and triforium is let into the soffit in the manner just described, and the roll on the tracery bar coalesces with that of the arch. Reims seems in many respects to have influenced the design of Westminster, and it was no

[1] Ed. Willis, Plate LXII.   [2] *Gleanings*, p. 19.

doubt closely studied by the English architect whom Sir Gilbert Scott imagines to have been sent abroad by Henry to see the great churches then rising in France.

The earliest traceried windows as at Reims and Earliest traceries two light

Fig. 121.

Westminster had only two lights. Consequently the Great width of lights are very wide; at Westminster from four to five lights feet; at Reims, according to Viollet-le-Duc, from 1 m. 20 to 2 m. 30[1]. Such an expanse of glass in

[1] *Dict. Rais.*, vol. v. p. 385.

leaded lights needed strong support not only against wind, but also on account of its own weight, and heavy

Ironwork supports

ironwork in stanchions and saddle bars had to be provided to hold it. The tall slender mullions also needed support by iron bars running through them from one jamb of the window to the other. This was inconvenient, and ironwork also is a bad ally for masonry, being apt by expansion and rust to flush the stone and split the mullions. The next step therefore was to

Four-light traceries

divide the lights and make the two openings into four by inserting two other mullions. At the Ste Chapelle in Paris, which was built by Louis IX and finished in 1247, a building where the Gothic theory of construction, reducing the space between the buttresses to a wall of glass, is carried out in perfection, there are four-light windows of geometrical tracery, in which the lights are

Subordination in tracery

reduced to 1 m. in width. But here a new element in the construction of tracery is introduced by *subordinating* these two additional mullions, and also the tracery they carry, to the original single mullion and circle.

Howden church

The transept window at HOWDEN church affords a good instance of this novel principle in the construction of window tracery[1]. It is a four-light window with tracery in two orders or planes (Fig. 122). The main order consists of the middle mullion with the two arches that spring from it and the great circle in the head. The sub-order consists of the two lesser mullions with the two arched heads of the lights and the lesser circles. This lesser order exists in embryo inside the larger in the jamb and mullion, and leaves it above the springing

[1] The design is almost the same as this in the Ste Chapelle, but the cusp points have bunches of foliage.

line. Each order has its own central and sight lines, Howden
as is shown on the right-hand half of the elevation, church

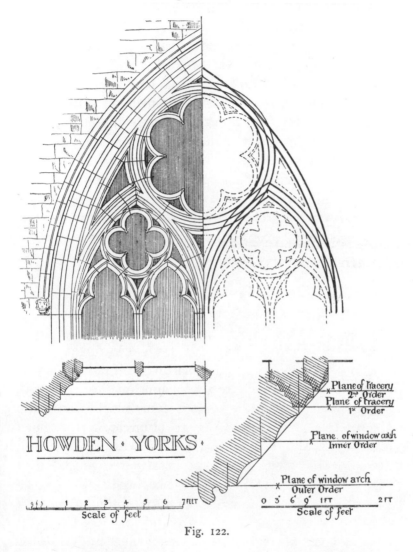

HOWDEN · YORKS ·

Plane of Tracery
2ⁿᵈ Order
Plane of Tracery
1ˢᵗ Order

Plane of window arch
Inner Order

Plane of window arch
Outer Order

Scale of feet

Scale of feet

Fig. 122.

where thick lines show the extra member of the main
order of tracery, and dotted lines the sub-order without

Howden
church

these members. The cusping again springs at a lower plane out of the inner order. The whole composition is enclosed in a window arch which has two orders and a label or hood-mould. All these orders—five if we count the cusping—represent successive planes, retired one within the other, exactly on the principle of subordination of orders which obtains in nave arcades, or doorways, and which has been claimed already as one of the *particular* principles which distinguish Gothic architecture from other styles.

Salisbury
cloisters
and
chapter
house

The cloisters of SALISBURY cathedral (Fig. 123) have regular bar-tracery in the upper part of their arcade with subordinated orders. The lower part of course does not belong to window construction, but the tracery and heads of the lights have grooves for glazing and were no doubt glazed as windows. The windows of the chapter house have bar-tracery fully developed (Plate LXXXV, *inf.*). They seem to date from the last half of the 13th century. All these traceries have soffit cusping, and the lights are not cusped.

Multipli-
cation of
lights and
orders

As the windows increased in width further subdivisions were made. The four lights might be subdivided into eight by a second sub-order springing out of the first, which springs as before out of the main order of tracery ; and as the great circle in the head grew larger and larger it was in its turn filled with tracery of its own, as in the east window at RIPON (Fig. 124) and at Tintern and Guisborough[1]. In France it seems that the preference was for an even number

---

[1] Guisborough and Tintern are illustrated in E. Sharp's *Decorated Windows*, Plates XII and XVII, and in Mr Bond's *Gothic Architecture in England*, pp. 475–6. These windows are in ruins, and the design is recovered from the remains.

Salisbury
cloister

Fig. 123.

of lights which gives a central mullion, but in England, where tracery shows more variety in the earlier styles, many of the larger windows have a central light.   This

RIPON
MINSTER
EAST
WINDOW

SCALE   0   5   10   15   20 FEET.

Fig. 124.

no doubt arose from our preference for a square east end and a great east window, in which the painted glass almost required a central panel for pictorial purposes.

This sometimes makes it necessary to have two thick Ripon
minster mullions together in the middle of the window, as in the seven-light east window of RIPON (Fig. 124). On the other hand in the south transept window at Hull there Hull are six lights which are divided by thick mullions of the main tracery order into three pairs so that a mullion of the sub-order comes in the middle. In the magnificent east window of Lincoln cathedral, the finest Lincoln
cathedral example of Geometrical tracery[1], there are eight lights, which of course places a large mullion in the middle, and it was the same in the east window of Tintern, now in ruins.

Although all traceries must be set out on the general principle shown in Figs. 119, 122, 124, they are capable of refinements. The mullion which generates the bar must be substantial, for it has to stand alone, unsupported except by such help as the ironwork affords; but when the figures in the head are close together the ramifications of the bar, if continued of the full width of the mullion, are apt to form heavy masses of stone work before they coalesce. In measuring one of the beautiful windows of CHARTHAM with its Kentish tracery, Chartham I found that this had been ingeniously prevented by making the bar taper from 6 inches in the mullion to $4\frac{1}{8}$ inches in the tracery. The difference is not obvious Diminu-
tion of
tracery bar to the eye and can only be detected by measurement (Fig. 125). My own practice is to make this reduction on the back of the head of the light, and to reduce the width of the fillet, making the splay of the moulding sharper. It results from this that the figures next the window arch have a sharper splay on one side than the other, for the section of the jamb cannot be altered

---

[1] See Sharp's *Decorated Windows*, Plate XI.

Chartham

Fig. 125.

in the arch.   But the irregularity is not noticeable, and like others of the same kind helps to obviate a too mechanical correctness.

The construction of soffit cusping, where the cusp Chamfer cusping is cut in thin stone and fitted into a groove in the soffit, has been explained already.   But this soon gave way to the more solid form of chamfer cusping (Fig. 126). According to this method the cusp exists in embryo in the chamfer of the tracery bar, emerges to form the figure required and subsides again into the soffit.   It

Fig. 126.

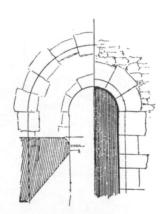

Fig. 127.

forms in fact a sub-order on a plane retired within that of the tracery bar, although as it dies into the splay of the bar it is not represented by any member of the jamb or mullion.

Enough has I think been said to make the constructional system of Gothic tracery intelligible.   It remains to explain certain fresh developments of the inner face of the window opening.

In Romanesque work of the earliest date the inner The inner window arch splay of the window was cut simply through the wall

Patrix-
bourne

Valence

E. Dere-
ham

and carried concentrically round the head as at PATRIX-
BOURNE (Fig. 127). Afterwards it was decorated on the
inside with colonnettes carrying an outer order round
the head as at VALENCE (Fig. 128). When the wall was
not very thick, in some cases the mullions were set in
the middle of it with an arch on both sides, as at
DEREHAM (Fig. 111, p. 9, *sup.*). But generally the
tracery is set on the outside of the wall as part of the
finished facing. The body of the wall, being of rubble

Fig. 128.   Fig. 129.

work behind the facing, required coigns of dressed ashlar
round the inside opening, in the jambs and also in the
arched head. The plan of continuing the splay of the
jamb round the head as at Patrixbourne (Fig. 127) was
soon abandoned, and the outer opening was raised to
the level of the inner, thus giving greater window light.
The inner arch therefore being no longer concentric
with the outer was quite independent and could be
treated with freedom. In simpler cases the soffit of

the inner arch was made horizontal at the crown, square The inner window arch
with the wall, and was run out to the inner wall face
and finished with a moulding or chamfer, as in Fig. 129,
where the coigns of the arched head bond back to the
rubble arch behind them.   In more elaborate work the
coigns are treated distinctly from the rubble arch and
made into a rib, on the back of which the rubble arch
may or may not rest.   The rib is the *scoinson arch*, and The scoinson arch and rear arch
the arch between it and the tracery arch is the *rear
arch*.   The wall being built of rubble faced with ashlar
on both sides, either over the whole surface or at all
events by coigns round the openings, the tracery forms
part of the outer ashlar facing and the scoinson arch
is a continuation of that on the inside, while the rear
arch corresponds to the rubble core of the wall between
the two sets of coigns.   This form of construction is
shown by the window at Chartham (Fig. 125).

The scoinson rib is often dropped so as to come The cusped scoinson
lower than the tracery arch, which of course it may
do without hiding it, as it is only seen from below.   And
often, especially in the west of England, it is treated
ornamentally and cusped, as in the north aisle at BITTON
in Gloucestershire (Fig. 130), Cheddar and Tintinhull
in Somerset, and many another place.   The windows
at HYTHE (Fig. 106, p. 5, *sup.*) and at Lydd in Kent
are examples from another part of England.

When tracery was fully developed it showed extra- Fertility of tracery
ordinary fertility of invention, especially in England,
during the 13th and following centuries.   Its variety
is amazing even during the Geometrical period, when
the limitation to certain definite figures imposed restric-
tions.   After these were removed the freedom of design
during the Curvilinear period knew no bounds, and when

somewhat later the French followed suit with their Flamboyant work it often bordered on extravagance.

At first the original idea of a circle as a central feature surmounting two pointed lights, as at Westminster and Reims, governed the design. When there were four lights as at Howden (Fig. 122) the two arches of the main order carry a central circle, and a smaller circle is carried by each pair of lights in the sub-order.

Fig. 130.

When there were three lights as in the sub-order at Ripon (Fig. 124) there were three circles fitted over them, and the main order carried its own single circle in the head. The three-light window at WINGHAM (Fig. 131) has three circles in the head, but the design is complicated by interlacing arches from the mullions, and the idea of a central figure is lost. It is however observed in the Kentish tracery at Chartham (Fig. 125), and generally in the Decorated windows at Exeter.

Plate LXXXIII

T. G. J.   BARNACK CHURCH—East End

In the fine east window at MERTON COLLEGE CHAPEL
the central circle is emphasized by being treated as a
wheel-window.   Here a novel feature is the introduction
of little pediments with a full complement of crockets
and finials into the head of the lights.   The same thing
occurs in the east window of BARNACK church (Plate
LXXXIII) in a simpler form, with the addition of

Merton
chapel,
Oxford

Barnack
church

WINGHAM

Fig. 131.

little pinnacles, and with a running scroll pattern up the
pediment instead of crocketting.   In this window the
idea of a central feature disappears, and the design
almost returns to that of a group of lancets like that at
Etton (Fig. 118).

In France, where Geometrical tracery lingered longer,
and lasted all through our Curvilinear period, the central
feature in the head was seldom forgotten.

One more form of Geometrical tracery must be described. In preceding examples it will be seen that the form of the piercings, whether quatrefoil, trefoil, or cinque or sexfoil, is given by the cusping, whether inserted in the soffit, or growing out of the chamfer. The quatrefoil, or whatever the figures may be, is in

Fig. 132.

these cases enclosed in a circle formed by the tracery bar. But in many instances, as at the Ste Chapelle for example, the figure is given by the tracery bar itself, which is curved into the required figure. In the

Chichester windows of the Lady chapel at CHICHESTER the cusping of the lights and the trefoils they support are treated

in this way (Fig. 132).   This is so also in the lovely
windows of S. Catherine's Chapel at LEDBURY (Fig. 133), Ledbury

Fig. 133.

all be-jewelled with ball-flowers, where the quatrefoils are
uncontained by any enclosing figure, and ramify into and

out of one another and of the arches, in the manner proper to bar-tracery.

Origin of cusping explained The notion of cusping, which is a peculiarity of Gothic, came, it seems to me, from the old piercings of plate-tracery. The plain shields were lightened and ornamented by cutting pretty figures through them of trefoils, quatrefoils, stars, circles, and other geometrical shapes. These figures it was desired to keep, although the shield in which they were pierced disappeared when bar-tracery was developed. Hence the bar had to accommodate itself to these figures, which were formed first by inserting thin slabs cut to the required form as soffit cusping, and afterwards by springing the chamfer cusp out of the solid of the bar and sometimes by bending the bar itself into foliation.

Lights not cusped at first It is confirmatory of this derivation that in the earliest traceried windows, as for instance those at Westminster, Salisbury chapter house, and the great east window at Lincoln, the lights are not cusped, but only the tracery above them in the window arch, which corresponds to the plate-tracery of an earlier period, when the shield of the window head was pierced with star-like figures while the lights below were plainly arched. The cusping of the lights followed later.

History of Gothic window summarised This then is the history of the development of the Gothic window. It begins with the gradual grouping of independent lights, at first severely distinct, then drawn together by degrees into alliance; next united under an arch on the inside, though still standing coyly aloof on the outside of the wall; then recessed within the interior arch till the divisions become piers of wrought stone, real mullions, clumsy and heavy at first, but afterwards of more slender proportions. Then comes the piercing of the solid shield in the head by History of tracery summarized independent figures, and the invention of plate-tracery, which led gradually to getting rid of the shield altogether, and the invention of bar-tracery by shaping the stone round the piercings on both edges, back as well as front.

This covers the whole history of the Gothic window down to the end of the Geometrical Decorated style, which corresponds to the second half of the 13th century. When once fully developed the style displayed, as I have said, infinite variety in the forms of its tracery, and the details of its decoration, but always within certain limits. It was in fact that period of fifty years during which, as Ruskin observes, equal attention was paid to the tracery bar and the piercings, to the solid and the void. Indeed we may go farther, and say that in the Geometrical style of the 13th century it is the opening that still gives the design ; the window is a composition of cusped figures, sexfoils, cinquefoils, quatrefoils, and trefoils, within circles, and circular curves, and the stone work is the mere setting that contains them. How this idea was subsequently modified we shall see when we come to the later styles of the 14th and 15th centuries.

CHAPTER XVIII

ENGLAND. GEOMETRICAL DECORATED

West-
minster
chapter
house

WITH Henry III's work at Westminster we pass, as I have said, from Early English to the Geometrical Decorated style. In the CHAPTER HOUSE which was begun in 1250, five years later than the choir, we find bar-tracery fully developed[1]. Seven of the eight sides are filled with large four-light traceries, of which six are real windows, the seventh is a blank window against the transept wall, and the eighth side contains a splendid doorway, reached from the cloisters by a low vaulted passage under the old dormitory. The shortened window above this doorway was originally of four lights, altered apparently in 1350 to a five light, and now altered back again. The chapter house was used from early times for meetings of the House of Commons, and when they moved to S. Stephen's Chapel it was made into the Record Office, the vault was removed, the windows were blocked or destroyed, the walls were lined with pens and cases, and a gallery and flat ceiling were inserted. From this state of desecration it was rescued by Sir Gilbert Scott, who may almost be said to have discovered it[2]. It is an octagon in plan, about

---

[1] Matthew Paris under the year 1250 writes " Dominus Rex aedificavit Capitulum incomparabile." It seems to have been finished in 1253.

[2] There is a view of the interior in this condition in *Gleanings*, p. 40. I remember when a pupil of Sir Gilbert Scott visiting it with him. We

Plate LXXXIV

W. S. WEATHERLEY

WESTMINSTER ABBEY—The Chapter House

58 feet in diameter, nearly the same size as the chapter West-minster chapter house houses at Salisbury, Lincoln, and York, all of them inscribed within a circle measuring, more or less, 60 feet in diameter. The central column of Purbeck marble, which fortunately survived the general disfigurement, is about 35 feet high, and the height to the crown of the restored vaulting is about 54 feet (Plate LXXXIV).

The entrance doorway had a central column and a medallion with sculpture in the head, which was cut away and has been restored. In niches right and left of the spandrels of the arch are two figures of the Virgin Mary and the Angel of the Annunciation. Scott tells us how he discovered them. " I was one day on the top of one of the presses, and on venturing to pull away an arris fillet which closed the crevice between it and the wall, I perceived the top of an arched recess in the wall behind the press, and on looking down into it I saw some round object of stone in the recess below. My curiosity being excited I let down into it by a string a small bull's-eye lantern, when to my extreme delight I saw that the mysterious object was the head of a beautiful full-sized statue in a niche.......The statue proved to be one of the Virgin, and in the spaces adjoining were angels censing. I afterwards found that it formed part of an Annunciation, the angel The sculpture having been on the other side of the door. This last-named figure has, however, been long since removed into the vestibule. Its wings are gone, but the mortices into which they were fixed remain. Both are fine

climbed up a heap of rubbish in one of the dark pens with a candle to see the paintings on the eastern wall-arcade. Chancing to look at what we were treading on we found the heap consisted of parchments in little rolls, or small boxes, some of them containing the building accounts of the fabric. These have been examined and preserved.

West-
minster
chapter
house
works, though not devoid of a remnant of Byzantine
stiffness[1]." Professor Lethaby finds an account in the year
1253 for two images, wrought by task work for 53s. 4d.,
which Professor Prior suggests may refer to these figures[2].

Sir G. G.
Scott's
restoration
In the restoration of this beautiful building Sir
Gilbert tells us there was little occasion for conjecture,
as enough remained to show the detail of every part.
The windows were restored from the blank tracery in
the bay next the transept, and it is remarkable as
marking a step in the development of the style that
the heads of the lights are cusped.   Scott points out
their resemblance to the windows of the Ste Chapelle
at Paris.

The
polygonal
plan
By the octagonal plan of his Chapter House, Henry
and his architect quitted French example.   Chapter
houses, circular or polygonal, are peculiarly English ;
in France they are rectangular as at Vézelay and Noyon,
and in Italy the round or polygonal plan belongs to
baptisteries.   One might wonder whether Abbot Ware
brought back the idea with him from Italy as well as
the stones of his pavement, but that the fashion is older
in England than his time.   Worcester has a round
chapter house of Norman date.   Margam had one,
round within, polygonal without, which probably set
the example for that at Abbey Dore, which was do-
decagonal both inside and outside.   Lincoln has a
decagonal chapter house built by Bishop Hugh of
Wells before 1235.

Polygonal
plan
abandoned
by
Regulars
Though the earliest of our round or polygonal chapter
houses are conventual, the monks seem soon to have
abandoned that form.   After Margam and Dore the

---

[1] *Gleanings*, p. 41.   The angel is now replaced.
[2] Lethaby, *op. cit.* p. 242.

Cistercians built no more chapter houses like them, and Polygonal chapter house abandoned by Regulars those at Buildwas, Byland, Fountains, Furness, Kirkstall, Netley, Tintern, and Valle Crucis are rectangular. Among Benedictine foundations Worcester and Westminster alone have a round chapter house, those at Rochester, Winchester, Canterbury, Chester, Gloucester, Norwich, and Durham are rectangular, the two last having apsidal ends. The Austin Canons have a polygon at Bolton, but rectangular buildings at Hexham, Oxford, Bristol, and Llanthony, the last with a polygonal end. There is an octagonal chapter house at Thornton Abbey (1282), and Evesham is said to have had a decagonal one. On the other hand the polygonal Popular with Seculars plan was the favourite with the Secular Canons, and though Ripon, S. David's, and Exeter had rectangular chapter houses, those at Hereford, Lincoln, Lichfield, Salisbury, Southwell, Wells and York are polygonal, as well as that of the Collegiate Church at Manchester. In Scotland, Elgin has an octagon, but elsewhere the chapter house seems to have been rectangular, as it is also at Christchurch, Dublin.

In all our polygonal chapter houses, except at York Vaulting of polygon where the roof is of wood, and at Southwell, there is a central column A from which the vaulting radiates (Fig. 134) as a conoid to a ridge BCH, etc., which forms a ring, octagonal or decagonal according to the number of sides the building has. The points of this ridge are intermediate with those of the building, so that there are formed lozenge-shaped vaults ABDC from centre to circuit, and the triangular spaces FBD between them are cross-vaulted to horizontal ridges of their own, BE and HG, etc., level with the crown of the vault. At Lincoln the ring BC, etc. is marked by a ridge rib, but the vault is later than Bishop Hugh's episcopate and was finished by his successor. At Westminster and Salisbury there is no ridge rib (Plate LXXXV).

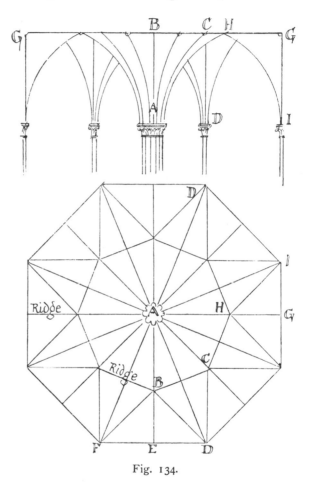

Fig. 134.

The Westminster chapter house, with its beautiful vestibule and sculptured decoration, is the finest example of the type, and when the paintings on the wall, of which only faint traces remain, were perfect it must have been

Plate LXXXV

SALISBURY CATHEDRAL—The Chapter House Vault

Plate LXXXVI

ELY CATHEDRAL. The Arches of Choir

superb. It still retains its original pavement of encaustic tiles.

The octagonal chapter house at SALISBURY and the cloister (Fig. 123, p. 23, *sup.*) are rather later, dating from the last quarter of the 13th century. The details are considerably more advanced, the mouldings much more developed and richer. The lights, however, are not cusped, and the cusping of the tracery is still of the soffit type. The wall arcading round the chapter house like that in the north porch has cinquefoil cusping in the head instead of the trefoil till then usual, and the spandrils are filled with well-known figure sculptures.

Salisbury chapter house and cloister

The door occupies one side of the octagon : on each of the other seven are eight subjects from the Old Testament, which were understood in the Middle Ages to have their antitypes in the New. After the Creation and Fall follow the story of the Flood, the Sacrifice of Isaac, and the history of Joseph, which were taken to typify Christian baptism and the life and death of Christ. The series finishes with Moses and the burning bush, a well-known emblem of the Virgin Mary[1], and the overthrow of the Egyptians in the Red Sea, typical of the final doom of the wicked.

The sculptures

In the canopied tomb of Bishop Bridport, which dates from 1262, Salisbury possesses a perfect gem of Geometrical Decorated work[2].

Bp Bridport's tomb

Coeval with the later work at Salisbury is the presbytery or "Angel choir" at LINCOLN in which the Geometrical style perfects itself (Plate LXXXVI). It was

Lincoln angel choir

---

[1]   "O mother maide, O maide and mother fre
        O bushe unbrent, brenning in Moyses' sight."
                                    Chaucer, *Prioresses Tale.*
[2] It is well illustrated in Dodsworth's *Salisbury Cathedral,* and there is a full-size model of it at the Crystal Palace.

Lincoln
presbytery

built between 1255 and 1280, to give better space for
the shrine of S. Hugh, and the influx of pilgrims who
resorted thither.   The apse of S. Hugh with its ambulatory and chapels was pulled down and the church was
extended five bays eastward and finished with a square
end (see Plan, Fig. 81, vol. i. p. 201).

The general design is magnificent, but it has not the
grace of Westminster; the bays are much wider in proportion, and the triforium, though beautiful, has not the perfect
refinement of Master Henry's work at the Abbey (vol. i,
Plate LXXVII and Fig. 100).   Westminster has some

The angels

fine angelic figures in the triforium of the transepts, and
those at Lincoln, which give its popular name to this part
of the building, are like them (Plate LXXXVII).   They
are variously occupied: one holds a little soul in the
usual piece of drapery, another plays the fiddle, a third
is driving our first parents out of Eden, while a fourth,
to our surprise, with falconer's gloves on his hands and
a smile on his face, holds a hawk on a lure[1].   The east
end is filled with one of those splendid traceried windows
that are among the glories of English architecture and
may well contest the claims of the continental apse to
be the finest termination of a great church.

Thornton
abbey

There is some excellent Geometrical work in the
chapter house of THORNTON ABBEY in Lincolnshire, where
in a blank bay the architect instead of copying, as a
dullard might have done, the forms of the window, has
substituted fleurs-de-lis for cusping (Fig. 135).   A somewhat similar liberty is very sensibly taken in the chapter
house at Furness Abbey.

Exeter
cathedral

To the same period belongs the work at EXETER

---

[1] There are casts of these figures in the Royal Architectural Museum at
Tufton Street, Westminster.

Plate LXXXVII

T. G. J.　　　LINCOLN CATHEDRAL—Figures in the "Angel Choir"

CATHEDRAL, where English Geometrical Decorated may be studied perhaps better than anywhere else. The plan is unusual ; a long interior as at Bourges unbroken by transepts, flanked by two massive towers where tran-

Fig. 135.

septs would have been, and where at Bourges are the two lateral porches. These two towers are the sole visible relics of the Norman church of Bishop Warelwast (1107—1136). The rebuilding of the eastern part by Bishops Bronescombe, Quivil, and Bitton occupied

Exeter
cathedral

thirty-seven years, from 1270 to 1307, and the nave was rebuilt between 1327 and 1335 in the same style

Respect
for
preceding
design

as the rest; one of the rare instances where, as at Westminster, the mediaeval architect respected and imitated the work of his predecessor, and worked in a style not his own.

The result is consequently as harmonious and consistent as that at Salisbury; but the difference between the two is like that between poetry and prose. The interior of Exeter has not the classic grandeur of Westminster, but I know none more lovely, though it is not easy to say exactly from what its especial charm arises (Plate LXXXVIII). It is long and low without any effect of depression; it is full of variety in window tracery without confusion of design; it is symmetrical without formality; and an extraordinary richness is given by the multiple shafting of the piers, by the solid marble of which they are made, by the contrasted tone of the arcades, and by the fan-like spread of the vaults with their thickly branching ribs. The whole has a mellow softness of line and colour, and a delicious harmony of parts; and not the least element in the beauty of the picture is the fine screen between nave and choir, and the lovely organ-case upon it, which divides and at the same time enhances the perspective length.

The vault

The vaults at Exeter afford a good example of the wide divergence of the English and French schools. In the diagram (Fig. 136) of the nave vaults at Lincoln there appear two pairs of intermediate ribs besides the transverse and diagonals, abutting on the ridge rib.

Multipli-
cation of
ribs

Thus AB and AC are the intermediates, which the French call *tierçerons*, AB abutting on the main longitudinal ridge, and AC on the cross ridge rib DC. At

Plate LXXXVIII

EXETER CATHEDRAL

Lincoln the cross rib stops short at C, though the Multi-plication of ribs longitudinal ridge rib runs continuously from end to end of the nave ; but in French work the ridge ribs generally stop short both at B and C. This short rib they call a *lierne*[1]. In France, however, this multi-plication of ribs is unusual in the 13th and 14th centuries, during which the simple quadripartite vault continued to prevail. Indeed in the French way of laying the ashlar courses of the panel there was nothing to invite it ; while in the English way, on the contrary, the lie

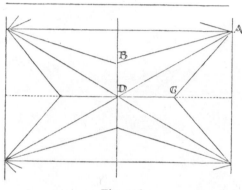

Fig. 136.

of the courses rather suggests it (Fig. 91, vol. I. p. 213). Suggested by the English way of coursing The English plan being to lay the courses more or less square with a line bisecting the panel, instead of parallel to the ridge in the French way, a fresh direction was given to the ashlar courses on each side of the intruded rib. At Lincoln there is only one intermediate or *tierçeron* in each panel, but the number soon multiplied, and at Exeter besides one pair in the main vault there are no less than three pairs in the cross-vault, which

[1] The word *lierne* seems to mean originally a trimming-piece in car-pentry. See Viollet-le-Duc, *sub voce.*

form a magnificent sheaf of ribs spreading out from the top of the vaulting shaft (Fig. 137). Now if the ashlars are laid square or nearly square with the bisecting line of each panel they will form half of a spherical cone attached to the side wall, and if the same principle is applied to the vault of a polygonal chamber, as for instance the chapter house of Salisbury (Plate LXXXV *sup.*) or to a building of two or more equal aisles like the retro-choir at Southwark, the vault forms a complete trumpet-shaped cone on the central shaft.

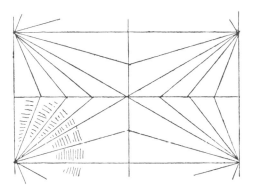

Fig. 137.

This multiplication of ribs gives a new character to English vaulting, and the circular plan of the ashlar courses led in the 15th century to construction of a totally different kind, as we shall see.

Another point to be noticed is that whereas in the transitional vault each rib came down entire on its own capital, as for example at Sens (Plate I, vol. I. p. 38), they now had to run together at the springing in order to find room on the capital; and the whole group was worked in solid stone for some way above the springing till the diverging ribs cleared one another. It is one of the most amusing tasks in masonry to bring a group of ribs nicely together at the springing, so as to form an agreeable figure on the impost, and to clear one another at the same level.

The chapter house at SOUTHWELL, alone among the polygons, is vaulted entirely from the side without a central column. It dates from 1294, and is coeval with that at WELLS, which was built between 1293 and 1302 upon a vaulted crypt begun in 1286. The Southwell chapter house has an internal diameter of 30 feet as against 50 at Wells. *Southwell chapter house* *Wells chapter house*

The Norman nave of Archbishop Thomas (1180) at YORK was pulled down and the present nave begun in 1291, and it was finished before 1324, except the upper part of the west front. It is a fair example of the last stages of Geometrical Decorated. All the windows above and below are Geometrical in design, and the triforium and clerestory are united into one composition. The clerestory passage has disappeared and the glass is brought to the middle of the wall. Vaulting shafts rise from floor to springing of the vaults, but the aisles alone are vaulted in stone, the nave having wooden vaulting imitating a stone construction with rib and panel. The nave arches are only of two orders, the capitals are small and poor, and the bases rather meagre. The whole has something of the air of thinness that I feel at Amiens. This nave cannot rank with the finest work of the period and is only saved from dullness by the fine 14th and 15th century work of the west front (Plate XCVII, *infra*). The outside is better than the inside, and the grand range of buttresses flanking the aisle reminds one of Reims. *York cathedral, the nave*

Far more beautiful was the church of the Benedictine
ABBEY OF S. MARY in the same city which remains in
ruin. It was begun by Abbot Simon de Warwick in
1270 and finished during his lifetime in twenty-four
years. It has that air of chaste severity in the
acute arches and the sharply profiled mouldings which

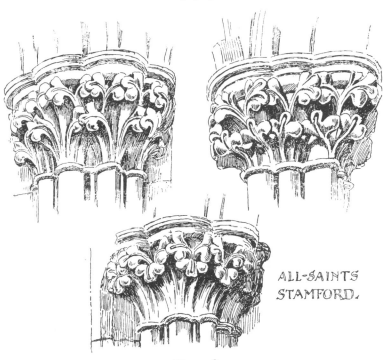

ALL-SAINTS
STAMFORD.

Fig. 138.

characterizes the Northern school of Gothic, and was
continued from the Early English of Rievaulx and
Byland into the Decorated period. To judge by what
is left of it this must have been one of the most beautiful churches in Christendom. The windows of the nave
aisle (Plate LXXXIX) are alternately of three lights
carrying three cusped circles and of two lights carrying

Plate LXXXIX

T. G. J.   S. MARY'S ABBEY, YORK—The nave aisle

Plate XC

T. G. J.　　SOUTHWELL CATHEDRAL—Capital in Chapter House

only one, but the two kinds of window are of the same size.

Edwardian Gothic, the last phase of the Geometrical Decorated style, has a singular grace and delicacy. The difficulties of construction that had given a tentative character to the earlier work had now been mastered, and it remained only to polish and refine the details. Sculpture advanced towards greater naturalism. The Early English leaf, which figures so largely at Lincoln, Edward-ian Gothic Sculpture

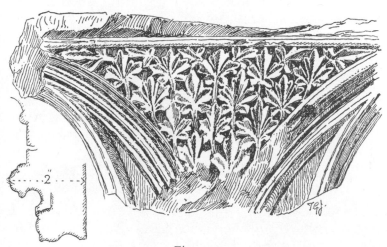

Fig. 139.

Westminster, Ely, Salisbury, and down to late in the century had attained a kind of perfection and could go no further. The capitals at ALL SAINTS, STAMFORD (Fig. 138), dating from the first half of the 13th century, are admirably composed, and show much greater skill in arrangement than earlier examples. This conventional foliage gave way towards the end of the century and the carving in the chapter houses at Wells and Southwell is exquisitely natural. The rendering of the

wild geranium (*Ger. pratense*) at SOUTHWELL cannot
be surpassed for truthfulness, combined with a suitable
decorative quality (Plate XC).   The Cantilupe shrine

at HEREFORD has in the spandrils of its beautiful
cusping some natural foliage prettily sculptured, though
it is arranged in a conventional manner (Fig. 139)[1].

In figure sculpture England at first lagged behind.
As I have already said, the Norman school, both here
and in Normandy, for want of good examples such as
Italy and the South of Gaul enjoyed in the remains
of Classic art, made little use of figure sculpture, and
its ornament was conventional.   Later still in the Early
English work at Lincoln, the nave of Wells, Ely, and the
Eastern transept at Durham, not to mention the Cistercian
buildings where it was forbidden, carving was confined
to freizes and capitals.   While in France during the same
period, from about 1180 to 1240, the great portals at
Reims, Paris, Chartres, and Amiens were gradually
being peopled with fine statuary, in our English churches
no preparation was made for any figures, and the only
statues were monumental effigies on tombs.

In decorative carving the Early English men attained a high degree of excellence, and their work shows
perhaps more originality than the French.   Bishop
Reginald's capitals at Wells, of which one is shown in
Plate LX, vol. I, p. 186, are older than those in the nave
at Chartres (Figs. 41 and 42, vol. I, p. 101), and surpass
them in technique and imagination.   Those at Stamford
(Fig. 138) show much more variety, and are more interesting than the *cap à crochet* (Figs. 47 and 48, vol. I.

---

[1] This is drawn from a fragment found in a loft over the cloister.   It
corresponds with the upper arcade of the Cantilupe shrine, and may once
have belonged to it.

Plate XCI

From Prior and Gardner

WELLS CATHEDRAL

Plate XCII

WELLS CATHEDRAL—West front—Figures of the Resurrection

T. G. J.

pp. 119, 120) which had been adopted generally in France, and of which to say the truth one gets rather tired.

It was not till nearly the middle of the 13th century that statuary began to make much show in English architecture, and it displayed at once considerable excellence. It was not a new art in England; recumbent figures had been carved for some time on monuments, and they were now set upright in niches, or carved in relief in spandrils and tympana as at Westminster and Lincoln; and the little figures that used to be introduced among the foliage of capitals came to be treated independently, and formed into subjects, as in the arcading at Salisbury chapter house towards the end of the 13th century. Early statuary in England

There are figures in the upper part of the west front at PETERBOROUGH, dating from the first quarter of the 13th century, which are stumpy in proportion, and rather barbarous. But those at WELLS in Bishop Jocelin's front, which was built before 1242, are fine works, and though not all of equal merit, many of them may be compared with the contemporary work at Chartres. Several of the niches have lost their population, but it is calculated[1] that out of some 200 about 130 still remain, and this is the largest collection of mediaeval statuary that we possess. They show a variety of handling; Messrs Prior and Gardner classify them into nine groups. So large a number of figures naturally employed a considerable number of sculptors, and occupied a considerable time; and many of them may not Statues at Peterborough Statues at Wells

[1] Messrs Prior and Gardner, *Architectural Review*, December 1903.

Wells
cathedral

have been finished so soon as the front itself, but have been inserted afterwards. They represent kings (Plate XCI), queens, doctors, and deacons of the Church, and have considerable variety of action and of expression in their heads deserving of all praise. Plate XCII shows part of the freize above the windows which represents the resurrection of the dead.

Advance
of
sculpture
towards
nature

From the statues at Wells, which have still the stiffness of an early school, the art progressed to the consummate art of William Torel's bronze effigies of Henry III and Queen Eleanor of Castile at WESTMINSTER, which have been described already, and which though perfectly well modelled are still conventional and do not attempt portraiture. At the end of the 13th and opening of the 14th century there is a further advance

Sculpture
at
S. Mary's,
Oxford

towards nature. The sculptures from S. MARY'S spire at OXFORD, which date from the beginning of Edward II's reign seem modelled from life; every head has its own character. S. Hugh of Lincoln, who is caressing the pet swan of which Giraldus tells us, S. Cuthbert carrying S. Oswald's head, and the other saints, bishops, and archbishops are treated with distinction and individuality, and seem to be portraits[1].

Lincoln
presbytery
door

The south doorway of the Presbytery or Angel choir at LINCOLN (1255—1280) is as rich in sculpture, and almost as grand in scale, as the French portals (Plate XCIII). The treatment, however, is very different. The figures are reliefs in the solid, firmly attached to the ground, and do not defy the laws of equilibrium

[1] The series of these statues is illustrated in my *History of the Church of S. Mary the Virgin, Oxford.* For the sake probably of reducing their weight and convenience of fixing, these figures are hollowed at the back so much that in some places the stone is only an inch thick, which has wrought the ruin of some of them.

Plate XCIII

LINCOLN CATHEDRAL—South door of Presbytery

Plate XCIV

The Synagogue

The Church

LINCOLN CATHEDRAL

like the French statuettes in their tabernacles as they come arching overhead.   The statues in the jambs are admirable, and there is nothing finer at Chartres or Amiens than the two figures of the church and the synagogue (Plate XCIV).   Alas! that they should be headless.   There is a magnificent figure of a Madonna belonging to the entrance of the chapter house at York.

CHAPTER XIX

ENGLAND. THE FLOWING DECORATED STYLE.
THE ENGLISH SPIRE

THE Geometrical Decorated style had not a very long life. Less than 50 years divides the chapter house at Westminster and the Angel choir at Lincoln, where the style first attained full development, from the chapter house at Wells where the first signs of a transition may be detected, and the choir of Dorchester abbey. The most obvious novelty is that of the window tracery. The geometrical window The geometrical window consisted of regular figures, juxtaposed, but united only at the tangential points, and retaining elsewhere their independent form of circle, sexfoil, quatrefoil, or trefoil. Each of these figures might in idea be detached complete from the rest (*v. sup.* Figs. 122--124). In these windows equal attention, as Ruskin put it, is paid to the bar and the figure of the opening. But at the beginning of the 14th century a change took place which is well shown by two windows that stand next to one another in Exeter cathedral. The left-hand window (Fig. 140) has geometrical tracery, where the circles and other figures are complete and theoretically detachable, united only where meeting at a tangent. This leaves the point of the sub-arch at A standing out rather awkwardly, and forming an inconvenient interval, only partially disguised by the little trefoil. In the right-hand window, where the same thing occurs, this is got over by repeating the curve of the circle reversed, so as to give an equal flowing line on both sides of the point. Here we have the parting of the two styles:

EXETER·CATH⁴
NO SCALE.

Fig. 140.

Fig. 141.

the left-hand window is in the Geometrical Decorated, and the right-hand one in the Flowing Decorated style.

Again in Fig. 141 A is a very common and simple form of a geometrical window, with a quatrefoil in a circle surmounting two trefoil-headed lights.   At B we have a 14th century version of exactly the same constituent parts, no longer, however, separate figures meeting

Fig. 142.

only at the tangential points, but run together by making the lines of the three figures flow without interruption into one another.

This was an important innovation. Instead of tracery composed as hitherto of simple circular curves we now have reversed, compound, or ogee curves; the figures of the openings are not merely juxtaposed, leaving accidental intervals where they do not fit, but are now shaped to fit one another exactly, leaving no intervals at all; and the tracery bar forms a continuous ramification throughout the window, instead of being broken into distinct geometrical figures, detachable in imagination without losing their completeness. The window from NEW ROMNEY church (Fig. 142) shows the principle of flowing Decorated tracery still better. It is an example of what is called reticulated tracery, the openings being equal and similar like the meshes of a net, and it is formed by the regular ramification of the tracery bar throughout. In this instance the ogee or compound curve is introduced into the cusping as well as into the tracery bar. The windows of the sacristy of MERTON COLLEGE chapel, built in 1310, are good examples of reticulated tracery.

The compound or ogee curve

New Romney

Sacristy, Merton college

Thus released from geometrical convention, window tracery blossomed out with a luxuriant growth, and a freedom of design hitherto impossible. The variety of curvilinear tracery seems inexhaustible, though it never ran to extravagance like French flamboyant a century later. The village churches of Northamptonshire are full of beautiful windows in this style, showing an infinite wealth of invention and freedom of fancy (Figs. 143, 144, 145).

Variety of curvilinear tracery

Reticulated tracery naturally admitted of only one order; but in other cases flowing traceries had the same subordination of orders as the geometrical. The south transept window at CHICHESTER (Fig. 146) has tracery

Chichester south transept window

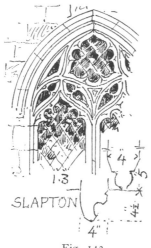

Fig. 143.

Fig. 144.

Fig. 145.

of three orders, with a combination of geometrical and curvilinear forms.   The great order is set out like a geometrical window, with a centre-piece consisting of a spherical triangle supported on three pointed arches, but the sub-orders are all drawn on curvilinear lines. In this window the construction of the orders is logical and consistent; that is to say each order is complete

Chichester cathedral

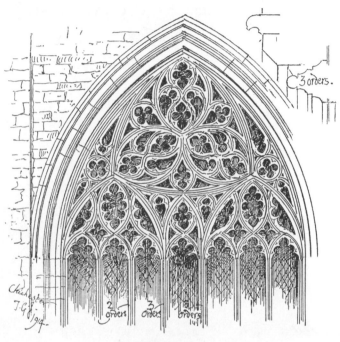

Fig. 146.

and would form a perfect piece of tracery by itself if the other orders were omitted.   This, which is an important principle, was not always respected.

The idea of a centre-piece which was commonly observed in geometrical windows prevailed also for some time in the curvilinear windows which followed. If we take by itself one of the three-light compartments

CAMROSE LUTHERAN COLLEGE
LIBRARY

of the Chichester window (Fig. 146) with its including arch, we have a perfect curvilinear window with an oval centre-piece. The same idea on a more important scale gives us the scheme of the fine east window at SLEAFORD[1], where the main lines are just like those of the three-light compartment at Chichester, though the number of lights is doubled. The east window of HAWTON church, in Nottinghamshire, is another of the same kind. The

Sleaford east window

Fig. 147.

Selby

east window of SELBY (Plate XCV) is another instance of the same general scheme; but the great order does not ramify logically over the whole window, being confined to the central oval and the arch over the three middle lights which sustains it, and it is therefore logically incomplete. There is a still more curious irregularity in the windows of the nave aisle at Selby (Fig. 147) where the central figure in the head is formed

[1] Sharpe's *Decorated Windows*, No. 40.

Plate XCV

T. G. J.   SELBY ABBEY—East end

partly on one order of the tracery and partly on another. Selby Not less remarkable is the reappearance of soffit cusping in a window of late Decorated design.   Cusping of the same kind occurs also in the flowing tracery of the stone screen round the choir.   The tracery that fills the spaces flanking the central oval of the great east window is almost flamboyant.   In the same way the east and other windows of HECKINGTON have a central oval in the head, Hecking-ton flanked by flowing curves[1].

The idea of a centre-piece is less positively marked in the great east window of CARLISLE, the finest curvi- Carlisle east window linear window in the country.   It has nine lights, the central one 2 ft. 10 in. wide, the rest 2 ft. 3 in., and it is 59 ft. 6 in. high and 33 ft. wide.   There are three orders: the great order is turned in an arch over the two side groups of four lights each, leaving the central light to run up and melt into the central oval, which thus loses its distinct character of a centre-piece.   This fine window has the fault of certain other windows with an uneven number of lights, that the great order does not meet in the middle, but is separated by a compartment of the sub-order.   The great order in fact is not logically complete in itself.   This defect is avoided at Chichester by turning the great order over the head of the middle light, so that it supports the centre-piece (Fig. 146).   At Carlisle it is indeed turned over the circle in the head of the middle light, but it carries Trinity church, Hull nothing.   In the great five-light window at HULL the great order does not meet at all but forms two detached arches over the two extreme pairs of lights.   For this

---

[1] Several windows from Sleaford and Heckington, etc., etc. are illustrated in Sharpe's *Decorated Windows*. Also the east windows of Lincoln and Carlisle.

reason windows with an even number of lights and a
central mullion are more easily managed.   The difficulty
is well surmounted in the curvilinear window of the
North-   beautiful late Decorated transept of NORTHBOROUGH
borough
church   church (Plate XCVI).

But in many, if not most, curvilinear windows the
idea of a centre-piece is abandoned.   In some the

Fig. 148.

figures spread out, and radiate from the centre in the
manner of foliage.   The window at SLAPTON (Fig. 145)
West   is an example of this.   The lovely west window at YORK
window,
York   cathedral (Plate XCVII) is filled with tracery of this
kind, where the figures spring to right and left from
a central stem like the leaves of a tree.   In the clerestory windows at SELBY there is a somewhat different
version of the same fancy (Fig. 148).   The tracery in

Plate XCVI

T. G. J.

NORTHBOROUGH CHURCH

Plate XCVII

this church is more flamboyant in its character than usual, and many of the windows almost anticipate the French traceries of the next century. An almost un- rivalled example of this kind of tracery, when the flowing lines and springing figures seem inspired by the natural growth of vegetation, is the west window of SNETTISHAM church in Norfolk, a church with many points of interest, and in particular a western porch of consum- mate delicacy and beautiful simplicity. *Selby* *Snetti-sham*

The same superb flow of line and suggestion of growth rules the design of the Southern Rose—the Bishop's Eye—at LINCOLN, which has all the easy flow of the French flamboyant a century later, without its license and extravagance (Plate LXXXII p. 11, *sup.*). *The Bishop's Eye, Lincoln*

The tendency to greater smoothness shown by softening off the angularities of geometrical forms in the tracery appears in the mouldings of the curvilinear period, which are simpler than those of the preceding style. We no longer get the deeply channelled hollows and slender rolls of the 13th century, but softer swelling surfaces and broader effects. *14th century mouldings*

The flowing curve now passed into general use not only in windows but in wall panelling, heads of niches, canopies and doorheads. In the choir screen at SOUTH- WELL, built between 1335 and 1340, we have Curvilinear Decorated at its best. The outside towards the nave (Plate XCVIII) has three arches under pediments with ogee cusping, and side panels with ogee arches. The inside of the screen towards the choir is much richer, with ogee heads to the arcading, flowing traceried panels, splendid crocketting, and in the central pediment a seated Madonna with the Holy Child, between two angels, but these figures are small and not remarkable. *Southwell choir screen*

In the later styles of Gothic statuary gives place to architectural ornament, and is comparatively rare.

Ely Lady Chapel

Rather earlier than the Southwell screen is the Lady Chapel at ELY, which was built between 1321 and 1349, under the direction of Alan of Walsingham, the Sub-Prior and Sacrist, by Brother John of Wisbech, one of the monks. The general design we may conclude is by Walsingham, but the marvellous detail of the interior must be due to some sculptor whose name is lost. The chapel stands apart, entered from the north transept, but only touching the cathedral at one corner. It is very large, 100 ft. long by 46 in breadth and 60 ft. high, with a stone vault very flat in section, and sustained in spite of its vast span by very moderate buttresses. The two end windows are not of the original date but were inserted by Bishop Barnett about 1373.

The walls below the windows are panelled with the most exquisite niche and tabernacle work in the whole range of Gothic architecture. Shallow niches with rounded backs are surmounted by pedimental canopies that project on a curved line, and are splendid with ogee cusping, delicately carved spandrels, crockets and finials. They are divided by pinnacled shafts, and the wall between and above the pediments was filled with imagery representing the life of the Virgin, now sadly mutilated. Nothing can surpass the beauty of the detail and the skilfulness of the technique here displayed.

The octagon at Ely

In 1322, a year after the Lady Chapel was begun, the central tower of the Cathedral, which had been begun by Abbot Simeon, and was finished after his death in 1093, fell down, destroying with it three bays of the choir, and also no doubt pulling down the adjoining bays of nave and transepts to the north, west, and south, as happened

Plate XCVIII

T. G. J.   SOUTHWELL CATHEDRAL—The Choir-screen

at Chichester when that spire fell in 1861. The wide Ely
cathedral empty space left after clearing away the ruins no doubt suggested to Alan of Walsingham the idea of the present octagon, a novelty on this side of the Alps. The plan (Fig. 149) is irregular, the four cardinal sides opening to nave, choir, and transepts being wider than the four oblique sides into which the aisles run. These four

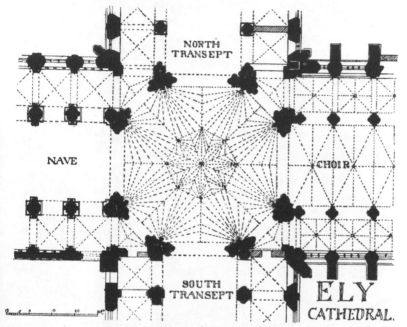

Fig. 149.

have large windows above the aisle roofs which light the central space admirably. The problem of covering Problem of
covering
the
octagon this great octagonal area, about 66 ft. wide[1], anticipated that which was too much for the successors of Arnolfo to solve, and which taxed the ingenuity of Filippo Brunelleschi a hundred years later at Florence. Earlier

[1] The published guide says 65 ft. 4 in.

The
octagon
at Ely

Its size
compared
with
others

Wooden
construc-
tion over
the
octagon

The
timbering

solutions were all on a smaller scale. The octagon of S. Vitale at Ravenna, covered by a hemispherical dome constructed with a spiral of earthenware jars, is only 50 ft. in diameter. Charlemagne's dome at Aix-la-Chapelle has an octagonal dome probably of brick with a diameter of 46 ft. 7 in. The oval dome at Pisa is no wider than the nave, 40 ft. or a little more ; the irregular hexagonal dome of Siena measures 55 ft. one way by barely 50 the other. None of these reach the dimensions of Ely. The idea of vaulting this great void in stone would not have commended itself to Alan : the thing was too great : nor would the support given by the converging walls of nave, choir, and transepts, cut up as they are by arcade, triforium and clerestory, have sufficed for so great a strain. The octagon at Ely therefore is covered by a wooden construction, of admirable design. Alan was no doubt familiar with the vaults of the octagonal chapter-houses at Lincoln and Ely, and they gave the suggestion for his great covering. Referring to the plan of a chapter-house vault given above (Fig. 134, p. 40) it will be seen that the ribs springing from the sides and centre meet on a ridge BCH, which is an octagonal ring set obliquely to the octagon of the walls. This construction, so far, was copied by Alan of Walsingham in wood, omitting all the structure inside the inner octagon, which may be regarded as the ring of a dome on pendentives. On this ring he erected his lantern stage with large windows to light the centre of the church, and covered it with lead. The ribbed pendentives, if we may so call them, are not the real construction, but an ornamental clothing concealing vast raking beams of oak that slope up from the angles of the great octagon to

Ely
cathedral
choir

Fig. 150. (*From* Fergusson.)

5—2

Ely
cathedral.
The
octagon

the angles of the octagonal ring on which the lantern rests. The whole of England we are told was searched for timber big enough for these mighty props, which was found with difficulty. The construction is curiously simple, almost primitive, but it promises to last as long as these great timbers themselves remain sound.

The octagon is said to have been finished in 1342, and the rebuilding of the ruined part of the choir soon after. The strain on the funds of the Abbey caused by this disastrous event did not interrupt the work in the Lady Chapel, which went on through the period of rebuilding. But the artist employed on the Lady Chapel cannot have had much to do with the ornamental details of the octagon, which are not very happy: the niches and corbels at the angles seem out of place, and the pedimented panels below the windows are ill-composed and unmeaning.

The choir

The three western bays of the choir which had been ruined by the fall of the tower and were rebuilt together with the octagon are much happier in their details (Fig. 150). Indeed the dainty traceries of the triforium and clerestory and the delicate ornamentation of the several parts are worthy of the companion work in the Lady Chapel, to which however they bear so little resemblance that they cannot be by the same hand. The traceries are of a peculiarly light and airy kind that is characteristic of the eastern counties, as at Little Dunmow and later at Dedham. At the same time the proportions of this part are rather squat and unsatisfactory, the levels being given by the presbytery eastward, which is in an earlier and different style.

Lincoln
cathedral

LINCOLN cathedral has some beautiful 14th century work, dating from the first half of that period. The fine

Plate XCIX

Sept. 18. 1860
J. S. J.

S. DAVID'S—Chimney in the Bishop's Palace

rose window of the south transept,—the Bishop's Eye,— Lincoln cathedral has been mentioned already. It dates probably from the first quarter of the 14th century (Plate LXXXII, p. 11 *sup.*). To the same period belong the choir screen, with its ogee canopy work resembling that at Southwell, and some other work of the same character at the west end under the south-west tower.

The work of Bishop Gower at S. DAVID's (1328— The palace at S. David's 1347) strikes rather a new note. In the palace which he built in that romantic dell which harbours the cathedral and S. Mary's college, as well as the group of prebendal houses, we have one of the rare instances of polychrome masonry on this side of the Alps. The Poly-chrome masonry palace, now roofless and ruined, when perfect must have been a particularly charming and original piece of mediaeval domestic architecture. Two great halls and a chapel with state apartments, and other smaller buildings for the offices, are grouped irregularly round a quadrangle, on the bank of the little river Alan which washes the walls on one side. The high pitched roofs have disappeared. They rose behind a massive embattled parapet pierced by open arcading, through the openings of which the roof descended; a singular feature, which occurs also in Bishop Gower's other houses at Lamphey and Swansea.

It is in this parapet that the polychrome decoration appears. It is faced with chequers of yellow freestone and purple stone from Caerfai on the neighbouring coast, with delightful effect (Plate XCIX)[1]. Whether any similar work was used elsewhere is doubtful: I think the rough walling was probably plastered: but the purple

---

[1] This chimney unhappily no longer exists. It fell, as my friend the late Dean Allen told me, in 1871 or 1872.

S. David's stone used in dressings to the windows and doorways is
The effective. The design of the main entrance to the King's
palace
porch Hall is graceful and characteristic of the period (Fig. 151)
and there is a pretty rose window in the gable end of
that chamber.

Fig. 151.

S. David's Bishop Gower lies in an altar tomb in a small chantry
cathedral.
The choir under the south end of the beautiful screen which he
screen erected between the nave and choir (Plate C). All
the work done for him at S. David's is marked by a

Plate C

T. G. J.   S. DAVID'S CATHEDRAL—Bishop Gower's Screen and Tomb

Plate CI

WINCHESTER CATHEDRAL—The Retro-choir

strong individuality, and has a singular grace of line and composition.

The Decorated work at WINCHESTER begins with the splendid stalls, which in style belong rather to the Edwardian Gothic of the end of the 13th century. They are among the earliest, and certainly among the best examples of mediaeval joinery in this or any country. The extremely beautiful canopied niches at the back of the feretory[1], which date from about 1320, resemble somewhat those of the Lady Chapel at Ely, with which they are contemporary. English Gothic is here at its very best (Plate CI). There are nine niches, originally holding two statues each of local saints, kings, and bishops, whose names are inscribed on the string below. In the centre of the wall is a small door leading to a chamber, generally known as the Holy Hole, where were deposited the saintly relics (*merita*)[2], its purpose being explained by two rhyming hexameters inscribed in fine Lombardic characters :—

CORPORA SANCTORVM SVNT HIC IN PACE SEPVLTA
EX QVORVM MERITIS FVLGENT MIRACVLA MVLTA.

At this period also the choir was rebuilt. The Norman choir ended in an apse beyond which was a narrower lady chapel. On the walls of this chapel De Lucy had based the piers of his retro-choir, which consequently

Marginal notes:
Winchester. The stalls

The feretory screen

The new choir

---

[1] The word "feretory," originally meaning a portable shrine, came to be applied to the chamber or chapel where such things were kept.

[2] Meritum. *Corpus alicujus sancti vel illius pars quaelibet.* Ducange. He quotes *fredas* (shrines) *quarum alia habebat merita S. Baudelii martyris, altera vero Pauli.* Also *Les merita d'une des onze mille vierges.* So in the mosaic at Parenzo we read

hoc fuit imprimis templum quassante ruina

     *   *   *

sed meritis tantum pendebant putria tecta.

The relics saved it. *v.* my *Dalmatia*, vol. III. p. 312.

was narrower than the choir. In order therefore to join the new choir to De Lucy's work the two last bays were inclined inwards, the pillars resting partly on the wall of the Norman apse in the crypt, and partly on piers added at the back of it. Although therefore the east wall is flat, and wide enough for a pair of arches below and a large window above, these inclined bays have something of an apsidal character, and the effect is admirable, combining the merits of both forms of termination.

In this new choir the triforium disappears, and its place is taken by prolonging the clerestory stage downwards with a wall passage, much in the same way as in the nave at Bayeux (Fig. 55, vol. I, p. 142). And this absorption of one of the three storeys, reducing the bay to two storeys only, became fashionable in Decorated and later work. In the choir at WELLS (Plate CII) the triforium is absorbed by the arcade ; in the choirs of Lichfield, Melrose, and Selby by the clerestory. In the Perpendicular nave of Winchester it is represented by a sort of balcony (v. Fig. 169 *inf.*) and in later buildings like Bath abbey it disappears entirely.

The triforium in fact comes to an end at this period, and its history is complete[1]. In the Early Basilican churches of Rome and Italy, which were not vaulted, there was a blank wall between the arcade and the clerestory, corresponding to the pitch of the aisle roof. This space was often decorated, and at S. Apollinare

---

[1] The derivation of the word *triforium* is hopelessly obscure. It is of ancient use. Ducange quotes from Gervais's account of Canterbury "*via quae triforium appellatur.*" He derives it from the triple opening formed by two colonnettes which *trinas fores seu aperturas praeferunt.* But a triple opening is not a very common form of triforium and the word is only found in old writers with reference to Canterbury, where the openings are by two and two (*v. New English Dictionary*). Viollet-le-Duc says it was brought into modern use by English archaeologists, *Dict. Rais.* vol. IX.

Plate CII

WELLS CATHEDRAL—The Choir

nuovo, Ravenna, is filled with the two processions of male and female saints in mosaic. When the builders arrived at vaulting the aisles this space, having little to carry because relieved by the clerestory window above, could safely be pierced (*traforato*) by openings, and became a triforium as at Caen (Fig. 14, vol. I. p. 42) lighting the space over the aisle. At Senlis, Noyon, Paris, and elsewhere this ceased to be a mere triforium, and became a gallery with a real triforium above it, thus making a bay of four storeys instead of three (*v.* vol. I. Plates II, VIII, and Fig. 30, p. 81). The next step was to give up the gallery, and the three-storey plan reappears at Chartres (Fig. 40, vol. I. p. 100), Reims, and Amiens (Plate XXX).

In England the three-storey plan had always been the rule, as at Canterbury (Fig. 78, vol. I. p. 192), Lincoln (Plate LXVI, vol. I. p. 202), and Wells (Plate LIX, vol. I. p. 185), for with us the four-storey plan never obtained.

The space for the triforium being given by the pitch of the aisle roof, when the aisle roofs became flatter the opportunity for a triforium diminished, and we get first the arrangement in the choirs at Lichfield, Selby, and Winchester, where it is absorbed by a prolongation downwards of the clerestory with an open passage below it passing through the piers, and finally the triforium disappears altogether.

The cathedral of BRISTOL has neither triforium nor clerestory ; the usual three-storey plan is abandoned entirely, and we have a choir and presbytery of three parallel and nearly equal naves, like the cathedral of Poitiers (Plate XLVI, vol. I. p. 165) or the hall churches of Germany. The eastern limb and transept alone were

Bristol
cathedral

included in Abbot Knowles's rebuilding, which began in 1306 : westward remained the Norman nave till its destruction after the dissolution of the monastery[1].

The aisle
vaults

Abbot Knowles's central vault, being much wider than those of the aisles, has its superior thrust ingeniously encountered by skeleton arches across the aisle, carrying a horizontal strut which abuts against lofty buttresses of plain masonry outside. The aisle vault is divided into two spans, their central springing being over the point of the skeleton arch, at the point where it might have risen under pressure. The result is not only scientific but picturesque and original (Fig. 152). By this arrangement great height is given to the arches, which reach from the floor to the top of the vault, no less than 52 ft., and the aisle windows reach as high, lighting the central nave so well that the clerestory is not missed.

The
decorated
ball-flower

The south aisle of Gloucester nave, built in 1318, retains more of the Geometrical character in its window traceries. They are be-jewelled with the Decorated ball-flower, an ornament particularly favoured in the western district. The windows at Ledbury, illustrated above (Fig. 133, p. 33), are full of it and so is the magnificent south aisle of the great church at Leominster. It studs the niches of S. Mary's steeple at Oxford, and occurs in that of Ashbourne in Derbyshire, but the west country seems to be its native place. It is a purely English ornament : I am not aware of a single example of it on the continent. The same may almost be said of the

The
English
dog-tooth

dog-tooth ; the nail-head is common enough abroad, but it was in England that it was glorified into the dog-tooth. I do not remember ever seeing it in France, but I found

---

[1] The present nave and aisles were built by Mr Street between 1868 and 1888 in the style of Abbot Knowles's work.

Bristol
cathedral

Fig. 152.

it, to my surprise, in the doorway of S. Maria at Toscanella, which has in many other respects a curiously English look[1], and it occurs also in the Norman work in Sicily (*v.* Plate CXC, *infra*).

Sculpture in capitals

The capitals of this period have natural foliage, chiefly of vine or maple leaves, generally disposed as wreaths round the bell rather than giving by their upright springing lines the same expression of support as those of the earlier styles. The leaves are much more twisted and bossed, and more crowded on the surface of the bell than those of the 13th century, and in many cases the result is a confused mass in which the structural meaning is lost. Several of them, however, have considerable beauty. Those in the choir at Selby (Plate CIII) are good examples.

Decorated tombs at Westminster

In nothing is the grace of our Decorated style shown better than in the screens and tombs of the period : and of the latter there are no finer examples than the three monuments on the north side of the altar-space at Westminster abbey, to Edmund Crouchback Earl of Lancaster, Aveline his Countess, and Aymer de Valence Earl of Pembroke. They are all surmounted by exquisite canopies, and the niches in the lower part contain beautifully sculptured little figures of mourners. The smallest and simplest is that of Aveline, who died in 1273, a girl of 21. Her husband Edmund Crouchback, brother of Edward I, whom he had accompanied to the Crusades, died in 1296. His tomb is the largest of the three, with a triple canopy. The most beautiful of them all is that

Tomb of Aymer de Valence

of AYMER DE VALENCE (Fig. 153), one of the most exquisite works of English art. Aymer, who played a conspicuous part in the troubled reign of Edward II,

---

[1] *v.* my *Byzantine and Romanesque Architecture*, vol. I. p. 222.

Plate CIII

T. G. J.   SELBY ABBEY—Capital in Choir

SOUTH ELEVATION

The Finial, the Pinnacles above a·a, {
the Caps'on the Brackets and
part of the west Buttress b
have been restored

·a.j.s
oct 1892

SCALE OF FEET

Fig. 153.   (From *Spring Gardens sketch book*.)

Tomb of
Aymer de
Valence

was son to William de Valence, half-brother on the mother's side to Henry III, and he died by a somewhat mysterious death in France in 1324.   He lies under a single-arched canopy, beautifully cusped and carved, with brackets from the pediment which have lost their figures of angels holding candlesticks.   In these tombs the effigies are fully in the round, not flattened at the back as if in relief, like those of Henry III and his daughter-in-law.   In the trefoils of the pediment of both the knights' tombs are figures of the knight himself armed, and with surcoat and housings, riding his war-horse, in the attitude with which we are familiar on the royal seals of the period.   All three tombs were richly decorated with painting and gilding on gesso, in which the armorial bearings were modelled, and with inlays of coloured glass which have now disappeared, though Burges believed he had formerly seen some of them.   As these tombs are on the raised platform of the presbytery they are lifted high above the ambulatory aisle, and the podium on that side is panelled and painted with figure subject now barely intelligible. The tombs have many details in common, and were all probably made at the same time at the opening of the 14th century, and Burges thinks very likely by the same artist[1].   Mr Lethaby suggests Master Michael of Canterbury, *cementarius*, who was then engaged in building S. Stephen's chapel[2].

Decora-
tion with
painting
and gesso

The Percy
tomb,
Beverley

The famous PERCY tomb at BEVERLEY (Plate CIV), a memorial to a Lady Percy who died in 1365, rivals in splendour of sculpture and delicacy of ornament the work in the Lady Chapel at Ely.   The amount of detail in it is astonishing ; every compartment has its figure

[1] *Gleanings*, p. 159, etc.   [2] *Op. cit.* p. 182.

Plate CIV

Percy Tomb
Beverley.
Aug 28. 1914

T. G. J.   BEVERLEY MINSTER—The Percy Tomb

with heraldic achievements, the very cusp-points are The Percy tomb, Beverley finished with hovering angels, other angels stand on brackets like those of Aymer de Valence, and in the apex is a figure of Christ seated and receiving the Lady's soul in a napkin supported by two angels according to the usual convention. The pediments are double, one above the other, and the lower is bowed forward to support the group of figures which fills the space in the apex of the upper. The beauty of the flowing lines thus given, and of the drawing of the cusping is beyond all praise. Attached to it on the east side is a turret with a stair leading to the loft over the screen or reredos.

Earlier in the century the nave at BEVERLEY was Beverley nave built in flowing Decorated work, but the design of the Early English bay (Fig. 97, vol. 1. p. 245) was followed including the curious alternating arcade of the triforium stage, a concession to the style of a preceding period unusual in mediaeval work. The lower stage of the two western towers has arcading of 14th century work, but the upper part of the fine façade and of the towers is Perpendicular.

The Easter sepulchres at HECKINGTON and HAWTON Hecking-ton and Hawton churches belong to the same class of work. The sedilia at the latter place are fine examples of late Decorated Gothic, and the windows show very well the transition from Geometrical to Curvilinear tracery, both systems being apparent in the design.

Vaulting was elaborated during the later Decorated Four-teenth century vaulting period by the continued multiplication of intermediate and lierne ribs, arranged so as to form regular figures, stellar, or square, or lozenge-shaped, as in the choir at Ely (Fig. 154). The intersections were enriched by bosses carved often with singular beauty, though so far away that from the floor their full merit can only be appreciated imperfectly.

Christ-
church
priory

The priory of CHRISTCHURCH in Hampshire has some valuable 14th century work. The massive screen between nave and choir happily escaped destruction at the hands of those whose passion for opening up vistas has done so much mischief. But it suffered considerable injury and defacement to make way for

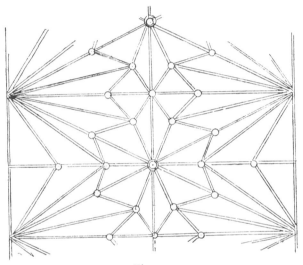

Fig. 154.

pewing during the period when Gothic was in disgrace, and its architectural features now only date from Mr Ferrey's restoration[1]. At the east end of the Perpendicular choir is the earliest of the four examples

The
reredos

in England of a great reredos-screen, the others at Winchester, Southwark, and S. Alban's being all of the

[1] The editors of Mr Ferrey's book claim the strictest accuracy for his restorations. *The Antiquities of the Priory of Christchurch* by Benjamin Ferrey. Edited by E. W. Brayley and J. Britton, 2nd ed., 1841.

Plate CV

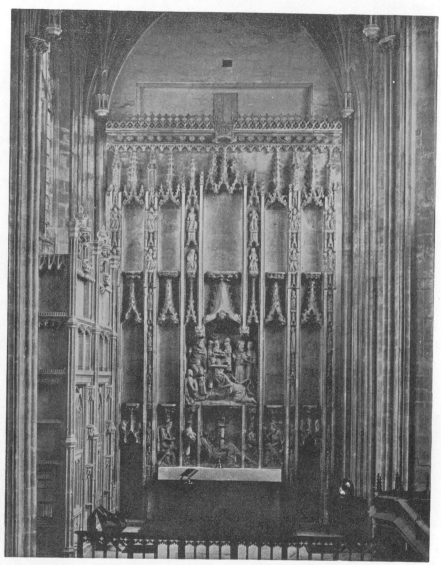

CHRISTCHURCH PRIORY—The Reredos

Perpendicular period. This at Christchurch is a 14th century work, and at the rebuilding of the choir was refixed against the 15th century east wall with iron cramps and very little bond. The sculpture represents the tree of Jesse (Plate CV). There are five compartments in the width, containing niches once filled with large figures, and divided by upright bands or borders containing smaller niches with little figures, most of which remain. A colossal Jesse lies prostrate at the foot, with David and Solomon on the lowest branches right and left. Above is now a group of the Holy Family with the Adoration of the Magi, which seems to be a later insertion, a mullion on each side being cut away to make room for it. This may have happened when the reredos was brought hither and refixed in the 15th century after the rebuilding of the choir. Christ-church priory reredos

The sculpture throughout is rather clumsy, but the lower stage with Jesse, David, and Solomon is better than that above. The latter, however, has been much injured, and when examining it for the purpose of repair I found that the figures of the Virgin and the Infant Saviour and many other parts were largely of plaster very badly modelled[1]. The cresting at the top of the reredos is in a later style, and seems to date from the refixing in the 15th century.

Towards the middle of the 14th century signs begin to appear of a new motive. At LITTLE DUNMOW PRIORY, of which only the south aisle remains, we have a Little Dunmow priory

---

[1] The rusting of the iron cramps had burst the stone and the whole was in some danger. In 1911 these cramps were cut out and replaced by copper, the old stone that was broken was replaced, and the whole is I trust now safe. I had no occasion to introduce any new pieces, and the plaster patches have not been disturbed.

Little
Dunmow
priory forewarning of the coming transition to the last phase of English Gothic (Fig. 155). The work is of that light and airy character which I have noticed already as belonging to the eastern counties; and the scheme of the delicate traceries so much resembles that of the choir at Ely, that there cannot be much difference in their date. The arches of the choir at Ely are depressed and not much above the semi-circle; at Dunmow one window only retains the acutely pointed arch of the earlier period, the others have a broken arch, struck from four centres though without the flowing line of the Tudor arch. In the central three-light window also we have a new motive in the tracery, for though the lights are cusped like the rest the head is filled with perpendicular bars instead of the flowing lines of the other windows, a premonition of the coming change, which indeed had already begun in other parts of the kingdom.

The
English
spire Space will not allow more than a brief notice of one especial glory of English Decorated Gothic. In nothing did we excel more than in our towers and spires. Towers belong more particularly to the next period, and the 13th and 14th centuries were more distinctly famous for their spires. In France, Normandy stands easily foremost in this class of design, and the spires of Coutances, Norrey, Caen, and Caudebec have been illustrated in a former chapter. But in England the spire plays a still greater Its greater
variety part in our church architecture, and is treated with still greater variety. For the two steeples of S. Pierre and S. Sauveur at Caen are alike in all but their height; that of S. Jean had it been finished would have been almost identical with them; and the same design serves for those of Norrey, Bernières, and the rebuilt tower and

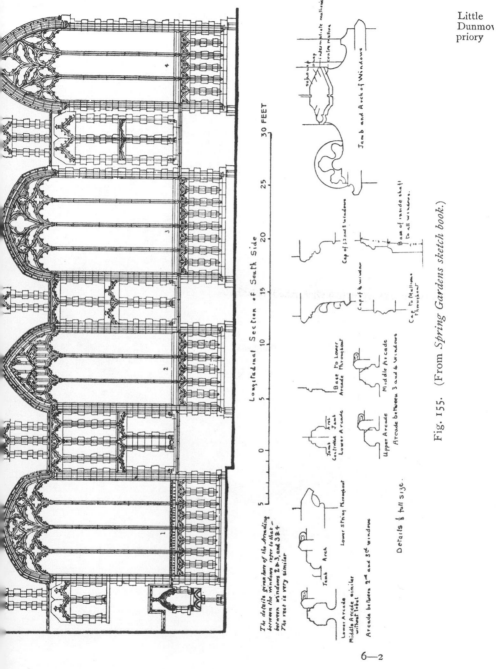

Little
Dunmow
priory

Fig. 155. (From *Spring Gardens sketch book*.)

spire of Bretteville-l'Orgueilleuse. With minor differences they might all six have been built from one set of drawings.

The
timber
spires   The prototype of the spire was a pyramidal roof of timber to protect the interior of the tower and the bells.

Fig. 156.   Fig. 157.

The country-side is still full of timber spires, covered with oak shingles, which give a charm to many a rural village. That at DARENTH is of the simplest type : a mere pyramid (Fig. 156).   That at MERSTHAM is a good example of the next form, where the square is brought to an octagon

Darenth
and
Merstham

Plate CVI

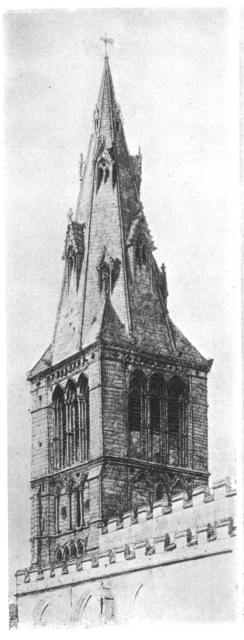

T. G. J.   S. MARY'S, STAMFORD   KETTON

(Fig. 157).   But there were also timber spires on a grand scale, like that which once crowned old S. Paul's, and the fine one covered with lead still existing at Sutton S. Mary. At Merstham the square of the tower is brought into an octagon by broaches, a feature easily constructed in timber : and when the design was translated into stone these broaches were carried by squinch arches across the four angles of the square.   The spires of Seaton, Etton, and Crick have broaches of this kind, based on the timber type.   An obvious improvement was to alter the form of the broach to a gable, which fitted the squinch arch better, and by saving material did not load it so much.   The beautiful spires of S. MARY's at STAMFORD and KETTON, which were added to Early English towers, have broaches of this second form (Plate CVI)[1].   They have spire lights also, to let out the sound of the bells, which reverberates in the hollow pyramid as under a sounding board.

The broach and squinch

Stamford and Ketton

A properly constructed spire, it should be noted, has no thrust, being built with horizontal beds on a system of corbelling, gradually oversailing till the courses meet some way below the apex ; a primeval form of construction as old as the Treasury of Atreus at Mycenae.   Each course being a self-supporting ring, the masonry may be very thin, and toward the summit even of the largest spires it is seldom as much as seven inches in thickness : even at Salisbury it is only nine.   In some cases the angle squinch is replaced by simple corbelling, as at All Saints', Stamford ; but the thrust of a squinch is in most cases practically negligible, for very little of the oblique side of the spire comes beyond the inner face of the tower wall, and the rest has a direct bearing.

Construction of spire

[1] The belfry lights of S. Mary's had originally central colonnettes like those at Ketton.

The tower stair

The regularity of the design is sometimes agreeably broken by enlarging one corner to contain a winding stair, which pushes the belfry window a little on one side, as at S. Mary's, Stamford. Often the stair is made to project a little from the tower as at NORTH LUFFENHAM (Plate CVII). The way in which this is done is generally very ingenious, and always delightful, giving just that amount of variety which relieves but does not mar the simplicity of the design. In structures of this kind outline is everything, and our men seem to have had an unerring eye for a good profile, which enabled them to play these tricks not only without harm, but with positive advantage.

North Luffenham

Angle pinnacles

The broach was before long ornamented with pinnacles, which added weight usefully on the angles of the tower : as at the CATHEDRAL of OXFORD (Fig. 158), and at WITNEY (Fig. 159).

Division of tower and spire

In all these examples the spire occupies the whole area of the tower, the division between the two being marked by dripping eaves with very slight projection, and generally an ornamented cornice or a small corbel course. This line of division, so essential to the logic of construction, is often ignored in continental examples, and its absence is a defect : it is always positively expressed in English steeples as it was also in those of Normandy.

Spires within parapets

The simple broach spire of the type already described is obviously unsuitable on a grand scale ; the effect would be too ponderous, and all our largest spires, at Salisbury, Norwich, Lichfield, Chichester, Grantham, and Newark are set within a parapet, with a walk round them on the top of the tower.

Pinnacles

In order to fill out the outline pinnacles are placed

Plate CVII

North Luffenham
24 aug. 1861.

T. G. J.   NORTH LUFFENHAM

either on the angles of the tower to carry up the lines of the buttresses, or else within the parapet.   At ASHBOURNE there are slender pinnacles set on the broaches of the 14th century spire, to break the angle at which the upright

Ashbourne

Fig. 158.   Fig. 159.

and raking lines come together (Fig. 160).   The corner turret containing the stairs with its spirelet adds a pictur-esquesness to the design[1].   In many cases the number of

[1] In this fine steeple at Ashbourne, "the Pride of the Peak," the squinches are placed unusually high up.   Their general place is in the belfry

pinnacles is doubled, one set being on the angles of the
tower, and a second set within them on the broaches of
the spire.   The richest cluster of spire-pinnacles in the
S. Mary kingdom is that of the church of S. MARY THE VIRGIN
the Virgin,
Oxford at OXFORD (Fig. 161).   Their composition is extremely
complicated, as will be understood from the plans at
various levels shown in Fig. 162, and the design has
successfully challenged and overcome many difficult
problems.   A well designed tower and spire ought to
have a tolerably regular conical and compact outline
from top to bottom, whether seen in direct elevation or
diagonally.   To make it look well from both these points
of view is not easy, for whereas the square tower is half as
wide again when seen diagonally as it is in direct elevation, the octagonal spire remains the same in both aspects.
Usually therefore the angle pinnacles are kept inwards
as much as possible, not exceeding the line of the parapet,
but at S. Mary's the projecting buttresses are boldly run
up outside the parapet and the pinnacles stand upon them.
On the diagonal line therefore the tower and pinnacles
have a width of 41 feet while the spire has only 20.   To
disguise this break-back of 10 feet 6 inches on each side
a massive pier is run backwards from the outer pinnacles, pierced in three cases by a passage, and containing
in the fourth the newel-stair ; and on these piers are set
the upper pinnacles, which are made oblong on the
diagonal line, and furnished also with quaint little triangular spirelets to fill out the profile.   These are so queer
and unusual that one may imagine the architect, looking
at his outline from below, and finding it imperfect, added

stage.   The construction is perilously slight: the wall passage at B leaves
only 18 inches for the outer wall and 14 inches for the inner.   In the late
repairs I found it necessary to wall up the angles.

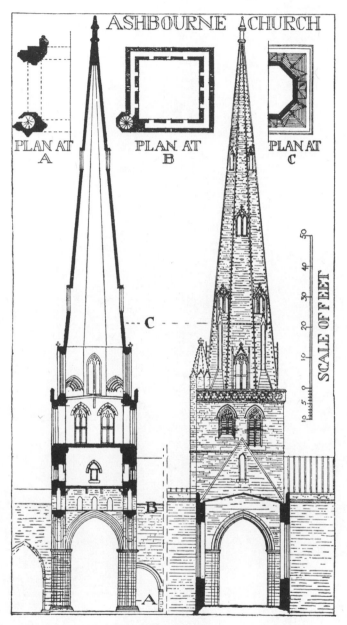

Fig. 160.

S. Mary
the Virgin,
Oxford

North Elevation

Fig. 161.

S. Mary
the Virgin,
Oxford

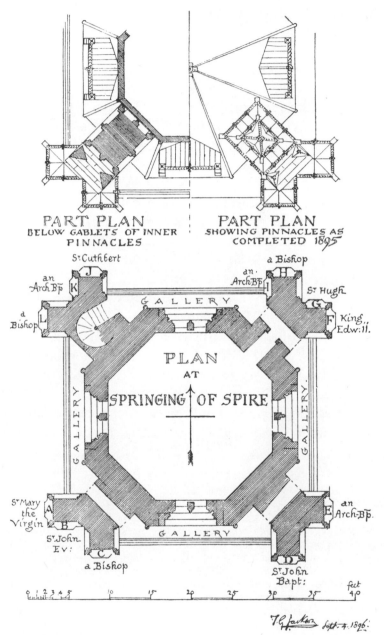

PART PLAN
BELOW GABLETS OF INNER
PINNACLES

PART PLAN
SHOWING PINNACLES AS
COMPLETED 1895

St Cuthbert

an
Arch.Bp

a Bishop

an
Arch.Bp

St Hugh

King
Edw:II.

d
Bishop

PLAN
AT
SPRINGING OF SPIRE

GALLERY

GALLERY

GALLERY

GALLERY

St Mary
the
Virgin

St John
Ev:

a Bishop

an
Arch-Bp.

St John
Bapt:

Fig. 162.

S. Mary
the Virgin,
Oxford them as an afterthought to correct his profile. The result is perfectly successful, and from either point of view there is no more satisfactory composition than this noble steeple[1].

Salisbury
spire The most famous steeple in the kingdom is of course that over the crossing in SALISBURY CATHEDRAL (*v. sup.* Plate LXXII, vol. I. p. 235). The preparation made there is so slight that only a very moderate structure could have been contemplated by Bishop Poore's architect. But in the bishopric of Robert Wyvil (1329—1375), the present lofty tower and spire was placed on these inadequate supports, and it has tried them sorely[2]. Signs Inadequate
supports of failure appeared at once; flying buttresses were thrown across the aisle, and a little later strutting arches were built across the transept arches, but the structure has been a constant source of anxiety ever since. More fortunate however than Beauvais, Salisbury still possesses the steeple which was the creation of this too daring venture. Whether Bishop Wyvil was the proposer of the scheme we know not. Godwin only tells us that he was an unlearned man, and " so unpersonable that if the Pope had seen him he would never have cast so high a dignity upon him." The architect seems to have been Richard de
Farleigh,
architect Richard de Farleigh, who entered into an agreement with the Chapter in 1334 to do all the work at the

[1] Further plans and details will be found in my *History of the Church of S. Mary the Virgin.* (Clarendon Press.)

[2] Mr Thompson of Peterborough, whose firm carried out the work of strengthening the foundations under the late Sir Arthur Blomfield, tells me the weight on the foundation is about 16 tons to the foot superficial, the total weight being about 7,000 tons. The foundation moreover is not good. Price says the footings are on a hard bed of gravel overlying a wet sand (*Observations on the Cathedral Church of Sarum,* 1753). But Sir Arthur Blomfield reported that they do not reach the gravel, but stand on a stratum of clay. The water lies near the surface and sometimes floods the church floor. It has done so this winter, 1914—1915.

Cathedral, notwithstanding his other engagements at the Cathedral of Bath, and the Abbey of Reading, which were not to hinder it. He was to have 6*d.* a day, and 100 marks a year paid quarterly, should he survive Robert the regular master of the works and succeed him as permanent guardian of the fabric[1]. Salisbury spire

As to the beauty of Master Richard's design there cannot be two opinions. The outline is perfect. The diminution of the upper stage of the tower is masterly, and the grouping of the pinnacles at the base of the spire is thoroughly successful. It fits so satisfactorily into the design of the older fabric that it is difficult to imagine the church without it. Some salient central feature must surely have been intended by Bishop Poore's architect, though he made but a poor preparation for it. Westminster and Beverley it is true have nothing in the centre, but they have each a pair of western towers. Salisbury has none, and without a central tower would have been a mere amorphous mass of building. Need of central feature

The subject of spires however might well have a treatise to itself, and it is only possible here to indicate generally the different types under which English spires may be grouped.

[1] Dodsworth's *Salisbury Cathedral.*

CHAPTER XX

ENGLAND.   THE PERPENDICULAR STYLE

French
and
English
14th
century
work con-
trasted

DURING the 14th century, when in England Geometrical Gothic melted into the softer forms of Flowing Decorated, it will be remembered that in France no corresponding change took place : that chapter in the Art is missing and the Geometrical style there continued from the 13th century onwards without any difference, except that it became more thin and mechanical, showing however no disposition to relax its geometrical rigidity.

But in England about the middle of the 14th century, before, as we might imagine, all the resources of Curvilinear Gothic were exhausted, our art underwent

End of
curvilinear
decorated

another and most unexpected change.   The graceful curves of the later Decorated style were abandoned ; the lines of the tracery suddenly stiffened themselves into rigid bars ; verticality superseded a more horizontal treatment ; square panelling took the place of flowing forms in wall decoration, and a certain dry severity extinguished the more genial freedom of the preceding period.

Perpen-
dicular
Gothic
peculiar to
England

The Perpendicular style is peculiar to this country ; for except in the Church of Notre Dame at Calais, which is full of Perpendicular tracery, and was built during English rule, I know no instance of it abroad.   It has been the fashion to decry it as debased Gothic : as Gothic in its decrepitude ; the work of mere mechanical designers,

Plate CVIII

Phot. A. H. Pitcher   GLOUCESTER CATHEDRAL

unworthy successors of the artists to whom we owe
the noble work of the 12th, 13th, and 14th centuries.
That in some respects it declines from the standard of _Its weakness_
Amiens and Westminster may be admitted.   It depends
less on sculptured ornament; its mouldings are less
effective, its details less varied; its panelling is somewhat monotonous, and its traceries are often repeated
till they become commonplace and tiresome.   But to
condemn as a decadent art the style which has given us _Its strength_
the glorious towers of Gloucester, Canterbury, Boston,
Malvern and Magdalen College at Oxford, those that
cluster round the Mendips or stud the vales of Somerset,
the splendid churches of the Fen country, the chapels of
Windsor, of Henry VII at Westminster, and of King's
College at Cambridge, than which one might say architecture can do no more, is surely to trifle with the
subject, and mere pedantry.   The psychological element _Its psycho-logical character_
is no doubt different from that which inspired the earlier
styles.   It is less religious and more secular, like the age
itself in which it prevailed; it is less careful of detail and
more given to broad sweeping effects; it has no mystery,
no depth of symbolism, and appeals to the purely artistic
sense rather than to any hidden meaning: but no style
shows on the one hand a more complete mastery of _Its mastery of technique_
technique, a sounder knowledge of construction, and a
more perfect appreciation of the problems of good
masonry, or on the other a truer sense of the beauty
of outline and composition in the mass.   And to turn to
purely decorative design, we may claim for the woodwork
of this period in screens and stalls an almost unrivalled
excellence, while the painted glass which plays a prominent part in the style is as lovely as any the world has
ever seen.

Various reasons have been suggested for the transition from Flowing Decorated to the Perpendicular style. It has been attempted to trace its origin to the two great events of the time, the Plague and the Hundred Years' War with France. The plague, travelling westward from China, spread round the shores of the Mediterranean in 1348. Boccaccio tells the story of its ravages at Florence, which drove Pampinea, Filomena, and her companions to their country villa and the pleasant distractions of the Decameron. It reached England in August, when the Black Death, as they called it, carried off half the population of London and two-thirds that of Norwich. More than half the entire population of the kingdom was swept away. All classes, noble and gentle, high and low, rich and poor, suffered alike. The convents were depopulated, for the mortality was greater among the monks than among the secular clergy. From that time constant outbreaks of the pestilence occurred during the next three centuries till its final appearance as the Great Plague of London in 1664, when 70,000, or some say 100,000, perished[1]. That this awful visitation must have affected every department of life may readily be understood, and it is suggested that the skilled workmen had been so much reduced in number by the Black Death that architecture declined, and had to adapt itself to a lower standard, which was expressed by the Perpendicular style[2].

This however is begging the question. In the first place the change had begun and made considerable progress before the advent of the plague, and in the next

The Black Death

Perpendicular architecture antecedent to the Plague

[1] Other countries fared no better. At Lyons the plague carried off 60,000 in 1632, and at Naples in 1656 no less, it is said, than 400,000. The great plague at Milan in 1628 forms the theme of Manzoni's novel.

[2] v. *Social England*, vol. II. p. 262.

place the architecture of the 15th century, as I have said already, shows no decline in constructive skill or inventiveness, but rather the reverse.   There was no lack of *Its fertility* life about it : the output of the new style was enormous ; there are very few buildings of the Middle Ages, great or small, which do not show some Perpendicular work in them.   The older churches were enlarged or remodelled in that style; Canterbury received a new nave and tower; Winchester had its nave transformed and its eastern chapels furnished with exquisite woodwork ; Gloucester threw a veil of Perpendicular tracery over the Norman fabric; Peterborough received a new eastern chapel ; new cloisters were built at Gloucester, Worcester, Canterbury and Norwich ; and great parish churches on a scale almost rivalling the minsters rose from their foundations in all parts of the kingdom, especially in the Eastern Counties; for the wars of Edward III in France *Effect of* and his relations with the Low Countries opened that *the French wars on* market to the English woollen trade, and the great *English trade* towns of Norfolk and Suffolk became prosperous centres of commerce.

Great revolutions in art cannot be traced to particular historical events any more than those in politics.   These events only precipitate changes for which society is already ripe.   The advent of Perpendicular architecture was no more due to the French wars or the Black Death than the reformation in Germany to the accident of Luther's picking up a Bible at Erfurt, or that in England to Henry's desire for a change of wives.   It would have come about anyhow for the same reasons that made the *Restlessness of* Early English of Salisbury pass into the Geometrical *Gothic* Decorated of Lincoln, and that in its turn into the Flowing Decorated of Selby and Ely.   It was the genius of Gothic architecture, unlike that of any other style, never to stand still, for it was the faithful reflexion of the society of the day ; and as the modern European world, unlike the ancient world of Egypt and Rome, was constantly changing, advancing, and developing a new character, so the Gothic art in which it found expression was constantly changing too.

Early Gothic in England monastic

English Gothic in its earliest phases had been a monastic art in a greater measure than that of France. In France, as we have already seen, the great burst of cathedral building in the 13th century which gave us the Gothic of Paris, Reims, and Amiens, was an anti-monastic movement, and the work of Secular as opposed to Regular clergy. But in England things were different. Here alone the two were united, and the Archbishop or Bishop was also the Abbot of the monastery, or Head of the Collegiate body. Those great Benedictine convents like Canterbury, Winchester, and Bath, that were attached to a church which was also a cathedral, were governed by a Prior, the Bishop being their real head, and to this day the Bishop of Ely has no throne but sits in what was the Abbot's Stall.

Decay of monasti-cism

But by the middle of the 14th century, when Perpendicular architecture first appeared, the decline of monasticism had set in. Never, we are told, had the spiritual and moral hold of the Church on the nation been less ; never had her wealth been greater. She was attacked from without by the baronage, anxious to seize her riches, and from within by the assaults of Wyclif, not only on her temporal abuses but on the very stronghold of her position, the dogma of transubstantiation itself. The day of monasticism was over, and the Parish clergy rose in esteem in proportion as the Regular orders sank into contempt.

The Monk in Chaucer was a fine gentleman, a sports- Chaucer's Monk
man, with greyhounds "as swift as foul of flight."

> "Of pricking and of hunting for the hare
> Was all his lust, for no cost would he spare."

The Prioress was a lady of fashion, with dainty The Prioress
manners and a brooch with the motto "amor vincit
omnia."

The Friar was a merry soul, "the beste begger in all The Friar
his hous," who would sing and play on a rote, and "lisped
somewhat for his wantonesse."

> "He was an easy man to give penance,
> Ther as he wiste to have a good pitance."

But the poor Parson of the town, on the contrary, was The Parson

> "riche in thought and werk,
> He was also a learned man, a clerk,
> But 'Criste's lore,' and his apostles twelve
> He taught, but first he followed it himself."

A little later when Bishop Fox proposed to found a Bp Fox and Corpus Christi College 1516
house in Oxford for young monks from his monastery
at Winchester, he was dissuaded by his friend Bishop
Oldham of Exeter. "What, my Lord," said he, "shall
we build houses and provide livelihoods for a company
of bussing monks, whose end and fall we ourselves may
live to see? No, no, it is more meet a great deal that we
should have care to provide for the increase of learning,
and for such as who by their learning shall do good in
the Church and Commonwealth." Corpus Christi
College consequently was founded for the education
of the secular clergy.

The tendency thus shown found expression in the Growth of the parish church
architecture of the day. No more conventual churches
were founded, no new cathedral arose, but the parish
church assumed dimensions unknown before. The

great churches of the Eastern Counties, Long Melford, Lavenham, Lowestoft, Lynn, Bury, those of Norwich, the Fen country, Dedham, East Bergholt, the great lantern church at Yeovil, Boston, Wakefield, Coventry, Ashbourne and others on a similarly grand scale, are all in the later Gothic style, some of them larger than many cathedrals, one of them in fact having now attained cathedral rank.

Perpendicular Gothic a secular style
The new style therefore was a secular style, with none of the mystery and symbolism of its predecessors, and with no hieratic pretensions. Why it took that special form which it did is another matter. It arose no doubt from the feeling that the Decorated style had lasted long enough, and that just as at the end of the Romanesque period, and again at that of the Early English style it was time to move on.

We can observe the new motive coming in even as early as 1326 at the east end of WELLS cathedral, where the window is divided in three by two perpendicular mullions running up to the head (v. Plate CII, p. 72). It Its advent at Gloucester seems however to have been at GLOUCESTER that the new pattern first appeared in a definite form. The Abbey had suddenly become rich. In those days the fortune of a monastery depended on the popularity of the local saint. At Canterbury the cathedral was eclipsed by the Abbey of S. Augustine, where the bones of the Roman missionary lay, till the murder of Becket happened as a blessing in disguise to give the monks of Christchurch the most illustrious saint of the Middle Ages. Durham had S. Cuthbert, Ely S. Etheldreda, Winchester S. Swithin, S. Alban's and Bury S. Edmund's had their eponymous saints, York had S. William, Chichester S. Richard, Whitby S. Hilda, Worcester

Plate CIX

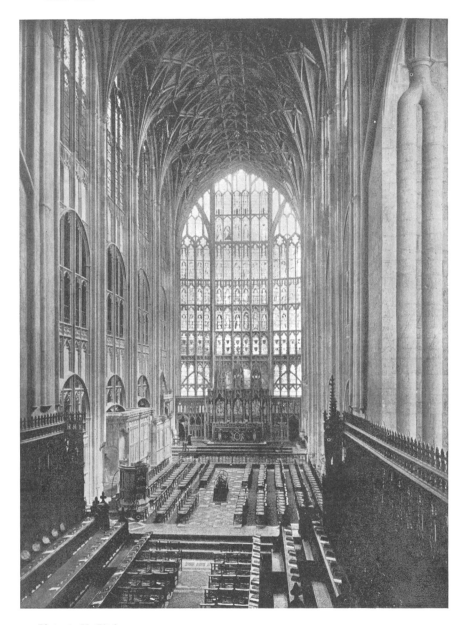

Phot. A. H. Pitcher

GLOUCESTER CATHEDRAL—The Choir

S. Wolfstan, and most of the great churches except Gloucester were well furnished with objects of pilgrimage. When therefore the body of the murdered King Edward II had been refused burial at Malmesbury and Bristol for fear of the Queen and Mortimer, Abbot Thokey (1307—1329) saw his chance, and enshrined him in his Abbey Church at Gloucester. Pilgrims began to flock to the tomb of the Lord's Anointed, miracles were soon forthcoming, and the abbey rapidly grew rich enough to rebuild the whole church had the monks pleased to do so.

Murder of Edward II 1327

Fortunately they did not do this, but set to work to improve the low-arched Norman work of the eastern part by illuminating it with larger windows, raising it much higher, and vaulting it. The south transept was cased lighted and vaulted by Abbot Wygmore between 1327 and 1337 : the choir was raised with a new clerestory, the lower walls encased, and a new east end built before 1377, by Abbot Stanton and his successor Abbot Horton (Plate CIX).

Gloucester cathedral. The new choir

Unlike the nave, which with its lofty columns and small triforium is very different from the general Norman type, the Norman choir at Gloucester has a low arcade and a large triforium, proportioned according to the more usual Norman fashion, like those at Ely, Norwich, Caen, and Walkelyn's work at Winchester. This proportion had long gone out of use, and in Early English and Decorated work the arcade occupied, more or less, half the total height of the bay. As he was told to retain the Norman work, Abbot Stanton's architect had the difficult task of disguising these unfashionable proportions as best he could, and of getting the effect of great height without altering the stumpy arcades of the lower part. He did

The Norman structure retained

it by drawing a veil of tracery work over the whole bay, so as to unite it into one composition and obliterate the horizontal divisions. To do this he cut back to a flat face the outer orders of the Norman arches and the front of the massive round columns, and applied his casing against the new surface so formed (Fig. 163), no doubt bonding

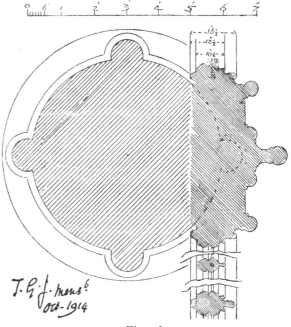

Fig. 163.

his new work to the old, for the new facing at the back of the sunk panels is not a foot thick. Above, he raised a splendid range of four-light clerestory windows, lifting the eastern part of the church to the height of 85 ft. from floor to vault, and 20 ft. above the Norman nave (Fig. 164).

The window mullions are produced downwards to the floor of the church, forming panels where the wall is

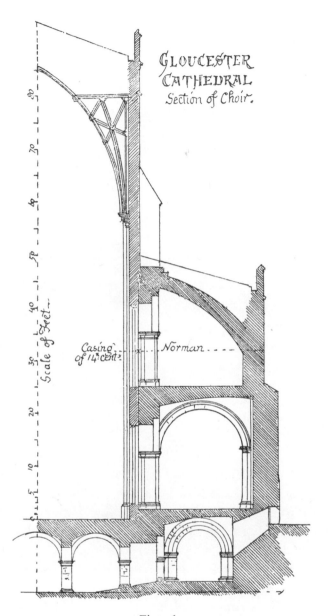

Fig. 164.

solid and open screens where passing in front of the
Norman arches of triforium and arcade.   Triforium and
clerestory had often been combined before, at Selby and
elsewhere, but the arcade had nowhere been united to
them in this manner.   The result is quite successful: you
ignore the stumpy proportions of the Norman work, and
see only the splendid height and soaring lines of pier
and mullion (Plate CIX).   The lofty clerestory is very
light in construction ; the piers between the windows are

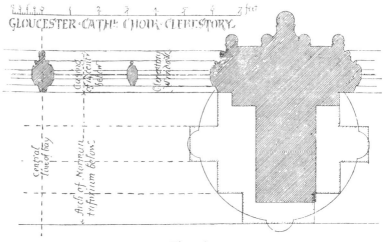

Fig. 165.

comparatively slender, and the vaulting which springs
from them is sustained without any flying buttresses by
simple buttresses of such moderate projection that room
is found for them on the massive wall of the Norman
triforium arcade (Fig. 165).

The east
end
     Not less audacious was the alteration at the east end.
The Norman crypt shows that the plan of the original
apse above was semi-circular.   But apses had long gone
out of fashion, and the typical English east end was

square, with a great east window. How was this to be managed on the rounded Norman foundation ? At Winchester we have seen the same problem solved by canting the last bays of the choir inwards, leaving a narrowed square end, enough for two arches into the retro-choir and a fair-sized window above. At Gloucester the method is something like it, but the whole east end is formed into one gigantic window resting on the outer ambulatory wall. It is divided into three by two massive mullions, or slender piers, with buttresses outside them, and the two side compartments are canted at an angle to accommodate them to the Norman substructure (Plate CVIII, p. 94 *sup.*). The effect of this wall of glass as one comes upon it on passing through the choir screen is astonishing, and the whole choir with its upward soaring lines and the intricate web of the vault has an airy magnificence that is most impressive. It is a real effort of genius. The glass with which this east window is filled is supposed to have been given by Lord Bradeston, governor of Gloucester Castle under Edward III, to commemorate the victorious campaign of Crecy, and especially his friend Sir Maurice de Berkeley, who fell at the siege of Calais. This would fix the date between 1347 and 1350. Lord Bradeston's arms and that of his friend appear in the glass[1]. As Winston observes, the glass is of Decorated character, from which it would appear that architecture progressed more rapidly than painting. The general scheme consists of figures painted on white glass enriched with yellow stain, set on grounds

---

[1] *Account of the Painted Glass in the East Window of Gloucester Cathedral*, by Charles Winston, Esq. *Gloucester Cathedral*, by the Very Rev. Dean Spence-Jones, p. 60. *English Church Architecture*, by E. Bond, vol. II. p. 656.

of ruby alternately with a beautiful blue.   In the side compartments of the tracery is a good deal of white glass in quarries with a simple pattern.   The general effect however wants the luscious glow of the painted glass at Wells.

The vaulting of the remodelled choir, seems to have been finished before 1351.   The idea of enrichment by intermediate and lierne ribs, of which the choir vault in Ely affords an early example (*v. sup.*, Fig. 154, p. 80), here runs

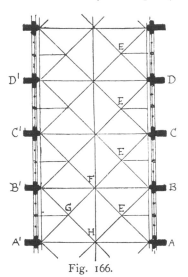

Fig. 166.

riot over the whole surface, forming an intricate network in which at first sight it is not easy to detect any system. Lengthways the vault is really a pointed barrel, for the cross-vaults are much lower, and cut into it like a Welsh vault[1] (*v. sup.* Fig. 164, p. 103). They are generated by making the diagonal traverse two bays instead of one (Fig. 166).   Thus the length of the bays being AB, BC and CD, and the transverse ribs being A.A′, B.B′, and C.C′, the diagonal is laid from A to C′ instead of from A to B′, and from B to D′ instead of from B to C′ and similarly from C to A′, and D to B′.   The points of intersection at E.E.E and those opposite, define the apex of the cross-vaults AEB, etc., and a diamond HEFG is formed on the main ridge uniting the points of the cross-vaults at E and G.   Within these main lines, which however are

[1] For the Welsh vault, *v.* Fig. 8, vol. I. p. 32.

Plate CX

WINCHESTER CATHEDRAL—The Nave Vault

not more strongly expressed than the rest, is a maze of other ribs ; and the effect of laying the diagonals at an angle of 45° to the transverse section instead of an acute angle is to spread the net more evenly over the surface, and make the meshes more open and more equal.

A similar system is adopted in the later roof over the nave at Winchester, though the diagonals do not traverse two bays, but stop on the ridge beyond the transverse line, after crossing one another ; but here too the vault is really a barrel with side vaults at a lower level (Plate CX)[1]. Winchester vault

Henceforth these elaborate lierne vaults prevailed till the end of the Gothic period : they are to be found in Bodley's tower and the proscholium of the old schools at Oxford, and are imitated in the gateways of Wadham College and the other Jacobean Colleges[2] there. The true lierne vaults like those at Gloucester and Winchester are miracles of masonry, needing very accurate jointing at their innumerable points of intersection, and very neat filling in to their innumerable panels. The least movement in the vault disturbed them, and made the shorter liernes, which cannot be very securely keyed, apt to fall out[3]. The junctions were often contrived on a boss, to disguise an awkward angle of intersection, and give opportunity for sculpture, and the wealth and variety of carving in these bosses is amazing.

In the choir and Lady Chapel at CHRISTCHURCH PRIORY, Christchurch priory vaults

[1] At Bitton in Gloucestershire the vault is actually a pointed barrel, on which ribs are traced in relief, merely as ornament.

[2] These latter however are constructed more in the manner of fan-vaulting.

[3] Those in the aisles of Winchester cathedral had become dislocated, and many of the liernes were loose. It was a troublesome task to secure them by wedging and grouting. The choir vault at Gloucester is now (1914) undergoing a similar repair for the same reason.

Christ-
church
priory
where the ribs and liernes form a stellar pattern as at Ely, the main ribs spring from a pendant which is bracketed out from the wall, leaving a narrow space, like a shallow barrel-vault, decorated with quatrefoil panelling, between the longitudinal rib and the wall.

Divinity
School,
Oxford
In the DIVINITY SCHOOL at OXFORD (Plate CXI), the idea goes further.   An arch of strong masonry is thrown across, from which the vault springs at some distance out, the space up to the wall having a narrower vault of its own.   A pendant worked in the solid of the arch marks the common springing of these two vaults.   In
Cathedral
vault,
Oxford
the cathedral at OXFORD the choir vault is similar, but the side spaces have longitudinal barrel-vaults, an amplification of those in the Lady Chapel at Christchurch priory.

Fan-
vaulting
From vaults like these it is but a short step to the fan-vault, the final achievement of the Perpendicular style.   It has been pointed out already (p. 45 *sup*., and vol. I, p. 212) that the English way of laying the ashlars in the panels of the vault resulted naturally in forming a conoid, while the French way preserved the rectangular plan.   The vault of Salisbury chapter house (Plate LXXXV, p. 40 *sup*.) was given as an example.   In the two vaults just described at Oxford there are complete conoids on the pendants of the Divinity School, and half conoids on those of the Cathedral.   In the former we have actually four polygonal conoids in each bay, meeting against a diamond-shaped space in the middle.   Make the conoid circular instead of polygonal and you have the fan.   But this was not all.   It was
Vaults in
solid
ashlar
discovered that the troublesome task of piecing together all the multitude of ribs and liernes might be avoided by simply working rib and panel on the same stone, which

Plate CXI

OXFORD—The Divinity School

Plate CXII

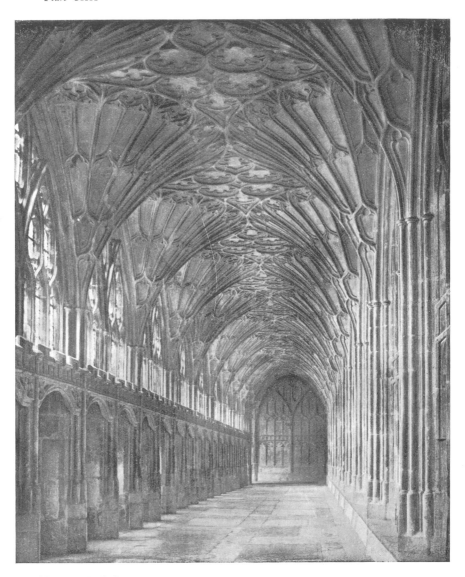

Phot. A. H. Pitcher

GLOUCESTER CATHEDRAL—The Cloister

could be jointed where you pleased in large or small Vaults in solid ashlar
pieces. The vault was thus simplified into a shell of
regular masonry, which might have been left plain and
smooth on the face, but was in fact adorned with sunk
panels and ribs worked in relief, doing nothing constructive but merely decorating the surface.

It was not at Oxford however that fan-vaulting was
invented. It had been done a century earlier at Gloucester, and it is to GLOUCESTER masons again that we
must give the credit of this discovery. The lovely and Gloucester cathedral. Cloisters
unrivalled cloister, begun in 1351 and finished in 1412,
is covered with fan-vaulting from end to end (Plate CXII).
The semi-circular conoids are complete, meeting on a
flat space at the crown, decorated like them with sunk
tracery. The precocity of this invention will be understood if we remember that when these cloisters were
begun in 1351 Geometrical Gothic was still in full swing
abroad, for the choir and transepts in that style at S. Ouen
in Rouen were not finished till 1339, and in England
the Decorated style was still flourishing elsewhere.

The fan-vault did not travel far from Gloucester for
some time. It was not till the end of the 15th century that
Abbot Aston (1438—1471) and Abbot Kirton (1496—
1528) added a retro-choir to their Abbey-church at Peter-borough retro-choir
Peterborough, over which the new type of vault appears.
The Norman apse is round, and fan-vaulting must be
square, so the architect planted two piers at points where
the corners of a square east end would have been, and
turned arches from them to the apse, which gave him the
square plan he wanted. KING'S COLLEGE CHAPEL at King's College Chapel, Cam-bridge
CAMBRIDGE (Plate CXIII), begun in 1447, was originally
intended to have a lierne vault, and the earlier chapels
are actually vaulted in that manner. It was not till 1512

that Provost Hacomblen and Thomas Larke, surveyors of the King's works, entered into a contract for the fan-vault with John Wastell, master-mason of the said works, and Henry Severick, one of the wardens of the same[1]. The fan-vault at S. George's Chapel, Windsor, was finished in 1508, and that of Henry VII's Chapel at Westminster some four years later.   The choir vault at Oxford Cathedral was finished in 1511.

Of these vaults those at Cambridge, Bath Abbey, and Peterborough are the simplest, being the Gloucester cloister vault on a grand scale.   That at Westminster is the most elaborate and wonderful, a masterpiece of construction.   The Windsor vault is almost a barrel-vault with side pockets, and the vault at Oxford Cathedral choir is perhaps the most picturesque and original.

In 1502, when the chapel at Westminster was begun, William and Robert Vertue were the King's chief masons.   William was concerned in the vault at Windsor, and it is probably by him or Robert, who may have been his brother, that the chapel was designed and executed[2].

---

[1] The indenture is given at length in Walpole's *Anecdotes*. The contractors are to " sett up, or cawse to be made and sett up at their own cost and charges, a good, suer, and sufficient vawte for the grete churche there, to be workmanly wrought, made, and sett up after the best handlyng and forme of good workmanship, according to a plat thereof made and signed with the hands of the lords executors to the Kyng of most famous memorye Henry the 7th, whose sowle God pardon."   They were to be paid £100 per severy, i.e. bay.   There are twelve bays—*v*. also Willis and Clark, *Archi-tectural History of Cambridge*, vol. I. p. 479.

[2] The Vertues were also architects of the choir of Bath Abbey with its fan-vault.   Bishop King writes in 1503 to Sir Reginald Bray, " Robert and William Vertu have been here with me that can make unto you Rapport of the state and forwardnes of this oure chirche of bathe.   And also of the vawte devised for the chancelle of the said chirche.   Whereunto they say nowe ther shal be noone so goodely neither in england nor in france.   And therof they make theym fast and sure."—*Proceedings of Somersetshire Archæological and Natural History Society*, 1915.

Plate CXIII

CAMBRIDGE—King's College Chapel

Plate CXIV

WESTMINSTER ABBEY—Vault of Henry VII's Chapel

The construction is very like that of the Divinity School at Oxford, which was finished in 1480. A great stone arch is thrown across the building, and room is got for large clerestory windows by springing the main conoids from pendants some way out from the wall (Plate CXIV). Here however the upper part of the rib is buried in the vault ; at Oxford it is exposed.
Construc-
tion of the
vault

The supports are managed in a highly original way. The outer wall of the aisle consists of a curtain of glass between massive octagonal piers from which flying buttresses spring to strut the high central vault, and the windows between them are broken out into semi-circular bays, in a manner elsewhere confined to domestic work (Fig. 167). The effect is extremely beautiful and original ; the whole chapel is a lantern of glass, and the fairy vault overhead seems to float on air, a gossamer web of unsubstantial intricacy.
Construc-
tion of
supports

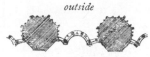

outside

Fig. 167.

The latest great fan-vault is that over the staircase to the Hall at CHRISTCHURCH, OXFORD, which was put up in post-Gothic times, about 1630, by Dr Samuel Fell " with the help of an architect from London of the name of Smith[1]." It is an extremely fine work, and an extraordinary production at that date.
Christ-
church,
Oxford

We must not leave this subject without mention of the exquisite fan-vaults on a miniature scale in the oriels of College Halls, and those at Eltham, those over the chantries at Winchester, Bath, and Christchurch Priory, and over the tombs at Tewkesbury Abbey.
Miniature
fan-vaults

[1] Ingram's *Memorials of Oxford*; Anthony Wood, *Colleges and Halls*, p. 456, ed. Gutch ; Peshall's *City of Oxford*, p. 126, " He (Dr Fell) made it as it is now by the help of —— *Smith*, an artificer from *London*, and built the most exquisite Arch that now is."

CHAPTER XXI

ENGLAND. THE PERPENDICULAR STYLE, *continued*

Win-
chester
cathedral.
Bishop
Edyngton

IF the Perpendicular style began at Gloucester it appeared almost at the same time throughout England. Bishop Edyngton of WINCHESTER in 1345 pulled down his Norman front, set it back forty feet, and on the back wall of the Norman towers raised the present west façade, at the same time remodelling in the new style two bays of the nave on the north side and one on the south. In the new façade, which with its nave gable between two slender turrets and its low aisles has a parochial rather than a cathedral air, the new style is already fully developed. The great west window is divided like that at Gloucester, with which it is contemporary, by two massive mullions into three compartments of three lights each. The mullions are steadied by three transoms in the side compartments and four in the middle one. All the tracery bars are severely rigid and upright, forming rectangular panels with cusped heads: the great order alone throws off an arch over the three side lights.

Develop-
ment of
perpen-
dicular
tracery

It is interesting to trace the steps by which flowing tracery gradually stiffened into the Perpendicular bar. We see the new type in its origin at GLOUCESTER in Abbot Wygmore's south transept window of 1330—1337, where there still are curvilinear forms in the tracery, but where the upright bar B of the second order penetrates the arched rib of the main order A, and runs up into the head (Fig. 168).   In the windows of the choir clerestory (1351) there still are faint traces of the flowing line.   The clerestory windows of the Presbytery at York (1361) still have some openings in the head which incline outwards from the centre (Fig. 98, vol. I. p. 253), like the foliations of the west window, but those of the choir next to them (1380), and evidently intended, as Prof. Willis observes, to be like them, have all the mullions

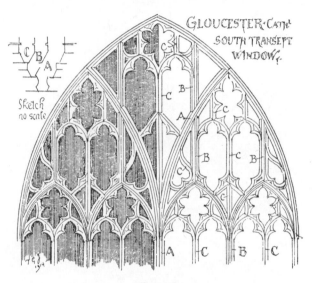

Fig. 168.

and panels upright.   The great east window also, though the mullions in the tracery are upright, has faint lingering traces of flowing lines between them.

Bishop Edyngton's intended reconstruction of the nave at WINCHESTER was interrupted by his death, and it was left to be continued by his successor, William of Wykeham, in 1366.   The problem was to do what had been done by William of Sens at Canterbury, that is to substitute a lofty arcade and a small triforium for the low Norman arches with a triforium almost of the same size.   What the Norman nave was like may be seen in the existing Norman transepts.   At Canterbury a clean sweep was made of the old building, but at Winchester the Norman fabric still remains under a disguise, as it does in the choir of Gloucester.   What

Fig. 169.

was done for William of Wykeham, by his master-mason William Wynford, was to cut out the Norman arches of the lower storey, throwing it and the triforium into one, to vault the aisles at the higher level of the new arcade, to substitute a vault over the nave for the Norman ceiling of wood, and to remodel the clerestory (Fig. 169).   The triforium is represented by a balcony

with two doors to the aisle roof space.   Behind it the
arch of the Norman triforium remains, and in some
parts of the church behind the vault may still be seen
the Norman pilasters that ran up to carry the tiebeams
of the former wooden ceiling.   The piers were at first
simply pared down to the new section, and towards the
west end of the nave the wide mortar joints of the
Norman masons remain up to where the Norman arches
started.   For some reason this plan was not continued,
and the other piers were re-cased.   The result is that
the piers retain their robust Norman proportion; and
this gives the nave of Winchester a character of massive
grandeur beyond any other of the same period, raising
it far above the Perpendicular nave at Canterbury which
was rebuilt at the same time.   There is no interior
in England more dignified and impressive than this
splendid nave.

About early Perpendicular work there is a certain
harshness, and a flavour of dry severity that produces
a curious sensation when contrasted with that of the
preceding periods.   The work done under Abbots
Stanton and Horton at Gloucester reminds one of a
whiff of east wind or a sip of dry sherry.   It is as if
the artists, satisfied with the luscious beauty of flowing
Decorated, had turned away from it in weariness, and
taken refuge in an ascetic negation of anything but
hard straight lines, sharp-cut mouldings, and purely
conventional and rather mechanical ornament.

Sculpture during this period is comparatively rare,
and though niches were used as decorative features they
were not always filled with figures.   HENRY VII's
CHAPEL however was well furnished with imagery; the
forty-eight figures of apostles and prophets have vanished

Statuary
in Henry
VII's
chapel

from the outside, but there still remain almost a hundred inside, more, as Professor Lethaby says, than anywhere else in England, after Wells. He attributes them to Master Lawrence Imber and others whose names appear in the accounts, and possibly some may have come from Master Drawsword of York, of whom we have already spoken. They are admirably sculptured and full of life and character, with none of the stiffness of the earlier Gothic schools. Their treatment is somewhat peculiar, and in many of them suggestive of the wood-carver rather than the carver in stone (Plate CXV). Bath Abbey has some good figures in the niches of the side turrets of the west front, though several of the set are sadly wasted away. There are statues also over the gateways of New College at Oxford and Winchester College, but statuary does not play so prominent a part in this as in the earlier styles of Gothic.

Decorative
sculpture
in perpen-
dicular
style

The same may be said of the decorative sculpture. We miss the beautifully foliaged capitals of Stamford (Fig. 138, p. 48 *sup.*) or Southwell (Plate XC, p. 49), or even the later type at Selby (Plate CIII, p. 76). Where foliage was attempted it was poor and insignificant, and the capitals as a rule were moulded, and moulded very simply, with none of the delicate grace of Salisbury or Westminster. At Bath Abbey the

Disap-
pearance
of the
capital

degradation of the capitals goes a step further : they are nearly gone altogether, being represented only by a moulded band round the four cardinal shafts of the clustered pier, while the intermediate mouldings run continuously from the pier upwards round the arch. Lastly, even this pretence of a capital vanishes, and the arch-moulding runs down without interruption to the base of the pier. In other features of the design the

S. MATTHEW

S. JOHN

S. ANTONY

W. S. *Weatherley*

WESTMINSTER ABBEY—Figures in Henry VII's Chapel

ornament was generally architectural, consisting of panelling with flat traceries; and on wall and screen, bench-end and pulpit, we have repetitions of the perpendicular windows, and miniature imitations of the buttresses and battlementing of the main structure. At the same time it is wonderful what a degree of splendour was attained in the interior by these simple means. The nave of LAVENHAM Church in Suffolk (Fig. 170) is a good example of what was done in this way with merely conventional forms and geometrical figures. That of Saffron Walden is something like it, and might be by the same architect. The neighbouring church of Long Melford is still more striking, and its long flank with the range of nineteen tall windows in the aisle and as many in the clerestory above is extraordinarily fine. At this church, and also in the grand church of S. Mary Redcliffe at Bristol, the wall below the clerestory is panelled like Gloucester choir by running the mullions of the clerestory windows down upon the back of the main arcade. At Bristol these panels are subdivided by a mullion and tracery. There is the same treatment in the churches of S. Michael and Holy Trinity at Coventry. The two great churches of S. James and S. Mary at Bury have enormously high aisles and arcades, with large side windows and a small clerestory, and without any positive ornament are extremely impressive.

In many parts of England flint from the local chalk formation suggested a very interesting form of polychrome decoration. The churches of Norfolk and Suffolk are full of it. At LONG MELFORD the whole of the south side is ornamented with flint inlay in geometrical patterns (Fig. 171), and the parapets have the names of benefactors worked in it on a frieze from

[margin notes:] Conventional ornament

Lavenham

Long Melford

S. Mary Redcliffe, Bristol

Bury S. Edmund's

Polychrome decoration in flint work

Long Melford

Lavenham
church

Fig. 170.

Long
Melford
church

Fig. 171.

Lavenham end to end of the building. At LAVENHAM the chapel built by the great family of Spring, rich clothiers who allied themselves with the noble Veres, bears their names interspersed with arabesques, sunk and filled in with flint chips in the same way (Fig. 172). A still

Ipswich. S. Laurence richer example is the tower of S. Laurence's church at IPSWICH, which is covered with this polychrome

Fig. 172.

decoration, and bears the initials of the Saint (Fig. 173). Though East Anglia is the principal scene of flint inlay, it occurs also in Surrey and Devonshire, and other parts of England where the chalk formation exists.

The English wooden roofs
Except in larger buildings the churches of this period had no vaults, for which indeed their slender construction was unfitted. S. MARY REDCLIFFE is exceptional; it is on the scale of a cathedral, and vaulted throughout with

Ipswich.
S. Lau-
rence

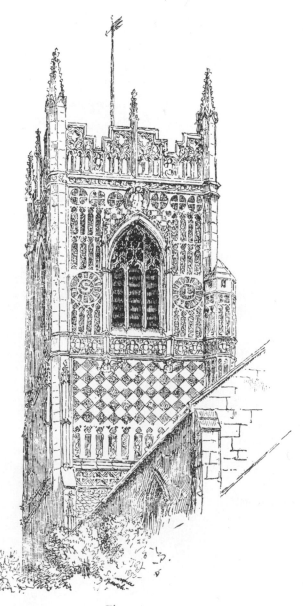

Fig. 173.

regular flying buttresses.   But as a rule the Perpendicular church has a wooden roof.   This was in fact a reversion to the basilican type of S. Apollinare Nuovo and S. Clemente.   In many cases, as at Long Melford, there was no chancel arch, but the roof ran unbroken from end to end, the chancel being defined by screens, and perhaps by a wider pier to receive the rood-loft, which is a remarkable feature of 15th century church architecture.

These English roofs are triumphs of carpentry, and may well be set against the vault which is common abroad, even in the smaller churches.   They are moulded and enriched with traceries and figures of saints and angels, and often painted and gilt.   East Anglia in particular abounds in magnificent roofs of

this period.   The grandest of all, and indeed incomparably the finest wooden roof ever constructed, is that put over Rufus's HALL at WESTMINSTER[1], in the time of Richard II, between 1394 and 1398 (Plate CXVI). Professor Lethaby believes it to be the work of Master Hugh Herland, one of the King's carpenters[2].   The construction is of a mixed kind.   Like the vault of the Divinity School at Oxford (Plate CXI, p. 108 *sup.*), it has a strong arched rib, which gives the main support, from which subsidiary arches spring with framing to carry the gabled roof.   On so gigantic a scale no timber construction by itself would suffice, and there are strong buttresses outside each truss.

[1] The dimensions of the Hall, perhaps the largest in Europe without central supports, are given by Fergusson as 239 ft × 68 ft.   Fabyan says Rufus on seeing it for the first time was "therewith discontented y^t it was so lytle."— Matthew Paris says "Cum alii eam dixissent magnam nimis esse et aequo majorem, dixit Rex eam debitae magnitudinis dimidia parte carere, nec eam esse nisi thalamum ad palatium quod erat facturus."—*v.* Britton and Brayley, *Palace of Westminster*, p. 17.

[2] *Westminster Abbey and Craftsman*, p. 217.

Plate CXVI

From Brayley and Britton

WESTMINSTER HALL—South end in 1834

Here we are introduced to the hammer-beam, an The hammer-beam
imperfect tiebeam of which the middle part has been
removed. All sound carpentry depends on triangulation,
the triangle being an unalterable figure, and therefore
the only perfect roof is that which has a tiebeam from
wall to wall, held up in the middle by a king-post to
prevent it from sagging by its own weight (Fig. 174A).
But the tiebeam is often inconvenient ; it demands very
long and large timbers, and in a church or hall cuts
awkwardly across the great end windows.   The
problem was how to omit it and yet keep the roof in
shape, for if you remove the base of the triangle the
sides tend to spread, and unless the walls are of
monstrous thickness, push them over.   Every other
form of roof-construction therefore is a device to do in
a complex way what was done in the simplest way by a
tiebeam ; or in other words a device to contain the thrust
of the disconnected sides of the triangle so that moderate
walls should suffice.   None of them do this perfectly ;
all have some points of weakness, and most of them need
some external support.

Thrust was not the only difficulty: the rafters, untied The trussed rafter roof
at the base, tend not only to spread but to bend under
their load, and they need support.   Fig. 174C shows a
form of roof common in country churches.   The rafters
are supported by the collar and the braces, which also
hold them together.   Here the strength obviously
depends on the tenons and pins where the timbers
meet, and when they give way, as they often do, the
rafters spread, and pivoting on the short ashlar kick up
from the plate, and the roof becomes in danger[1].

[1] I have known many instances of this.   The remedy is to draw the rafter
foot back by bolts to the inner plate.   For the unprofessional reader I must

English
wooden
roofs

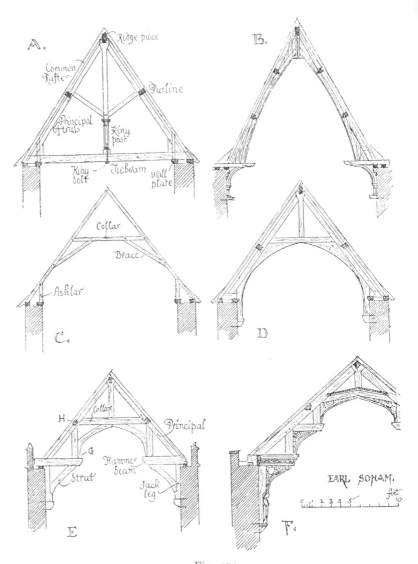

Fig. 174.

The transept roof at ELY (Fig. 174 B) has the principal rafter strengthened by a curved timber below it, to receive which at the foot a pad-piece is run out on the plate, and is itself supported by a strut from below. Here the principal is stiffened, but it is obvious that nothing is done to confine the thrust, and the roof only stands safely because it rests on a very massive Norman wall; otherwise it would open from the apex where is the hinge. Another expedient is by means of curved braces to bring the thrust lower down the wall where it is less likely to yield (Fig. 174D). The hall at the Hospital of S. Cross has a roof of this kind. Here again everything depends on the tenon and pin holding good, instead of on the tensile strength of the timber as in the tiebeam.

The hammer-beam roof was an improvement on this (Fig. 174 E). The hammer-beam may be regarded as an imperfect tiebeam, of which the middle part is removed. The principal framed into it tends to drive it outwards, but this is resisted by the strut below, which presses firmly against the jack-leg, and so brings the thrust lower down the wall, where superior weight comes into play to steady it. From the point G, thus fortified, an upright post is framed into the principal, and from it spring curved struts to the collar, which is often hung up by a king-post to the ridge.

The roof of the hall at ELTHAM PALACE (Fig. 175) is a fine example of this construction, and unfortunately also of its defects. The common history of hammer-beam roofs is that the hammer-beam drops under the

explain that in the Roof C every rafter is so framed ; in the others only the trusses are framed, at intervals of 10 or more feet, and the common rafters between are supported by purlines.—v. Fig. 176 inf.

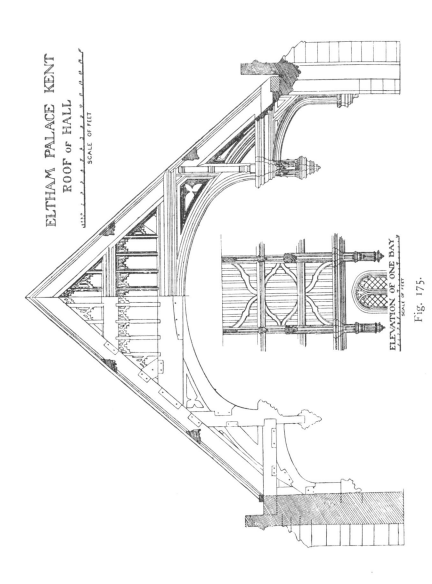

ELTHAM PALACE KENT
ROOF OF HALL
SCALE OF FEET

ELEVATION OF ONE BAY
SCALE OF FEET

Fig. 175.

load at G (Fig. 174E), and the principal bends at the Eltham
Palace
roof point H which is the hinge[1]. This of course involves a disturbance of the wall, and often, as at Eltham, the fracture of the corbel on which the wall timber rests. A hammer-beam roof really needs support almost as much as a vault, and that at Westminster is strongly fortified by flying buttresses. Failing such support, one constantly finds roofs of this kind have had to be tied together by iron rods from side to side of the church. Those that have stood without this aid generally owe their stability to the unusual thickness or strength of the walls.

In the Eastern Counties many church roofs have Earl
Soham more than one tier of hammer-beams, as for instance that at EARL SOHAM, which has however sunk considerably and is secured by iron ties in the manner above indicated (Fig. 174F).

Happily, however, in spite of these inherent weak- Enemies
of wooden
roofs nesses, and of the dangers to which timber is exposed by wet, the larvae of beetles, and attacks from fungus and dry-rot, we have innumerable fine timber roofs in all parts of the kingdom, dating from the Perpendicular period. The Eastern Counties are especially rich in them. One of the finest is that at Wymondham Wymond-
ham (Fig. 176), which is a compromise between a regular hammer-beam roof and one like that at Ely (Fig. 174 B). It has an alternation of main and intermediate trusses, the former, between the clerestory windows, having stronger arched ribs and wall-posts or jack-legs down

---

[1] At Eltham, which I had occasion to repair, the principal timbers were of enormous scantling but they had bent considerably. The pierced casing round the pendants does not now exist. The design is preserved by a drawing of Mr Buckler in 1814, which is reproduced in Garner and Stratton's *Domestic Architecture of England during the Tudor Period.*

Wymond-
ham
church

Crest
of plate

Truss

Purline

Fig. 176.

the wall, which are curtailed in the latter for the window Wymond-ham
head. The projecting pad-pieces that carry the arched
ribs are fashioned into angels; great star-like groups
of leaves cut out of thin boards adorn the meeting of
purline and ridge with the trusses; and the wall-plate is
faced with a crested panel on which are planted angels
with wings displayed. The common rafters are exposed.
MILDENHALL Church has another fine roof of this kind.
The figures that jut out horizontally to carry the arched
trusses are cleverly carved; those in OUTWELL Church Outwell
shew a masterly treatment of the material, unlike what
would have been proper for stone. The wall-plate
here too has angels with wings displayed like that at
Wymondham. The roof of Wolsey's Hall at HAMPTON Hampton Court, 1530
COURT is a magnificent structure, and most of the college
halls at Oxford and Cambridge have fine timber roofs,
that at Christchurch being the grandest. These roofs, Christchurch Hall, Oxford, 1529
with modification of details, continued into the post-
Gothic period, as at Longleat House, Wadham College,
Oxford, and the Hall of the Middle Temple.

It is not only the window tracery that gives the Vertical line insisted on
name Perpendicular to this style; a tendency to insist
on the vertical line runs through all design during the
period. It is enough to compare the upper part of the
south-west tower at Wells, built by Bishop Harewell
(1366—1386), where all the features are vertical, with
Bishop Jocelyn's Early English work below, where the
horizontal line is at least as strongly emphasized as the
vertical (Plate LXXIV, vol. I. p. 239). This too was the
great time for the tower, in which vertical expression The late Gothic tower
is especially wanted, and there are no more successful
towers anywhere than those of England during this
period. It is no easy matter to build a tower with

The late
Gothic
tower

perfection of outline, as anyone who has tried it knows very well.   To profile your buttresses so as to escape a fatal concave, and yet not overdo the delicate convex line ; or if not buttressed to set in the various stages just enough and not too much ; to contrive your pinnacles so as to defeat the dangerous optical illusion that makes them seem to spread outwards, all this demands no little skill, judgment, and experience.   Very few modern towers achieve success in this respect, but the men of the 15th and late 14th centuries had an extraordinary gift that way, and seldom if ever made a mistake.   The

Gloucester
cathedral.
Tower

tower of GLOUCESTER cathedral (Plate CVIII, p. 94, *sup.*) reigns supreme over that noble church.   The upper part above the roof was built in the time of Abbot Seabrook, between 1450 and 1457, the architect, it is said, being Robert Tully, a monk of the abbey, who was afterwards Bishop of S. David's.   His performance is recorded above the western tower arch :—

" Hoc quod digestum specularis opusque politum,
Tullii haec ex onere Seabroke Abbate jubente."

Here the vertical line rules the design with magnificent effect.   The construction is very slight and daring, and the inner leg of the great pinnacles, having no wall to rest on, is carried audaciously on a slender flying rib like those across the north and south tower arches in the choir.

Gloucester is a buttressed tower.   The lovely tower

Mag-
dalen
tower,
1492–1505

of MAGDALEN COLLEGE, Oxford, is unbuttressed but has an octagonal pier projected at each corner, and its perfect outline is secured by delicately setting in the various stages.   Plain below, it gradually increases in splendour as it rises like Giotto's Campanile at Florence ; and the management of the parapet and pinnacles is very happy.

Plate CXVII

CANTERBURY CATHEDRAL—The central Tower

Plate CXVIII

T. G. J.   WELLS—Tower of S. Cuthbert's

Coeval with this was Bell-Harry tower at CANTERBURY (Plate CXVII), which was built by Prior Goldstone in 1495. This, like the last, is unbuttressed, and has projections at the corners : these are strongly marked with upright ribs at the angles, and the vertical line is even more vigorously emphasized than it is at Gloucester. Of the two towers this is rather the higher : as to their comparative merits opinions may differ, but it may safely be said that they need in their own sphere fear no rivals.

Somerset is as famous for towers as Northamptonshire for spires. They cluster thickly round the Mendips, those of Banwell, Cheddar, Chewton Mendip, and Wrington being among the best. There are others not less fine at Evercreech, Ilminster, Leigh on Mendip, Mells, and North Petherton, and two still more magnificent at Glastonbury and Taunton. None however excel that of S. CUTHBERT'S at WELLS, which is designed by a master hand, though Wrington and Evercreech run it very close (Plate CXVIII).

There are many towers of this period elsewhere in England not less remarkable, though the Somerset group form a school by themselves. The twin towers of the west front at YORK (Plate XCVII, p. 63 *sup.*), finished between 1432—1470, are a worthy complement of the design ; and there is a magnificent pair in the west front of Beverley. On the whole the latter façade is perhaps a better composition than that of the metropolitan cathedral. The tower at S. Neot's in Huntingdonshire is good, and also that at Evesham, which formed the gateway to the vanished abbey, and is covered from top to bottom with panelling. One of the grandest, and perhaps the richest of all is at Wrexham, which was finished in 1506. All these show infinite variety in the management of

[margin: Canterbury tower, 1495]

[margin: S. Cuthbert's, Wells]

[margin: York]

[margin: Beverley]

[margin: S. Neot's and Evesham]

[margin: Wrexham]

buttress and pinnacle, and deserve very careful study. There are many graceful Perpendicular spires also, generally set within a parapet between angle pinnacles, from which frequently flying buttresses spring to the spire. That at Louth is perhaps the finest of them, and there is a splendid pair at Coventry, and a pleasing one at All Saints, Stamford.

Louth

15th century glass

The part played by painted glass in Perpendicular architecture is so important that the invention of Perpendicular tracery has been attributed to the desire for upright rectilinear compartments, better suited for single figures than the irregular spaces inclined out of the upright, afforded by the curvilinear windows[1]. The wish for painted glass may have had a great influence on the expansion of windows to receive it, and without painted glass the excess of light in these late churches is troublesome. But the earlier windows are just as suitable for single figures in the lights as the later, and the little figures in the tracery are not important enough to have influenced the architecture. It is more reasonable to suppose the design of the glass adapted to the space it had to fill than the reverse. One concession evidently made to the glass painter is the omission of cusping in the heads of the lights in many churches, as for instance at Hatfield in Yorkshire, for to fit glass nicely into the cusps is troublesome. At Bath Abbey the windows alternately have cusped and un-cusped lights. The glass of this period is extremely beautiful, the painting delicate, the grounds clear and transparent,

---

[1] E. Bond, *Gothic Architecture in England*, p. 491; and *Introduction to English Architecture*, p. 654. Mr Bond suggests that the passion for painted glass in the 15th century caused the design of the tracery to be neglected because the glass obscured any beauty of tracery when seen from inside. But surely it is the outside effect of tracery that matters.

the colouring restrained, the drawing less archaic, and often excellent. The general effect is to subdue glare without darkening the church; the dim religious light of Chartres, Reims, and Canterbury was a thing of the past.

In the 15th century both in England and France *Domestic architecture* domestic buildings first began to play a great part in Gothic architecture. The days of the military strong-hold,—the *château fort*,—were past; the Lord and his Lady no longer lived in gloomy chambers, lit only by a narrow slit except where a tolerable window could safely be opened on an inner court. The Tudor mansions have large mullioned and traceried windows like the churches, for there was but one style in existence, and there was no difference between civil and ecclesiastical architecture: the details were alike in both, and the arrangements were only varied by considerations of convenience. Many of the manor-houses were still moated, as Hever, Igtham Mote, and Kentwell, for the days of private war were not yet quite over; but this slight protection sufficed, and the house could safely be made light and cheerful. After the Reformation the grant of the monastic buildings to private owners occasioned a vast amount of building to convert them into a more habitable form. Palaces of a splendid type began to arise under the Tudor kings; we still have Wolsey's magnificent building at Hampton Court, though the great palace of Henry VIII at Richmond has almost entirely disappeared. Some of the earliest *Oxford and Cambridge* domestic Gothic on a large scale is to be seen at our ancient Schools and Universities, at the Colleges of All Souls, Magdalen, Christ Church, Brasenose and Corpus Christi at Oxford, at the Colleges of Winchester and Eton, and at Queens', Christ's, S. John's, and

The
Tudor
manor-
house

Trinity Colleges at Cambridge. The great manor-houses of the 15th, 16th, and 17th centuries are planned much on the same lines as the colleges, that being the accepted domestic arrangement of the day. They have their great hall with buttery and kitchen, their with-drawing room like the common and combination rooms, generally at the end of the hall; often they have their chapel; and the fine gateways of Trinity, Christ's and S. John's Colleges at Cambridge (Plate CXIX) have their parallel in those of Little Leigh's Priory, Cowdray, Titchfield, Oxburgh, and Layer Marney. Sometimes there is a separate gatehouse in advance of the house, as at Lullingstone in Kent and at Westwood. The whole of England is full of domestic work of the 15th and two succeeding centuries, to an extent that has hardly been realized: in some counties there is hardly a village without its ancient manor-house, great or small, still habitable and inhabited[1].

Interior
decoration
panelling

In the interior greater attention was paid to comfort. Instead of hangings of tapestry, or in humbler dwellings of say or darnix[2] on bare walls, the chambers were lined with panelling in oak, often richly moulded and carved, and decorated with linen-pattern, or medallions of heads

Chimney
pieces

in relief. The fireplaces had fine chimney pieces, often carried up to the ceiling, and adorned with pilasters and heraldry carved and painted[3]. On the outside the

Chimneys

chimneys were treated ornamentally in late Gothic

---

[1] See the fine volumes of Messrs Garner and Stratton, *The Domestic Architecture of England during the Tudor Period*, 2 vols., 1911, and Mr Niven's volumes on *Old Houses in Staffordshire, Warwickshire, and Worcestershire*, and Mr Gotch's *Architecture of the Renaissance in England*.

[2] Darnix is cloth of Tournay.

[3] At Queens' College, Cambridge, in 1531, John Ward is paid xvi^d for eight escutcheons, and Dyrik Harison vj^s viii *pro* 4^{or} *maioribus skochyngis et armis* (Willis and Clark, *Architectural History of Cambridge*, vol II, p. 62).

Plate CXIX

CAMBRIDGE—Gateway of S. John's College

Plate CXX

KNOLE—The Cartoon Gallery

buildings. There is a fine range of them at the Hospital of S. Cross: Preston, near Yeovil, has a good one treated architecturally, and there is another something like it on a cottage at Harringworth in Northamptonshire (Fig. 177.) The later chimneys are of brick, a material which came into general use in the 15th century in those parts of the country like Surrey and Sussex and the Eastern Counties where there is little or no stone, and they are formed into shafts twisted, fluted, and embossed in a variety of ways.

Chimneys

Brick work

Fig. 177.

Ceilings

The ceilings were not neglected, but were enriched with moulded work in plaster. The library and combination room at S. John's College, Cambridge, has a fine ceiling of this kind, the work of an artist named Cobbe, in 1600[1]. There are excellent examples at Knole (Plate CXX). Lord Cobham's steward writes to him to suggest that

> "the plasterer would be sent for to come to bring to y^{r} Lo. modells or paternes of the maner of the sealing that y^{r} Lo. maie make yor choice of that kind of work that shall best like yo^{u}, and some care would be had that he be a good workman and the price reasonable[2]."

The same ceilings are repeated in various parts of England, showing that the plasterer travelled with his patterns from place to place. In the house where I

[1] Payd also unto Cobbe for frettishinge the gallerie and the great chamber 30 li. Willis and Clark, *op. cit.*, vol. II. p. 260.

[2] Paper by Mr Gotch in *The Builder*, Mar. 12, 1892.

write these lines is a ceiling of about 1610 or 1613 which occurs also with little variation at Audley End.

Coming of
the Re-
naissance

Towards the middle of the 16th century we begin to find signs of the coming Renaissance of Classic Architecture.   Foreign artists were invited to England by Henry VIII, as they were to France by Francis I.   In 1512 the king engaged Pietro Torrigiano to make his father's tomb, and Italian work began to catch the English fancy.   The Salisbury Chapel in Christchurch Priory (1541), though Gothic in design, has Italian arabesques in the pilasters and friezes, and they are to be found in the De la Warr tombs at Boxgrove, and in the terra-cotta work at Sutton Place near Guildford. Before long Classic forms invaded the actual structure, and we have Gothic design with Classic details in the Tower of the old Schools at Oxford, and in the great houses at Longleat, Bramshill, Kirby which is the most beautiful of them all (Plate CXXI)[1], Burleigh (Plate CXII) and Audley End.   At Brasenose Chapel

Tenacity
of Gothic
at the Uni-
versities

there are traceried windows between Corinthian pilasters. Gothic tradition died hard at the Universities.   The chapel of Wadham College at Oxford has windows of tolerably correct Perpendicular Gothic, made by John Spicer for so much apiece in 1612[2].   Nevile's Court at Trinity College, Cambridge, which is in a mixed style, dates from the same year, and in 1618 Trinity College, Oxford, began a Gothic Hall only a year before Inigo Jones started building the Banqueting House at Whitehall, in purest Classic.   Twenty-one years later still,

[1] The window in the tower at Kirby is an insertion by Inigo Jones, who also remodelled the wing through which the court is entered.

[2] He was paid £6 for each side window and £20 for the great East window, labour only.   v. my *History of Wadham College*, p. 155.

Plate CXXI

KIRBY HOUSE

Plate CXXII

T. G. J.   BURLEIGH HOUSE

about 1630, Dr Fell put up the Gothic fan-vault over the staircase to the Hall at Christchurch.

In fact the sentiment of Gothic can hardly be said ever to have died out completely in this country. It affected all that was done in the earlier days of the Renaissance. Wren's plan of S. Paul's is a Gothic plan, forced on him by national sentiment, and the beautiful towers and spires with which he and his successors Gibbs, Flitcroft, and others have embellished London are really more Gothic than Classic, and are as alien to Vitruvian rule as Westminster Abbey itself.

Duration of Gothic in England

CHAPTER XXII

FRANCE. THE FLAMBOYANT STYLE

The Flamboyant style

THE last stage in the history of French Gothic is that represented by the Flamboyant style. Throughout the 14th century, a period disastrous in French history, the Geometrical forms of the 13th century continued, and there was no sign of anything like the Flowing Decorated of England. The Lady Chapel of Rouen in 1302, and the eastern part of S. Ouen, built between 1318 and 1339, which are purely Geometrical, are contemporary with Abbot Knowle's choir of Bristol (1306—1332), where Curvilinear tracery is fully developed, and Alan of Walsingham's work at Ely (1321—1349) where it reached its zenith. But towards the end of the 14th century, when in England the graces of the Decorated period had yielded to the more ascetic rule of Perpendicular, France suddenly without any preparation blazed out into flaming lines, and developed the brilliant style which we call Flamboyant, with which French Gothic at last expired in the middle of the 16th century

Its sudden appearance

Its English origin

The suddenness of its appearance, without a transitional stage, naturally suggests adoption from some foreign source, and M. Enlart, M. Colfs, and other writers derive it from English example. This conclusion has been manfully contested, but it is hard to account for the origin of the movement otherwise. The flowing

Plate CXXIII

ABBEVILLE

Plate CXXIV

ROUEN—S. Maclou. West front

ROUEN CATHEDRAL. West front

line, which is the principal elementary idea of the style, Its English origin had been in vogue for at least seventy years with us before its appearance in France; during that period a great part of France had been under English rule, and the intercourse between the two countries, though not always amicable, had been continuous. Many buildings in France had been built by the English; and though, as Viollet-le-Duc observes, the architecture remained French even in the English provinces, it was inevitable that some influence from across the channel should have made itself felt. It was, we know, contrary to the nature of Gothic ever to stand still, and in France the Geometrical style had long outstayed its time. It had French Geometrical exhausted become dull and mechanical; the later buildings of the period suggest weariness and lack of interest; and it is easy to imagine the architects seizing with avidity on the suggestions conveyed by the very different work then running its course in England.

The output of architecture in France during the Fresh life given by Flamboyant disastrous 14th century was very scanty; but with the advent of the new style a fresh building epoch set in, even though the country was still exposed to English aggression, and partly still under English rule. The Flamboyant church at Caudebec was begun in 1426 and S. Maclou at Rouen in 1432, while Normandy was still Advent of Flamboyant English, and the gorgeous church of Notre Dame de l'Epine near Chalons was begun only four years after the battle of Agincourt. When the English had finally been driven out in 1456 the new style spread everywhere; new churches were founded and old ones rebuilt or embellished in all parts of the country; and Flamboyant architecture pervaded the kingdom of France as universally as the Perpendicular style did that of England.

In the lateral chapels of the nave at Coutances, built between 1371 and 1386, in those at Amiens finished in 1375, and at the end of the century in the nave of S. Quentin (Plate LII, vol. I. p. 172), we have the latest French Geometrical Gothic, free from any sign of the coming change. The suddenness with which it did come is remarkable: as early as 1412 we find the Flamboyant style fully developed, and this is the strongest argument for the adoption of the curvilinear motive from outside.

True to national instinct however the new style took from the first a national character, and it is chiefly in the window traceries that it borrowed directly from the English. If the traceries from S. Germain at Amiens (Fig. 178), built early in the 15th century, are compared with those at Selby (Fig. 148, p. 62 *sup.*), which are a century older, it is impossible to doubt whence the inspiration for the French Flamboyant window came. That marked A is actually a version of the Selby window in all its figures, but it is the Selby window spoilt. In purity and delicacy of design the 15th century French tracery will not compare with our 14th century Decorated work. It often deviates into extravagance; sometimes it takes fantastic forms unsuitable to masonry, such as the Fleur-de-Lys traceries, of which Fig. 178 D is an example from the back of the Hôtel de Ville at S. Quentin; at others it lapses into figures that are positively ugly, as in Fig. 178 C and F. Reticulated tracery is common, but the foiled figures are pulled out lengthways as in the example from S. Etienne, Beauvais, (Fig. 178 E), and have not the beauty of that for instance at New Romney (Fig. 142, p. 56 *sup.*).

The character of the mouldings underwent a great

Marginal notes:

End of French Geometrical

Sudden development of Flamboyant

Influence of English tracery

Inferiority of the Flamboyant window

The Fleur-de-Lys tracery

Reticulated tracery

The mouldings

A. S Germain Amiens.

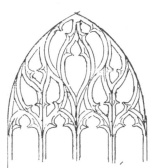

B. S. Germain Amiens

C. S Germain. Amiens.

D. Hôtel de Ville. S. Quentin.

E. S Etienne
Beauvais

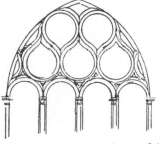

F. S. Etienne. Beauvais.

Fig. 178.

change. At the end of the Geometrical period they had
become thin and reedy, but in the Flamboyant style
they were extraordinarily keen and deeply undercut to

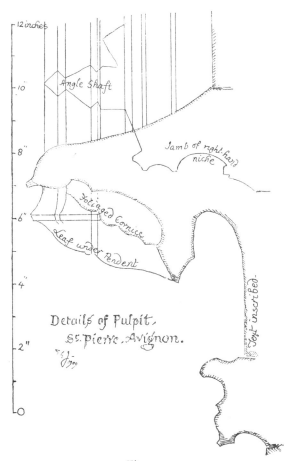

12 inches

10

Angle Shaft

8"

Jamb of right-hand
niche

6"

Foliaged Cornice

Leaf under Pendent

4"

Details of Pulpit,
S⁺ Pierre, Avignon.

Text inscribed.

2"

0

Fig. 179.

give brilliant sharp edges and deep shadows. The
sections (Fig. 179) of the lower cornice of the pulpit at
S. PIERRE, AVIGNON (Plate CXXV), give a good idea
of Flamboyant detail. One can conceive nothing more

Plate CXXV

T. G. J. AVIGNON—Pulpit in S. Pierre

Plate CXXVI

T. G. J.   LISIEUX—S. Jacques

novel or unlike the mouldings of the preceding period, which seldom went beyond a roll on the angle of the order. The treatment of alternate light and shade in moulding of arch and cornice is masterly.

In bases the tendency on the other hand was towards The base simplicity. The scotia of the quasi-attic base never appears, the mouldings are shallow and superficial, the members are elongated and the whole is lifted high above the floor (Fig. 182 *inf.*).

In some particulars the style underwent changes like Disappearance of the capital those already described in our English Perpendicular. The capitals disappeared, and the arch-mouldings were carried without interruption down to the base. The church of S. MACLOU at ROUEN is a good example of Flam- S. Maclou, Rouen boyant architecture in its rather earlier stages (Fig. 180). It was begun about 1432, and the design is of that earlier date, though the church was not finished till the next century. The triforium is united to the clerestory, an arrangement that had now become regular; the windows have flowing tracery of a very good type; the mouldings are sharp and divided by wide and deep hollows, and they run from the arch down the pier to the base without interruption by capital or string-course. The whole is light and elegant, and without any appearance of weakness or insecurity.

The most striking part of S. Maclou however is the The west porch well-known west porch, which indeed quite dominates the façade. It is canted in five bays, to accommodate the plan to the streets adjacent, and this adds much to its picturesqueness[1]. All the resources of the style are lavished upon it, and though the front arches have lost

---

[1] The stone spire is modern. There used to be a pyramidal spire of much less height, of timber slated.

S. Maclou,
Rouen

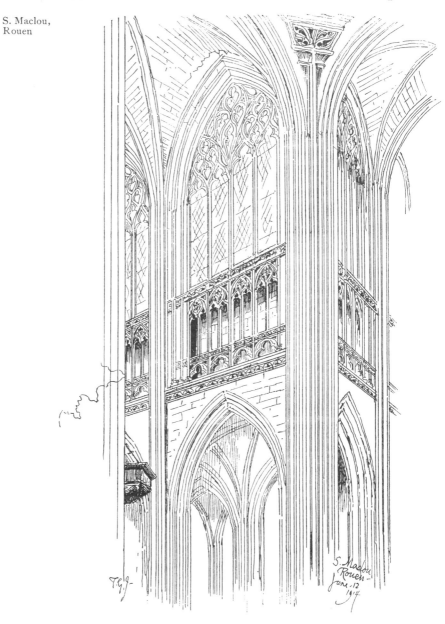

Fig. 180.

their statuary these portals, with their pierced and
traceried pediments, open parapet-work and pinnacles,
have an extraordinary magnificence (Plate CXXIV B).
There are somewhat similar porches, not less splendid,
at Vendôme and Alençon.

There is a tendency in all late styles towards in-

no scale.

Fig. 181.

genuity and clever tricks, often at the expense of more
serious design, and Flamboyant architecture affords
flagrant examples of it. Now was the time for elaborate
problems of interpenetrating mouldings, conceived to
meet and pass through one another, and emerge at the
proper point, which was calculated with the nicest geometrical accuracy. The bases of clustered piers gave

favourable opportunities for display of the mason's cleverness in this field. Those of the piers in S. WUL-FRAN at ABBEVILLE (Fig. 181) afford a good example of these tricks of masonry, but there are many still more curiously ingenious.

The same geometrical problems evidently delighted

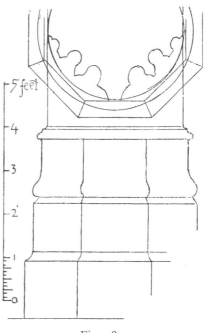

Fig. 182.

the masons at the fine church of S. JACQUES in LISIEUX, where elaborately moulded arches are made to die into or spring from circular columns (Plate CXXVI). The section of the arch may be conceived to lie in embryo within the round pillar, and each rib of the moulding and each hollow that divides rib from rib has to clear itself in turn as the curve of the arch brings it forward, to emerge

Plate CXXVII

T. G. J.   S. LÔ—Interior of East end

Plate CXXVIII

S. OUEN—The Central Tower

from the circular drum of the column, which is continued S. Jacques, Lisieux
vertically (Fig. 182).

This fine church, which is late in the style, is
interesting in many ways.   It is ten bays long, without
transept, the division between nave and choir being
marked only by more massive columns, one on each
side, one of them containing a stair.   The apse has three
cants, and the aisles end square at the chord of the apse.
The vaults are quadripartite.   The triforium as usual is
united to the clerestory, and the clerestory tracery is
devoid of cusping.   The church contains some good late
glass.

The church at S. Lô (Plate CXXVII), which like the S. Lô
last is in Normandy, has a 14th century nave and front
with two towers and spires.   The capitals are poor, like
those at S. Quentin (Plate LII, vol. I. p. 172).   There is
no triforium or clerestory, the aisles being nearly as high
as the nave.   The choir is Flamboyant of the 15th
century; it has a double aisle on each side, continued
round the apse, with very shallow chapels opening from
the outer aisle.   Both aisles are of the same height.
The choir has no triforium, but a wide-pointed clerestory
without tracery.   On the south side the aisle widens out
obliquely, with a side wall all a-skew, following the line
of the street, and this gives room for a fine window
facing east.   The irregularity of the plan causes a
charmingly intricate grouping of pillars, extremely
picturesque and unusual.   The vaults are all quadripartite, with sharply-moulded ribs, and the arch moulds
die into the circular columns in the same way as those
at S. Jacques, Lisieux.

The west front of the cathedral at ROUEN, which Rouen cathedral. West front
finds a place in Turner's illustrations of the rivers of

France, is perhaps the most gorgeous work of the Flamboyant style (Plate CXXIV A).   As at Lincoln the old Romanesque doors remain embedded in later work. Here they are enclosed in the most elaborate screen conceivable of Flamboyant panelling, pediment, pinnacle, tracery, arcading, niches and statuary.   The façade proper covers the width of nave, aisles, and chapels between the buttresses ; but beyond on each side is a tower, which expands the front like that of Wells.   The

Tour S. Romain on the north is Romanesque : the Tour de Beurre on the south is clothed from top to bottom with Flamboyant panelling, niches, and canopies, and finishes with an octagonal pinnacled stage between four tourelles.   The richness of the tower is almost bewildering.   It is perfect in outline, and one of the happiest creations of the style.   Begun by Guillaume Pontifs about 1481, it was finished after his death in 1492 by Jacques Le Roux.

No less splendid is the central tower of S. OUEN (Plate CXXVIII), which however is less happily placed than its rival ; for while that is seen from the ground upwards this stands over the crossing, and from some points of view seems too small for the great church below.   The octagonal stage here plays a more important part than in the Tour de Beurre : it is placed in the same way between four octagonal tourelles, from which flying buttresses are thrown to the eight angles of the lantern.

The cathedral of ALBI, begun about the middle of the 14th century, is a vast pile of brown brick, with bastions for buttresses, externally more like a fortress than a church.   But it has on the south side a very picturesque Flamboyant porch of surprising magnificence,

Plate CXXIX

ALBI CATHEDRAL—The Choir

Plate CXXX

ALBI CATHEDRAL—Side Screen of Choir

and the interior is enriched with painting, and with screens, canopies, carving and statuary almost beyond belief (Plate CXXIX).

The plan is peculiar: it consists really of one vast nave from end to end, vaulted, and with chapels on each side in two storeys, between the great buttresses. The choir is not defined in the main fabric, but formed by screens of elaborate masonry within the nave, leaving a passage on each side by way of aisle between the screens and the side walls. There is a similar arrangement at the interesting church of S. Bertrand de Comminges, on the foot-hills of the Pyrenees, and in the abbey of Moissac.

The screens consist on their inner side of canopied stalls of stonework elaborately carved, and on the outside of panelling and niches filled with excellent statuary (Plate CXXX). The intricacy and delicacy of the Flamboyant crockets is extraordinary: their long wiry thistle leaves interlace and twist over and under one another in a way that speaks volumes for the ingenuity of the carver and his dexterity in stone-cutting, though in spite of all their cleverness they will not bear comparison with the simpler and broader effects of the earlier sculptors (Plate CXXXI).

The crockets at the Hôtel de Cluny in Paris are good examples on a less ambitious scale (Fig. 183A). Another from a house at Chinon is shown in Fig. 183B. In these crockets the foliage is less wiry than that at Albi, which is based on the long, deeply-indented leaves of the thistle or artichoke. But the character of Flamboyant foliage generally is sharp and angular, deeply undercut, and depending on brilliant contrasts of keen and bright outline with black shadows. With

this object the ground is deeply sunk, the leaves are
wide apart, and a great deal is made of the rough

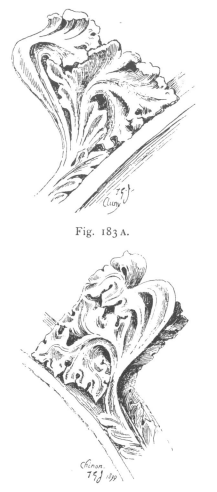

Fig. 183 A.

Fig. 183 B.

Fig. 184.

twisted stems with knots, and angles. The form of the
leaves is of less consequence, and they are often very
Abbeville shapeless, as in the example from ABBEVILLE (Fig. 184),

Plate CXXXI

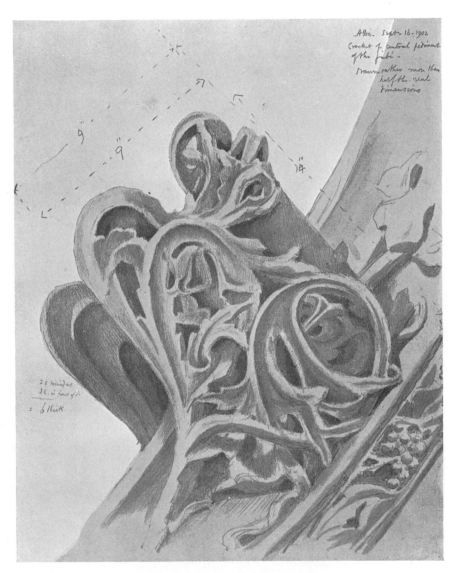

T. G. J.   ALBI CATHEDRAL—Crocket on Jubé

Plate CXXXII

T. G. J.   CHARTRES CATHEDRAL—North-West Steeple

Plate CXXXIII

T. G. J.   CAUDEBEC

where brilliant spots of light between dark shadows was all the carver cared for.

The spires of this style share the general luxuriance. The north-west steeple of the cathedral of CHARTRES, built by Jean Texier of the Beauce and finished in 1512, is a fine composition, ingeniously planned with stages that recede between pinnacles with flying buttresses to fill the outline, which in spite of all this complicated arrangement is well preserved (Plate CXXXII). *Chartres, north-west steeple*

The spire of pierced tracery at CAUDEBEC, if I am not mistaken, has been taken down and rebuilt, but the original design of 1426 is retained. The fluted pyramid, girdled with coronals that cast shadows on the recessed faces, is curious and original (Plate CXXXIII). At NOTRE DAME DE L'EPINE near Chalons is a gorgeous church of Flamboyant architecture, begun in 1419, with two western towers and spires, wonders of rich detail, but not artistically successful. *Caudebec steeple* *Notre Dame de l'Epine*

The fine church of S. Wulfran projected at ABBEVILLE is incomplete. It has a short and lofty nave of five bays, and beyond was to have been a transept, of which the west wall only is built ; and it was also to have had a central tower, for which the two massive western piers were prepared, with an undulating section like the late piers in the cathedral and the choir of S. Etienne at Beauvais (v. Plate XXXIV, vol. I. p. 128). The nave vault is quite English, quadripartite, with intermediate ribs, ridge ribs both lengthwise and across, and bosses at the intersections. The piers have no capitals, but the mouldings are continuous with the arch. The triforium has bold Flamboyant tracery and a pierced parapet, and the clerestory has four-light windows of the same kind. *S. Wulfran, Abbeville, 1480*

The west front is extremely beautiful, and as a

Abbeville composition can hardly be surpassed. The proportions are admirable, the buttresses well defined and profiled, and there is plenty of plain wall to give value to the richer ornamentation, which is abundant but not exaggerated (Plate CXXIII, p. 138 *sup.*). This front is, for me, quite the most lovely piece of Flamboyant architecture in France.

S. Riquier   A few miles away from Abbeville is another great Flamboyant building, the abbey church of S. RIQUIER, begun in 1457, restored after a fire in 1487, and finished in 1517. The design of the interior, with round piers and attached colonnettes, and with sculptured capitals, seems to belong to the earlier date. At the west end is a great tower, with a portal surmounted by pediment and niches in all the extravagant profusion of Flamboyant architecture at its height. The result is interesting, but the church is inferior in design to its beautiful neighbour at Abbeville.

Flemish influence in sculpture   In the figure sculpture of both these churches there is a decided trace of Flemish influence, and this runs through all that district. It is perceptible at Amiens, for the famous sculptures with scenes from the gospel and the legend of S. Firmin on the choir screen and in the transepts bear an unmistakeable resemblance to the art of the great masters of the Low Countries. S. QUENTIN

S. Quentin, Hôtel de Ville   has a charming Hôtel de Ville (Plate CXXXIV), which, though on a smaller scale, belongs to the same class as the municipal buildings of Bruges, Oudenarde, Ypres, Louvain and Brussels, and reminds us that we are near the Flemish border and the great cities of the Netherlands with their fine civic architecture.

Civil architecture in France   In France, as in England, during the 15th century civil and domestic buildings first began to play an important part in the architecture of the day. At

Plate CXXXIV

S. QUENTIN—Hôtel de Ville

Plate CXXXV

T. G. J.   BOURGES—Maison Cujas

BOURGES there are many notable examples. The Hôtel de Ville was once the HOUSE of JACQUES CŒUR, the unfortunate finance minister of Charles VII, who bought the site in 1443 and built himself a magnificent palace, resting at the back upon the old Gallo-Roman wall. Three of the bastions are worked into the building, and their irregular position causes an irregularity in the plan, which adds much to its picturesqueness. Through a gateway, over which is the chapel decorated with fresco painting by Italian artists, one enters a court surrounded by buildings. Facing the entrance is the principal block, containing great halls on two floors, and flanked by towers crowned with pointed roofs and containing winding stairs, for the day of stately staircases in straight ramps was yet to come.

The house built by the lawyer CUJAS, turned at one time into the Gendarmerie and now into a museum, is another typical example of the residence of a well-to-do citizen in the 15th century (Plate CXXXV).

The Musée de Cluny at Paris, once the town house or hôtel of the abbot of that great Burgundian monastery, is a fine 15th century palace; but it is significant of the age that the jeweller and financier at Bourges was able to house himself in a style not less magnificent than that of the greatest prelates of the Church.

Bourges has another fine Flamboyant building, now converted into the Lycée, but formerly according to tradition the HOUSE of CHARLES VII during the English occupation of France, when he was little more than *Roi de Bourges*. It has a beautiful tower (Plate CXXXVI) containing a winding stone staircase, and adorned with panelling, ogee crocketed pediments, and little figures of watchmen represented as on guard at the windows.

Hôtel
Lallemant,
Bourges
The Hôtel Lallemant in the same city is somewhat later, and the great chimney-piece with the porcupine of Louis XII and the ermine of Anne of Brittany has Renaissance capitals and arabesques.

In the treatment of their dormer windows the Flamboyant architects ran riot with a vengeance. Those Palais de
Justice,
Rouen of the PALAIS DE JUSTICE at ROUEN are so overdone with pinnacles, pierced tracery and flying buttresses, that the window proper is smothered and lost (Plate CXXXVII). But many dormers of this period, such as those in the earlier part of the Chateau at Blois, built by Louis XII and finished about 1515, are more soberly treated and delightful. The dormers of the Early Renaissance are treated in the same way, with pinnacles and flying buttresses, as for instance in the later part of the Chateau at BLOIS (Plate CXL *inf.*).

Senlis and
Beauvais.
Beauvais
cathedral.
Transept
The transepts of Senlis and Beauvais are fine examples of Flamboyant architecture. The southern transept at BEAUVAIS was begun in 1500 and finished in 1548; it rises to the full height of the choir, and is perhaps the most imposing monument of the style (Plate CXXXVIII). Two massive buttresses, covered with panelling and canopies, enclose the portal which is storied with sculpture, and a great rose-window filled with flowing tracery. The gable above is also covered with tabernacle-work. The tympanum of the south door is filled with niches, not with the usual sculpture, and that of the north door has a Jesse-tree, now statueless.

Senlis
The transept at SENLIS is very like those at Beauvais and probably of the same date. It is an insertion, and interrupts the original unbroken arcades of the nave and choir[1].

---

[1] *v. sup.* vol. I, p. 68.

Plate CXXXVI

BOURGES—Maison de Charles VII

Plate CXXXVII

ROUEN—Palais de Justice

In these elaborate compositions there is a certain heaviness in the mass that assorts ill with the delicacy of the detail, which indeed by contrast accentuates the ponderous air of the buttresses. There is also a great contrast at Beauvais between the Flamboyant transept and the lighter and more graceful architecture of the 13th century choir. [—]

Contrast of heavy mass and light detail

In spite of the splendour of the parts and the beauty of the execution the general effect fails to be entirely satisfactory.

At the end of the 15th century the influence of the Italian Renaissance of Classic architecture began to make itself felt in France, as it did at the same time in England. As in the Salisbury chapel at Christchurch Priory Italian arabesques appear in a design otherwise purely Gothic, so at the abbey of S. RIQUIER Classic ornament is mingled with Gothic details. The statue of S. Christopher near the west door stands under a Gothic canopy, but there is Renaissance ornament in the capital of the twisted shafts on which it rests (Plate CXXXIX). So also in the west front of Rouen cathedral, built by Jacques and Rolland le Roux between 1507 and 1530, there are twisted shafts with Renaissance details in the recesses, serving as pedestals to carry statues.

Coming of the Renaissance

S. Riquier, Renaissance detail

Rouen cathedral, Renaissance detail

Francis I invited Italian artists, Primaticcio, il Rosso, and even the great Lionardo, to France, as Henry VIII did the Florentine Pietro Torrigiano to England, and the Renaissance took root there and began to flourish. But in France, as in England, there arose a mixed style in which features of Classic origin were introduced into designs that in principle were really Gothic. The great chateaux on the Loire, Blois, Chambord, Chenonceau,

Italian artists in France

Gothic
design
with
Classic
detail

and Chaumont, and those of Fontainbleau and Azay-le-Rideau, correspond to Kirby, Longleat, Burleigh, and Audley End in our country. For all their columns, Doric, Ionic, Corinthian, and Composite, and all their architraves, friezes, cornices, and balustrades, they are still essentially Gothic buildings, free from Palladian formula, and designed with the same frank individualism as the purer Gothic of preceding generations. In the eyes of the Purist all these buildings stand self-condemned because they are irregular. For the Neo-Goth they are corrupted by the intrusion of features foreign to the art of the Middle Ages : for the neo-Classic they are debased by the retention of motives belonging to mediaeval semi-barbarism. For those who sit loose to convention and strict dogmas of orthodoxy in Art they are interesting as works of an eclectic period, striving, in the true Gothic spirit, after something new, but unable or unwilling to shake themselves quite free from the traditions of the past. So regarded the very irregularities of the style are the sign that it was really alive and moving onwards. It was not till it finally stiffened into the convention of pure Palladianism, and the Gothic element dropped out of it, that architecture died in those countries where Gothic was born, had grown up, and had flourished as being germane to the soil.

Chateau
of Blois

In the building of Francis I at Blois therefore (Plate CXL) we find the mullions and transomes of the Gothic window, though they are set between flat pilasters which have Classic detail. We find also dormers treated with the picturesque pinnacles and flying buttresses of the Hôtel de Ville at Rouen and Cujas's house at Bourges, though simplified and modelled into semi-Classic forms.

Plate CXXXVIII

BEAUVAIS CATHEDRAL—The South Transept

Plate CXXXIX

T. G. J.   S. RIQUIER

The great winding stair with its ramping openings Blois
is designed with all the freedom from convention
of the 13th century, and is as far removed from strict
Classic rule as the purely Gothic stair-tower at Bourges
(Plate CXXXVI). For it cannot be too strongly
maintained that the true difference between Gothic True
and Classic lies not in the forms employed but in difference between
the way you employ them. It is quite possible to Gothic and Classic
use Classic forms in the Gothic manner and Gothic
forms in the Classic manner, and it is to the latter
process that the unreality of so much Neo-Gothic work
of the 19th century is due. It is the spirit and not the
letter that matters and makes the difference.

In the chateaux on the Loire we see the mixed style
—Gothic in spirit in spite of its Classic details—in its
application to secular buildings. In the churches of
S. Eustache and S. Etienne du Mont at Paris we have S. Eu-
it applied to church architecture. In every respect of stache, Paris
plan, and every particular of construction, S. Eustache
is as much a great Gothic church as Notre Dame itself,
though every detail about it is based upon a Classic
model.

The same may be said of the eastern part of S. PIERRE S. Pierre,
at CAEN (Plate CXLI). Here we have the traceried Caen
window of Gothic, though under a round arch and with
uncusped openings. We have the regular plan of a
chevet, with ambulatory aisle and chapels which had been
in use throughout France from the time of Senlis, Reims,
and Amiens. We have the regular construction of vaults
sustained by flying buttresses, springing from massive
piers loaded with lofty pinnacles to annul the thrust.
But while every feature belongs to Gothic construction
the details of the ornament are quite novel, and if not

good Classic, which they certainly are not, they aspire at all events to be in the fashion of the Neo-Classic School.

National
character-
istics
reflected in
architec-
tural
history

It is interesting to trace in the course of the later styles of Gothic in England and France the different character of the two nations.   In England the progress of the art was steady, regular and continuous.   From Geometrical Decorated in the 13th century we passed almost insensibly into the Flowing Decorated of the 14th ; and thence towards the latter part of that century into the Perpendicular style, which ran its course till it was submerged by the incoming tide of the Renaissance. In France no such easy transition took place.   The Geometrical style of the 13th century, fully developed at Chartres, Reims, and Amiens, endured with little change throughout the 14th century, except that it became stale and monotonous because it had overstayed its time.   At the end of the 14th century there came violent revolution ; the old Art was brushed aside in a moment, and architecture suddenly blazed out into Flamboyant novelties.

Political
parallel

Is it fanciful to see in this contrast a parallel to the political history of the two countries ?   In England free liberal institutions modified our constitution slowly and regularly.   Our revolutions have been less violent, less sweeping, and less bloody.   We have taken our reforms in small instalments, without any serious convulsions of society, and some of them have passed over us almost without our noticing them.   In France change and reform was deferred too long ; the *ancien régime* outstayed its time : effete institutions and old abuses were tolerated till they could be endured no longer ; therefore when the revolution came it was sudden and violent, and

Plate CXL

BLOIS—The Stair Tower

Plate CXLI

Cliché Maillant phot. à Caen, Calvados

Cliché Maillant phot. à Caen, Calvados

the changes it made in politics and society were far more sweeping and destructive of the past.

In the same way we can trace the different temperaments of the two countries in the very different character which Gothic architecture took in its last stage in France and England.

In England Perpendicular architecture never lost that air of severity and restraint with which it began at Gloucester. As time went on it became elaborated and gorgeous to a degree beyond anything in the preceding styles; but its splendours are all kept within the bounds of order and regularity. So much is this the case that though in broad features of design it has plenty of variety, there is a want of variety in window, moulding, and panelling which causes a certain monotony in the details. From first to last, from Gloucester to Windsor and Westminster, the style has a regularity of form, and an austere dignity which is not impaired by the magnificence of its decoration. *English character in Perpendicular*

The sentiment of Flamboyant architecture in France is very different. Here all is gaiety and luxury. Dignity is forgotten; all must be joyous, fanciful, and clever. This no doubt often ran riot in extravagance and even meretricious gaudiness, but the style is so lively and piquant, so surprising and amusing, that we forgive its faults and think only of its charms. Above all, it must be admitted, even by those who regard it as architecture in its decadence, that it came to give new life to a worn-out art that had nothing fresh to say, and nothing to offer to the world but stale repetitions. *French character in Flamboyant*

CHAPTER XXIII

ITALIAN GOTHIC

Decline of
art in 7th
and 8th
centuries
WITH the end of the exarchate and the cessation of
the direct influence of Eastern Rome the arts in Italy
suffered a decline, and nothing was produced there in
the 7th and 8th centuries comparable to the splendid
work of Honorius, Theodoric, and Justinian. In the
9th and 10th centuries art began to revive; the churches
of S. Ambrogio and S. Satiro at Milan, and the early
buildings of S. Mark's at Venice, and Torcello in the
lagunes, showed fresh development of architectural style
and fresh promise for the future. At the end of the
Italian
Roman-
esque
11th and beginning of the 12th century Italian architecture reached a point of refinement and execution
which had nothing to approach it in transatlantic lands.
S. Miniato at Florence is of the same age as the little
wooden church at Greensted in Essex; and the Duomo
of Pisa, with its delicate arcading and mosaic panels, is
coeval with the rude Norman work of the Conqueror at
Caen, and older than that of Lanfranc at Canterbury
or Walkelyn at Winchester.

Rapid
progress
of the
northern
schools
But during the succeeding period Italy did not main-
tain an undisputed pre-eminence. The fine Romanesque
basilicas of Hildesheim, Cologne, Maintz, Tournay,
Worms, and Speyer in Germany, the great Norman
cathedrals in England, the churches at Caen and

Vézelay, those of Auvergne, the cathedrals of Chartres, Rapid progress of the Northern Schools
Sens, and Paris, and the domed churches of Perigord and
Aquitaine in France were all begun and either finished
or well advanced before the end of the 12th century.
In point of scale they excelled the average size of
similar buildings in Italy, and they soon began to rival
them in sculptured decoration, if they could not match
their splendour of marble and mosaic, for which neither
materials nor skill in working them were to be found
north of the Alps.

The rapid progress of the Northern Schools during Divergence of North and South
this great building age led them ever farther from the
style of Italy, resulting, as we have seen, in a new art,
based on the new social and economic conditions of the
time, which found expression in the novel forms of
Gothic architecture.

But in Italy many of these impulses were wanting. Classic tradition in Italy
It is true the Italians could not under new conditions
go on building as their Roman ancestors had done, but
many of those conditions were not so far removed from
life under the later Empire as to demand a fresh departure in art. Classic tradition was naturally stronger in
the Mother Country than in the provinces. The remains
of antiquity were more abundant, the conditions of
climate and material were unaltered, the skill of the
artist had never been entirely lost during its temporary
eclipse, and the feeling was still alive among the people
that the arts of their forefathers descended properly to
them together with their laws and their civil and
municipal institutions. It was not strange, therefore,
that, in spite of all changes in population and civilization,
Classic art should cling with tenacity to its native soil. Tenacity of Classic in Italy
It was inevitable that the architecture of mediaeval Italy

Tenacity of Classic in Italy

should differ widely from that of Imperial times, but it never took that fresh departure which resulted in the Gothic of France, England, and afterwards of Germany. The Gothic of Italy is Gothic with a difference, and the round arch never gave way entirely to the pointed. The tower of S. Gottardo at Milan, coeval with the Perpendicular work at Gloucester, is still purely Romanesque though forty or fifty years later than the Gothic of Orvieto and Siena, and the Romanesque apse of the Duomo of Lucca bears the date 1320.

Gothic regarded as German

To the Italians Gothic was the German style,—*lo stile Tedesco*,—always a foreigner and not always understood. Some Italian buildings in this style were, we are told, actually designed by German architects, like the great church at Assisi and the cathedral of Milan, though the designs were so modified and Italianized by local artists that they are very unlike anything in Germany; for there is very little northern feeling in either of these churches.

Survival of Romanesque

With these influences at work it is not wonderful that Romanesque architecture was for a long while practised in Italy with little change ; and though during the 11th and 12th centuries Italy was being rapidly covered with buildings that still excite our wonder and admiration, the progress in architecture was not so much towards novelty in style as towards greater skill in design and execution and superior refinement in detail. The churches of Pisa, Pavia, Zara, and Lucca, though the façade of the latter is coeval with that of Peterborough, are still mainly Romanesque in design, and even when they employ to some extent Gothic details they show no trace of anything like the Gothic then being developed on the other side of the Alps.

Other influences helped to give a peculiar direction Italy not a nation to architecture and the arts generally in Italy. Italy was not a nation like France and England, but a geographical expression. Nominally it formed part of the Empire, and the Emperor had to be crowned at Monza or Milan, as well as at Aix-la-Chapelle, and Rome[1]. But the Imperial power was rarely supreme; the Emperor was an alien; his interference was resented, and finally overcome at Legnano by the League of Lombardy. In the absence of a strong central power the old Roman municipalities, left to shift for them- selves, became semi-independent States, each with its The Italian communes own territory, its own laws, and its own communal government. The great Lombard cities, Milan, Cremona, Pavia, and the rest, became powerful self- governed communities, sometimes leagued together, but nearly always at war among themselves. Pisa and Genoa grew into great sea-powers, rivals till the triumph of Genoa at Meloria broke the power of Pisa and led to her subjugation by Florence. Venice stood mostly aloof, and looked to the East rather than the West, till her acquisition of territory on the mainland of Italy involved her in Italian politics. In the south was the kingdom of Naples,—*il regno*,—and in the centre were the States of the Church; but the Pope himself, whatever his world-power, ranked in Italy only as one of many political units. Nowhere else, except in ancient Greece, do we find a country thus divided among a number of

---

[1] Originally also at Arles, for that kingdom :

> Primus Aquisgrani locus est, post haec Arelati,
> Inde Modoetiae regali sede locari,
> Post solet Italiae summa corona dari.

> Godfrey of Viterbo—Cited Bryce, *Holy Roman Empire*.

small autonomous republics, aristocratic at Venice, demo-
cratic at Florence, warring or making peace with one
another like Athens and Sparta of old, entering into
leagues and making treaties like sovereign states, and
defying foreign interference with their liberties.

All this, so different from what was going on in
France and England, influenced the architecture of Italy,
which is essentially a civic style.   In these independent
communes, where national spirit ran high, nothing could
exceed the patriotic zeal of the citizens in embellishing
their city with beautiful buildings.   The spoils with
which they returned from successful wars were spent in
raising vast cathedrals for the people and stately palaces
for the magistracy.   The treasures which the Pisans
took from the Saracens of Palermo in 1063 were
expended on magnifying and adorning the Duomo[1];
the bronze horses which the Venetians brought from
Constantinople in the fourth crusade were mounted where
we see them over the portico of S. Mark's; and the
precious marbles with which the church is made splendid
within and without are the choicest spoils of the arms
and the commerce of the Republic.   The ducal palace
at Venice, the Broletti or town-halls, and the public
markets of great Italian towns such as Como, Brescia,
Cremona, and Udine, the Palazzo Vecchio at Florence,
and the Palazzo Comunale at Siena,—buildings that
have no parallel except to some extent in the great free
cities of the Empire and the Netherlands, where similar

---

[1] On the West front we read

> Intrantes rupta portum pugnando catena,
> Sex capiunt magnas naves opibusque repletas.
> Unam vendentes, reliquas prius igne cremantes,
> Quo pretio muros constat hos esse levatos.

municipal liberty prevailed,—all speak of strong civic ardour and the patriotic fervour with which each Italian commonwealth strove to do honour to its mother-city.

This sentiment, among others, served to give archi- Character of church architec- ture in Italy tecture in Italy a less religious character than in the North. The great church was to the Italian not only a place of worship but a monument to the glory of his home. That passionate and blind devotion which drove the nobles and delicate ladies of Chartres and S. Denis to harness themselves to carts and draw building materials to the sacred site would have been very unlikely in Italy. The Italian had none of that superstitious faith in the sanctity of ecclesiastical architecture which surrounded the northern cathedral with holy legend, mystic vision, and saintly miracle. The Church itself had for him less mystery and inspired less awe. He was behind the scenes and saw the working of the machinery and the manufacture of the thunder. Popes at whose nod Trans-Alpine Christendom trembled were not always masters in their own city; at one time driven away by the citizens, at another summoned back by the municipal authorities to their duty as bishops of Rome. This temper of the Italian mind is reflected in the church architecture. It Italian Gothic not mysterious has none of the mystery of the northern cathedral. Even S. Mark's is simple in plan, with no dim recesses like Chartres or Canterbury. The cavernous lower church at Assisi is exceptional, and was perhaps designed by a northern architect; but generally the Italian church is light and airy and the façade flat and superficial, where beyond the Alps we should have had shadowy recesses and deep over-arching portals.

But it was not only this attitude of the Italian mind that gave a distinctive character to the architecture. It

was very largely influenced by the materials at the
command of the builders.   One peculiarity of Italian
architecture is the use of marble, which affected the
whole style.   Marble is one of the regular building
materials of the country.   It is quarried in many parts,
but especially in the Carrara mountains, whence we get
not only white marble for statuary but a great variety of
breccia and other coloured sorts.   The abundance of this
beautiful material had an enormous influence on Roman
art, not less than on that of the Middle Ages.   The
Romans ransacked the world for precious marbles, and
we are still ignorant of the quarries whence some of them
were taken.   Pliny cries out upon the madness with
which men's lives and treasure were expended that
Romans might sleep within walls of variegated stones[1].

Spoils of   The Italians, therefore, besides the example of their
Roman
buildings   ancestors, had the vast accumulation of marbles of all
kinds remaining in the temples, villas, and public buildings with which the land was covered, many of them
ruined and deserted.   From these, as from an inexhaustible store of ready-worked materials, they pilfered without
scruple columns, slabs, architraves, and cornices, and
worked them up in their own buildings, at first in a hap-
hazard way, and afterwards with better skill and taste.
On this supply they had to depend for many centuries.
In particular the red and green porphyry used in their
pavements of *opus Alexandrinum* must all have come
from ancient columns and plaques, sliced into sections or
broken into tesserae, for the porphyry quarries were
unknown during the Middle Ages, and were only
re-discovered a very few years ago.

In the Byzantine buildings at Ravenna of the 5th and

[1] Plin. *Nat. Hist.* XXXVI. I.

6th centuries marble was used for interior decoration only, while the outside of the buildings remained of plain and rude brickwork.   Afterwards in the plain of Lombardy, where stone is scarce, a refined style of brickwork was developed, mixed with terra-cotta, which is only a kind of brick, and beautiful work was done in those materials; but even there marble was used for the more delicate features.   In the greater part of Italy from the early part of the 11th century the outside of the great churches began to be cased in marble as well as the inside, and afterwards a marble facing seems always to have been intended, though not always achieved.   Besides numerous structures in which this intention was realized, Italy is full of great churches with unfinished fronts of rough brickwork, where toothings are left to receive the marble front which has never come. *(Byzantine use of marble inside)* *(Lombard brick and marble)* *(Marble facing outside)*

This constant regard for marble had, of course, a powerful effect on the design.   It disposed, once and for ever, of the adoption of the Gothic details of the North. The deeply undercut hollows and complicated mouldings of our 13th-century work, natural and easily wrought in free-stone, were out of the question in hard marble, which demands much more delicate treatment and greater regard for surface.   In designing for free-stone masonry one thinks only of line and shadow, for which the material is merely the vehicle.   But in designing for marble the beauty of the material itself has to be regarded, and should not be obscured by cutting it up with dark hollows, even if the difficulty of working them in so stubborn a material allowed such treatment.   In all the details of Classic mouldings, with their shallow quirks and fillets, their broad flat soffits, and their simple curved members, we find expressed the nature of the *(Effect of use of marble on style)* *(Classic detail based on marble)*

Classic detail based on marble

material, which only lends itself readily to plain surfaces, and which only shows its full beauty when so treated. Classic architecture is essentially a marble architecture. Only with marble or the hardest stone resembling marble was a trabeated style possible, and in the laboriousness of working it is to be read the explanation of the greater respect paid to surface and the severity and restraint of the architectural details.

Italian Gothic a marble style

The Gothic of Italy therefore had to be a marble Gothic, and the details suitable to that material naturally differed much from those of Gothic on the other side of the Alps.

Accusation of Italian Gothic

It has been the fashion with many writers to decry Italian Gothic, and to say it is not Gothic at all, but only a bastard style undeserving the name. It is quite true that Northern Gothic never found a home in Italy, and that the churches of Siena, Orvieto, and Assisi are not like Amiens or Salisbury ; but how else would these critics have it ? To expect that Gothic would take the

Its unfoundedness

same forms in Italy as here or in France shows an entire misconception of the nature of the art. In a former chapter I have tried to explain that the essence of the style is its freedom to adapt itself to its environment, and the very difference of Italian Gothic from the northern style is its justification, and constitutes its claim to the title. Amiens cathedral in the plains of Lombardy or on the banks of the Arno would be as ridiculous as Giotto's campanile in Fleet Street or Cheapside. That the Italians indeed carried their Gothic style to the same perfection that they achieved in the Romanesque that preceded or in the style of the Renaissance which followed it, cannot perhaps be maintained ; and yet there is no more impressive interior than that of Milan, there are no cathedrals that dwell in the memory more vividly than those of Siena and Orvieto, and there are no more lovely cloisters than those of Pisa, Ragusa, Curzola, and Monreale.

With the use of marble came also the habit of design- ing in polychrome masonry, which is another point of difference from the northern styles.   In the South of France, at Le Puy, Clermont Ferrand, and the other Auvergnat churches, the outside walls are inlaid with patterns of black basalt and yellow stone, and in England there are buildings, like S. Peter's, Northampton, and the Bede-house at Higham Ferrers, which are banded with white and dark orange stone ; there is Bishop Gower's work at S. David's with chequers of purple and cream- colour ; and there are the flint inlays of the Eastern Counties ; but polychrome masonry is rare on this side of the Alps, and simple.   The command of coloured marbles as a material for wall decoration gave the Italian architect a much fuller palette, and polychrome masonry from the 11th century onwards played a principal part in his architecture both inside and outside.

It was used in two ways : either, as at Venice, by thin slabs applied to the walls like a veneer, or else, as at Como, Brescia, Bergamo, and Cremona, by building marble into the wall, like any other stone, in regular courses.   Mr Street[1] condemns the first method as unconstructional, which has no doubt been proved in some cases, though its duration to our day in the majority of instances helps to justify it.   His unqualified approval is reserved for the other method.   But it must be re- membered that these two modes of using marble had different objects in view, and that while the Lombard

Poly-chrome masonry in France

In England

In Italy

Two modes of poly-chrome masonry

Their different objects

[1] *Brick and Marble in Italy.*

Poly-
chrome
masonry
plan aimed at the agreeable variation of the surface by
bands and chequers, the Venetian mode, which is, in
fact, the Byzantine mode of Constantinople, Ravenna,
Salonica, and the Istrian churches, aimed rather at display
of the veining and blots of lovely colour in the material
by using it in large slabs. Often plaques were put
together from the same block reversed, so that the figure
of the veins made a regular pattern, a common device
at Constantinople and Ravenna, where red cipollino is
used in this way with splendid effect. For outside work
no doubt the Lombard plan is the better, but inside, out
of reach of weather, the Venetian use produces a much
finer effect.

Individu-
ality of
Italian
Gothic
The Gothic of Italy was much more individual than
that of the North. "Unfortunately," says Fergusson,
"in this style we know the names of all the architects."
I do not know why this is unfortunate. Our ignorance
of the names and personality of most of the Northern
Gothic architects is accidental, owing to their living in
an age and a country which were illiterate compared
with Italy. They have had no Vasari to embalm their
memories, and for the most part

> illacrumabiles
> urgentur ignotique longa
> nocte, carent quia vate sacro.

It is not to be supposed they were less proud of their
work than other people or less desirous of being remembered, and in fact we have seen in former chapters that
it is possible with a little trouble to recover the names,
and sometimes more than the names, of the architects of
several among the great churches of France and England.

In Italy there is seldom the same difficulty. And more
than that, whereas even when we do know the names of

northern architects, like William of Sens at Canterbury and Robert de Luzarches at Amiens, we know little else about them, in Italy, on the contrary, we do know a good deal about Buono, Arnolfo, Niccola and Giovanni Pisani, Margharitone of Arezzo, and scores more from the 12th century downwards, whose lives may be read at some length in the gossiping pages of Vasari ; and we know, too, pretty well to whose hand most of the famous buildings in Italy are to be attributed.

Our knowledge of the architects

There is, however, no doubt, some difference between the part played by the architect in Italy and that of his northern brethren. Although he naturally worked in the style of his day, the personality of the artist may be traced more distinctly in Italian work than in ours, and as time went on the influence of the man triumphed more and more over that of the school, so that we may often recognize the work of this artist or that, much as we can at the present day, when the individuality of the artist is everything and the school no longer exists. And so, while elsewhere we watch the steady progress of the art from style to style without being able to detect the personal influence of any single artist, we see at once in Italy how single artists like Niccola Pisano and Filippo Brunelleschi turned the current of the art of their day into new channels pretty much by their own personal influence.

Personal influence of individual architects

The more perfect history of architecture in Italy results, no doubt, in great measure from the superior standard of education there, and from the records being in civil hands and not solely in the cloister. But the strong civic feeling of each commune had also much to do with it, and the pride which each little State felt in the prowess of its sons in arts no less than in arms.

Their place in small societies

In small States the individual counts for more : each citizen of the commune felt a sense of proprietorship in its public buildings, and an interest in his fellow-citizens who designed them. In so small a society each artist would be widely known, and his career from apprentice to master watched by friendly eyes. It is hard in our cosmopolitan age to realize the intense devotion of the Intense communal patriotism Italian to his mother-city, and his ardour in beautifying it by every means in his power. The merchant galleys of Venice were charged to bring home marbles for the public buildings, and when the Pisans wished to reward the Florentines for their friendly protection while the flower of the Pisan manhood was away fighting the Saracens, no more welcome gift could be thought of than the two porphyry columns that now stand at the Baptistery gate[1]. City vied with city in the splendour of its buildings. When Arnolfo del Cambio was commissioned to build the cathedral of S. Maria dei Fiori he was The Duomo of Florence charged by the Signoria of Florence to make it " of such noble and extreme magnificence that the industry and art of man shall be able to invent nothing grander or more beautiful." No plan was to be accepted " unless the conception were such as to render the work worthy of an ambition which had become very great, inasmuch as it resulted from the combined desires of a great number of citizens, united as in one sole will[2]. Patriotic love for the very stones of his mother-city breathes in Dante's *il mio bel San Giovanni.* It was his passionate Foscari at Venice attachment to Venice that drew the younger Foscari back from exile to torture and death.

---

[1] One hopes the story is not true that the Pisans, out of jealousy, damaged them before they were sent.

[2] Richa, cited Trollope's *Hist. of Florence,* vol. I. p. 230.

Guard.	And can you so much love the soil that hates you?
Jac. Fosc.	The soil! oh no, it is the seed of the soil
	Which persecutes me; but my native earth
	Will take me as a mother to her arms.
	I ask no more than a Venetian grave,
	A dungeon, what they will, so it be here[1].

One more characteristic of the Italian school is brought out by our closer acquaintance with the individual artist. We find constantly that not only were the decorative arts of painting and sculpture allied to architecture in close co-operation, but the practice of more than one, sometimes of all three, was united in one artist. Margharitone of Arezzo practised all the arts; Niccola Pisano was equally eminent as sculptor and architect; Giotto excelled both in architecture and painting, and Vasari quotes Ghiberti to the effect that he also designed the sculptured panels on his great campanile at Florence; "and this," he adds, "may readily be believed, for drawing and invention are the father and mother of all these arts, and not of one only[2]." *Union of the arts in one artist in Italy*

Though this conjunction of the arts in one person may have been more usual in Italy, perhaps if we knew as much about the craftsmen in England, France, and Germany we should find that the profession of art as a whole was common also there. It was the case with Erwin von Steinbach at Strassburg, and half the sketch-book of Wilars de Honecort is filled with studies of the human figure, both nude and draped, and rules for drawing and composing it, as well as studies of animals drawn, as he tells us, from the life, done for use in his practice. *Also in other countries*

It follows from what has been said, that one feature which distinguishes mediaeval architecture in Italy from

[1] Byron, *I due Foscari.*   [2] Vasari, *Vita di Giotto.*

Impor-
tance of
secular
architec-
ture in
Italy
that of most European lands is the vast amount of civil and domestic work.   In the great trading communities of the Netherlands, whose history to some extent resembles that of the Italian Communes, we have the nearest approach to the wealth of secular architecture in Italy. They have their town-halls, exchanges, and not a few residences of wealthy merchant-princes and well-to-do citizens.   But in France remains of domestic work earlier

Secular
architec-
ture rare
in France
and
England
than the end of the 15th century are rare, and French Gothic is mainly ecclesiastical.   In England this is still more the case.   Examples of civil architecture, till Tudor times when church-building was almost at an end and private splendour took its place, are very rare indeed, and the only secular buildings of any consequence that have survived even in ruin are feudal castles, in which

Abundant
in Italy
art plays a small part.   But in Italy architecture bears a far less ecclesiastical aspect, and secular architecture is as important as that of the churches.   The streets of Siena are lined with Gothic palaces; every great city has its public buildings; at Venice, except the basilica of S. Mark, there are no buildings comparable to the Ducal Palace or the hundred splendid homes of Venetian nobles which adorn the banks of the Canals.   The streets of Cremona, Pavia, and Bologna still abound in private dwellings dating from the Middle Ages, as well as those of Florence, Viterbo, and the towns of Sicily; and in no other country can the secular architecture of mediaeval times be studied so well.

Plate CXLII

T. G. J.   COMO—The Broletto

CHAPTER XXIV

NORTH ITALIAN GOTHIC

DURING the earlier part of the 13th century Gothic Slow advent of Gothic in Italy made its way into Italy slowly, and for some time was practised side by side with Romanesque. Pointed arches and Gothic capitals appear in the lower storey of the Broletto at COMO, which dates from 1215 (Plate CXLII), though the windows of the upper storey have round arches; and even when the system of window tracery was fully adopted in Italy we find the round arch used in conjunction with it.

Gothic architecture was not a spontaneous growth on Italian soil. It filtered through gradually from beyond the Alps; rather, it would seem, from France than from Germany; for though the Italian always spoke of Gothic as *lo stile Tedesco*,—the German style,—the influence of France is much more apparent than that of any other country.

The church of S. Andrea at VERCELLI was founded S. Andrea, Vercelli in 1219 by Cardinal Guala dei Bicchieri on his return from England, where he had been Papal legate. He is said to have peopled it with monks from S. Victor at Paris and to have brought with him on his way through France a Parisian priest skilled in architecture, who built this church and became first abbot of the monastery. The monument of Abbot Tomaso Gallo remains in a

S. Andrea, chapel of the transept.   Another account has it that the
Vercelli   architect was an Englishman named Brigwithe[1], and
there is something English in the plan (Fig. 185), with
the square east end and the two apsidal chapels on the
east side of each transept, one longer than the other,
like those at Selby and S. Mary's Abbey at York as
originally planned, and those in the Confessor's Church
at Westminster, which was still standing when Cardinal
Guala was in London[2].   Apsidal chapels on the transepts,

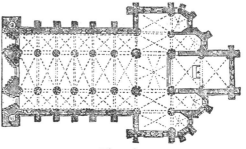

Fig. 185.

however, are more common in France than in England,
where they are more often square, and the details of the
lower parts of the church at Vercelli are more French
than English.   Indeed, the design up to the nave capitals
might pass for French Gothic: the bases are of the
quasi-Attic form like those at Reims with carved toes at
the angles, and there are deeply moulded bands to the

[1] Fergusson, *Hist. of Architecture*, and Enlart, *Origines Françaises de
l'Architecture Gothique en Italie*, p. 17, who cites Count Arborio Mella, to
the effect that a resemblance has been traced by a Rev. Dr of Winchester
between this 13th century church and the transept at Winchester.   He
probably means De Lucy's retro-choir, and M. Enlart can hardly have seen
Winchester or he would not have passed this mistake.

[2] Recent excavations show the same arrangement in Bishop Osmund's
church of 1192 at Old Sarum; but the longer transeptal chapels though
ending in a semi-circular apse inside were square outside like the end of
Carilef's choir aisles at Durham.

Plate CXLIII

VERCELLI—S. Andrea

Plate CXLIII

T. G. J.

VERCELLI—S. Andrea

shafts, and capitals with foliage *à crochet* (Plate CXLIII). S. Andrea,
Vercelli
The arches of the great arcades have square orders, and
are pointed, and so is the vault, but all the other arches
are round, and the rest of the structure upwards is Italian
in style. Over the crossing is an octagonal cupola on The
cupola
angle tromps, into which a colonnette rises from the
capital of the piers,—a thoroughly Italian feature which
is repeated on a larger scale at Siena. A passage under
brick arcading on marble colonnettes surrounds the interior of the drum above the squinches, and other shafts
of marble run up the angles to take the vault. This is
enclosed in an octagonal tower of brick surmounted by The
central
tower
a smaller stage. The outside of the church has cornices
of brick, and arcading with practicable passages in the
manner of Pisan Romanesque (Plate CXLIV), and the
detached campanile of brickwork, which is said to have
been built by Piero del Verme in 1399, is entirely
Romanesque in style. In the exterior, at all events,
there is no trace of Trans-Alpine feeling.

Stone was rare in North Italy; brick, the traditional Stone
rare in
Lombardy
material inherited from Roman building, was in general
use throughout the plain of Lombardy during the Middle Lombard
brickwork
Ages, except in the case of a few more important build-
ings, such as the cathedrals of Milan and Como. The
Gothic of North Italy, therefore, is essentially a brickwork style, and never in any other land did brick play
so important a part in decoration. Cornices were worked
with interlacing arches of brick, and enriched with brick
dentils; attached half-columns were constructed in brickwork, with capitals in the same material; and even
columns inside the churches were made of it. The
church of the Carmine at Pavia has columns, a full yard The
Carmine,
Pavia
in diameter, of dark-red brick, so finely jointed that the

Lombard brickwork

beds are hardly perceptible. The bricks were sometimes shaped to fit curves, as at S. Gottardo in Milan, where they are of various sizes, sometimes as large as 12 in. by 6 in. by 3 in., and they are put together with very fine mortar and thin beds. Stone or marble was only used for shafts too small to be worked in brick.

Terra-cotta

Before long, terra-cotta, which is only glorified brick, came into use, and gave a distinctive character to North Italian work during the mediaeval period and also that of the Renaissance. In this material elaborate traceries could be modelled, and delicate ornaments cast, to surround the arches of doors and windows. The facility it affords for

Abuse of terra-cotta

loading a building with cheap ornament is a snare to the vulgar, and lends itself to meretricious splendour; for when a mould is once made it costs no more to turn out ornamental pieces than plain. Since the manufacture of terra-cotta has been revived in modern times we have seen it so abused as to be offensive, and this has

Its proper use

brought discredit on the material. But when used with restraint and discretion,—used, in fact, as it was by the Italians of the 14th and 15th centuries,—no artist need despise it.

Inconvenience of brick for pointed arches

The use of brick is probably one reason why the round arch held its own so tenaciously in North Italy. To construct a pointed arch in brick involves some difficulty in making a good junction at the apex: if the joints radiate, as in masonry they would, to the two centres, the topmost bricks would be imperfect. A round arch presents no such difficulty, as all the joints radiate from one point and the voussoirs are all alike.

Italian mode of jointing them

This difficulty was generally got over in Italy by making the joints of the pointed arch radiate to one point in the centre of the springing line, instead of to the two proper

Plate CXLV

The Duomo   S. Gottardo

MILAN

points from which the arch is struck. In the example (Fig. 186) from a palace at CITTÀ DELLA PIEVE the pointed arch is jointed in this manner. In the window from LUCCA (Fig. 187) the same system of jointing is applied to the trefoil heads of the window lights. The defect of this is that the brick voussoirs, instead of a square end, come to a feather edge on one side, which, unless the brick were very hard, would break off with the slightest pressure. The strength of the arch is also impaired, and it was probably for this reason that the Italians frequently increased the depth of the arch as it rose, by striking the extrados with a longer radius than the intrados. In some cases the intrados is made semi-circular, and the extrados pointed. The doorway of the convent at ASSISI is an example of this (Fig. 188).

It is curious to find the same mode of jointing pointed arches followed when the arch was of stone, where there was no reason why the joints should not radiate from two points in the normal way (v. Fig. 195, p. 205).

The tower of S. GOTTARDO (Plate CXLV), which is enclosed in the Royal Palace at MILAN, was built by an architect from Cremona, who recorded his name by an inscription—

MAGISTER FRANCISCVS DE PECORARIS DE CREMONA
FECIT HOC OPVS

Though built in the 14th century by Azzo Visconti, who was lord of Milan from 1328 to 1339, it is quite Romanesque in style, with round arches moulded in brick, and a spire of bricks with rounded ends set outwards, so as to form a sort of scale pattern. Brick spires are not uncommon in North Italy: S. Agostino at GENOA has a fine one, octagonal with four square pyramidal pinnacles at the corners which are covered

Città della
Pieve

Fig. 186. (*From* Anderson.)

Lucca

Fig. 187. (*From* Anderson.)

with red, white, and green tiles in chequers and borders, Brick
and patterns of the same work are inlaid in the tower spires

Fig. 188. (*From* Anderson.)

below. There is another at Genoa something like it, and
there is a good example of a square spire in brickwork in

the Valle Crucis, near Rapallo. CREMONA has fine brick campaniles with spires of brickwork to the churches of S. Agostino, S. Agata, and S. Abbondio. At S. Agostino the shafts of the belfry lights are worked in brick : as a rule the detached shafts are in white marble, even when the attached half-shafts in the jambs are of moulded brick.

The church of the CARMINE at PAVIA has an elegant campanile with a brickwork spire formed, like those at S. Gottardo at Milan and S. Agostino at Cremona, of heading bricks with rounded ends. The façade of this church (Fig. 189) is a good specimen of Lombard brick and terra-cotta architecture. The pedimental cornices are of rich detail with interlacing arches, dentils, and running scroll. The great rose window has several orders of similar ornament, and the wheel-tracery is of terra-cotta with white marble spokes. The traceries of the other windows are worked in terra-cotta, but the circle does not mitre and coalesce with the head of the lights as in regular Northern Gothic.

The church of S. Francesco, also at PAVIA, and the Ducal Castle there, abound in rich work of brick and terra-cotta dating from the second half of the 14th century.

The front of the cathedral of CREMA, built late in the 13th or early in the 14th century, is a still more interesting design, divided into three by massive half-columns with cushion capitals all worked in brick[1]. The windows are surrounded by an unusually large number of brick orders. These orders in all this Italian work are very shallow, very slightly receding within one another,

[1] Illustrated by Gruner, *Terra Cotta Architecture in North Italy*, Plate 16.

FACADE OF THE CHURCH
OF THE CARMINE AT PAVIA
FROM
GRUNER'S "TERRA COTTA ARCHITECTURE"
SCALE OF FEET

Fig. 189. (*From* Gruner.)

so that the whole has a superficial effect, very unlike Northern Gothic, where the depth of an order is generally equal to its height, or nearly so (Fig. 190).

S. Maria, Monza

In the church of S. Maria della Strada at MONZA a new motive appears in the more Gothic design of the arcaded and canopied stage below the rose window. The building dates from the middle of the 14th century, and is attributed to Bonino di Campione, one of the architects at Milan cathedral. The tympanum of the great door and the spaces enclosed by the arcading were decorated with painting (Plate CXLVI). Gruner[1] remarks that the little ornaments in the squares of the borders containing the rose and other windows are all modelled separately, instead of being cast from the same mould as is too commonly done in cheap modern work.

The cupola

A central cupola over the crossing, such as that at Vercelli, is a characteristic feature of North Italian churches. At Vercelli it is enclosed in a tower with

Bergamo

one diminished stage above. At Bergamo the church of S. Maria Maggiore has the cupola covered by three receding stages decorated with arcading, the topmost being crowned with a little spire[2]. A finer example is

Chiara-valle

that of the abbey of CHIARAVALLE, near Milan, founded in 1135, and named after the abbey of Clairvaux, in honour of S. Bernard, who visited it the year before. The church was consecrated in 1221[3]. The cupola and the great tower above it are later, and are attributed to the same Francesco Pecorari[4] who designed the campanile of

---

[1] *Op. cit.* p. 53.

[2] Illustrated in my *Byzantine and Romanesque Architecture*, vol. I. Plate LXVIII.

[3] Anno gratie MCXXXV XI Kalendas Februarii constructum est hoc monasterium a beato Bernardo Abbate Clarevallensi. MCCXXI consecrata est ecclesia ista. Enlart, *op. cit.* p. 15.

[4] Calvi, cited by Gruner.

Crema
cathedral

Fig. 190. (*From* Gruner.)

S. Gottardo at Milan in the first half of the 14th century
(Fig. 191). The square area is brought into an octagon
by squinches of several orders, on which is set an
octagonal dome within an octagonal drum which rises

Fig. 191. (*From* Fergusson.)

as high as its apex. On this rests the tower with three
receding stages. The construction is extremely daring,
and is only partially justified by success. We are told
that it has been restored from time to time, and the

Plate CXLVI

MONZA—S. Maria della Strada

Plate CXLVII

T. G. J. BERGAMO

construction has been strengthened by iron bands and Chiara-
valle
flying buttresses[1].

The design of Pecorari's cupola and tower, if the design be really his, like that of his tower at Milan, has round arches throughout over the windows and arcaded openings, except in one of the stages where the windows are bluntly pointed. The cornices are of delicate brick interlacing arches, some of them round, others pointed, with trefoil cusping in the intervals; this seems to make it later than S. Gottardo, and it is dated by Street in 1370.

The weak point of the Romanesque churches of The
Lombard
porch North Italy was the west front, which was flat, bald, and uninteresting. Such façades as those of S. Pietro in Cielo d'Oro and S. Michele at Pavia, pierced with three doors and a few scattered windows in a flat wall, and only decorated with a ramping arcaded gallery in the gable, give little pleasure. Those of S. Zenone at Verona and the cathedral at Parma, as originally built, were not much better. It was a happy inspiration which suggested the projecting porch, often in two storeys, with columns resting on magnificently conventionalized lions, which relieves the flatness of the front and gives a dignity and picturesque charm to the entrances of many Lombard churches. We have it at Parma, at Modena, at Verona, at Cremona, at BERGAMO (Plate CXLVII), Bergamo and at BORGO SAN DONNINO, where are the finest lions of all[2], in every case redeeming the façade from dullness and giving it architectural value.

[1] Gruner, *op. cit.* p. 17.
[2] Illustrated in my *Byzantine and Romanesque Architecture*, vol. I. Plate LXXX.

CHAPTER XXV

THE GOTHIC OF CENTRAL ITALY—ITALIAN TRACERY

Fig. 192.

Two years after his death in 1226 S. Francis was canonized by Gregory IX, and the great convent Assisi and church of Assisi were begun by Elias, the first general of the order. According to the rule of the founder the brethren were to possess nothing, to live on alms, to be itinerant hedge-preachers with no fixed habitation; their services were to be conducted with the greatest simplicity, and they were limited to one mass in the day. But Francis was scarcely cold in his grave before his rule was violated, and the poor hedge-preachers housed themselves in one of the most sumptuous convents of Christendom.   As with the Benedictines at Citeaux and Clairvaux, attempts were made from time to time to revert to primitive poverty, but it was in vain.   The severity of the rules was relaxed by Papal authority, the order waxed rich, and Matthew Paris in 1249 complains that in three hundred years the monastic orders had not degenerated so much as the Friars in the forty years of their existence.

According to Vasari, Fra Elias had begun a church at Assisi two years before the death of S. Francis and while he was away preaching.   But after his death and canonization the rush of pilgrims was so great that it was decided to make the building much grander and finer. There being, says Vasari, a dearth of architects at that time, and the site presenting unusual difficulty on account of its precipitous character, an architect was invited from Germany, whom the Italians accordingly style Jacopo d'Alemannia.   But at that time the Gothic style had made no impression on German architecture and the design of Assisi could not have come from that source. It is said the archives contain no mention of Vasari's German architect[1].

The architect, whoever he was, levelled up the slope of the mountain by enormous substructures like the Septizonium of Severus at Rome, in order to form a platform for his buildings (Fig. 192).   On this he raised a double church, one church above the other; the lower

[1] v. Enlart, op. cit.

Assisi.
The
double
church

gloomy and cavernous, the upper light and cheerful with traceried windows and vaulting of rib and panel work. From the Piazza Superiore, by which the upper church is entered, a long flight of steps descends to the Piazza Inferiore, some 30 or 40 feet below, which is also reached by an inclined plane, the continuation of the Via Superba. Here is the entrance to the lower church under a fine Renaissance portico (Plate CXLVIII). The interior is

The lower
church

low and crypt-like, with vast cylindrical piers like towers, dividing it into nave and aisles, and with groined ceilings of which the arches seem to spring from the ground. Through the entrance door the afternoon sun pours a flood of light on the floor, kindling the traceries of the marble monuments and lighting up the dim frescoed vaults with reflected brilliancy. Beyond this streak of radiance the church melts away into a perspective of gloom and darkness like some vast grotto at Bethlehem or Hebron. Dimly seen in the distance is the apse, vaulted with a semi-dome. From the small stained-glass windows of the chapels outside the aisles the light hardly reaches the great cavernous nave, the darkness of which is increased by the depth of the fresco painting with which the whole church is covered on wall, pier, and roof, and which, whether in light or shade, invests the whole interior with the richest tones of colour. The pavement seems to fall gradually as you advance, and the gloom grows thicker; a screen crosses the church, beyond which you catch glimpses of marble, mosaic, and rich tabernacle work, lighted candles, the smoke of incense, and mysterious figures flitting about in rich vestments, while from out of this obscurity comes rolling the music of voices and instruments, the musicians themselves being invisible in the darkness.

The upper church, in marked contrast to the lower, is cheerful and brilliant. It is a simple cruciform building without aisles, articulated like all pure Italian Gothic buildings, into very large bays, and lit by two-light windows with geometrical tracery high up in the walls, each of the enormous bays being square in plan and covered in the simplest way by a quadripartite vault. The effect of this interior is very pleasing: the proportions are admirable, the light well placed high up in the side walls, so that though the windows are filled with coloured glass all the paintings with which the walls are covered can be well seen. The glass is original and extremely interesting: it is very light in tone, and largely composed of white metal.

The paintings, as every one knows, are by Cimabue and Giotto. Regarding them generally as surface decorations without closer investigation, as one stands at one end of the church and looks with half-closed eyes, the general effect is exquisite, and the whole building seems draped in tender tones and subtle harmonies of colour.

The work of Messer Jacopo—Lapo for short[1]—if there were such a person though not a German, has no doubt something of northern Gothic about it, not only in the gloom and mystery of the lower church, so foreign to the usual Italian sentiment, but in the upper church, with its apse vaulted in rib and panel work, in the simple geometrical traceries, in the horned capitals, and the gallery passages round the building in the thickness of the walls. And yet after all it is not much like the Gothic either of France or of Germany; and indeed in

---

[1] Secondo l' uso, che hanno i Fiorentini, e più havevano anticamente d' abbreviare i nomi, non Jacopo ma Lapo lo chiamarono in tutto il tempo della sua vita. Vasari, *Vita d' Arnolfo.*

Northern
modified
by
Southern
feeling
Germany, as I have said, Gothic had hardly at that time
begun to affect the current Romanesque[1]. The great
doorway of the lower church (Plate CXLVIII) is divided
by a central column like the French portals, and the
tympanum is filled with a graceful wheel window; but
the shallow orders, the inlaid decoration of archivolt and
jamb, the spirally twisted shafts of the wheel, all betray
local influences, and have little in common with northern
schools of architecture. What share any northern architect had in giving the general design, we can only guess.
It is said that a brother of the order, Fra Filippo di
Campello, was associated with him as joint architect,
and this will account in great measure for the thorough
Italianizing of the Trans-Alpine plan, while the rest will
be explained by the native artisans being left to work
out the details in their own way.

Vasari on
Jacopo
Tedesco
According to Vasari, Messer Jacopo, or Lapo, was
summoned to Florence in consequence of the reputation
he had earned at Assisi, and he spent the rest of his
life there. Among other works which Vasari attributes
to him is a design commissioned by Manfred for the
tomb of Frederick II at Monreale. The Emperor's
tomb, however, is not at Monreale, but in the Duomo
of Palermo, and is in a style quite unlike anything in the
manner of Jacopo. Vasari has also been shown to be in
error in making Arnolfo, whom he calls Arnolfo di Lapo,
the son of Jacopo, and "the heir not less of the virtue
than of the ability of his father."

Genoa.
S. Loren-
zo
At GENOA we are met again by distinct traces of
northern influence, modified, however, as at Assisi by
passing through an Italian medium. The fine church

---

[1] The lower church was built between 1228 and 1232, and the upper part
in 1253.

Plate CXLVIII

ASSISI

of S. LORENZO, which was consecrated in 1118, has Genoa.
S. Lorenzo undergone many subsequent alterations, and was extensively restored in 1307 and 1312. Under the north triforium of the nave we read in Lombardic lettering :—

⊻ MCCℂVII° PASTONVS DE NIGRO · ET · NICOLAVS DE GOANO · FECERVNT · RENOVARI · HOC · OPVS · DE · DECRETO · LEGATORVM · ⊻

Another inscription on the south side gives the other date.

The church has a nave of nine bays, carried by eight The arcade mono-cylindric columns of claret-coloured marble, varied with streaks and blots of other colours and white, and the shafts are diminished with an entasis. Each has a course of white marble next the base. In the western responds this white course is omitted, and the capital dropped an equal distance, so that that side of the arch is stilted. The arches are pointed and well moulded in two orders, and are banded with black and white voussoirs alternately. The splendour of these colonnades is almost unrivalled; this was the first marble church I saw in my student days, and I well remember the astonishment with which it struck me.

The capitals are very Classic, and have a deep abacus The
capitals like those at S. Mark's in Venice. Three capitals next the east end have figures of angels at the corners instead of foliage and volutes. Above, in the place of a triforium, is an arcade of round arches on wide piers The upper
arcade alternated with single shafts. The arches have two plain unmoulded orders in white marble, and all the capitals are foliated and have a strong abacus. There is no triforium storey, but this upper arcade is open to the aisle, as at Rochester, and the cathedral of Rouen, and the aisle has a plain barrel vault tied in with iron, as is also that of the nave.   There is a simple clerestory of single round-headed lights perfectly plain.   The aisles are lighted by tall round-headed lancets high up in the wall, opposite the quasi-triforium arcade.

The
transept

The transepts, choir, and dome show only Renaissance work inside, but the transept has Gothic arcading without.

At the west end is a gallery on a vault with ribs and panels, all constructed in black and white marble.

Dimensions and
details

The bays of the nave, at a rough measurement, are about 13 ft. long by 42 ft. wide, and the aisle is about 30 ft. wide.   The columns near the base have a diameter of 2 ft. 6 in. or 2 ft. 7 in.   They have a quasi-Attic base, well profiled, the lower torus overhanging the plinth in the centre of each face ; and there are carved toes at the angles, in one case a human hand turned back towards the shaft, in others heads of a lion or an ox, and some are simple spurs, fluted.

French
influence

All these details betray a French influence, modified, of course, by Italian feeling, and by the use of marble instead of free-stone.   This mixture of sentiment is still more plainly seen in the magnificent west portal

The Portal (Plate CXLIX), where the capitals might have been carved by a Frenchman from Burgundy, and the twisted columns remind one of Avallon, though the marble and inlaid work of the jambs is purely Italian.   The admirable sculpture of some of the panels of the podium is more like French work in free-stone than Italian work in marble (Fig. 193).   This doorway appears to date from the restoration at the beginning of the 14th century, when the church was probably nearly rebuilt from the 12th-century columns upwards.

Plate CXLIX

GENOA—S. Lorenzo, West Portal

The influence of Northern Gothic is shown very plainly
in the church of S. Galgano in Tuscany (A.D. 1218), now
a ruin, which has arcades of pointed arches in two orders
on clustered columns, of which the shafts next the nave run
up to take the vaulting, as they do at Sens (Plate I, vol. i.
p. 38) and S. Alpin at Châlons (Plate VI, vol. i. p. 72).
There is even a triforium, though the opening is very

Fig. 193.

small, and the east end has two tiers of three single lights
surmounted by a rose in a high-pitched gable, reminding
one of Laon, Chartres, and Châlons-sur-Marne, and not
unlike Byland, Elgin, and the south transept of Westminster. The design must have come from a northern
hand, though it is modified to some extent by local
methods. The high vaults of the nave were of regular
rib and panel work, but instead of flying buttresses there

S. Gal-
gano

are substantial piers outside the clerestory which rest partly on the aisle vaults. The church belonged to

Cistercian
influence
on Italian
Gothic

a Cistercian abbey, and 'it seems to have been through the Cistercians from Burgundy that Gothic architecture made its way in Italy to a great extent.

The foregoing description of S. Galgano will apply generally to the Cistercian churches of Fossanova which was consecrated in 1208 and Casamari in 1217, both of them farther south, to S. Martino near Viterbo, and to several other churches of the same Order in Italy[1]. They all have pointed arches and the Cistercian square east end, but their central octagonal lantern towers are Italian rather than French. Their vaults have no flying buttresses, and M. Enlart says it would be hard to find seven churches in Italy with them.

These churches seem to mark the beginning of Gothic work in central Italy[2]. They were followed by the Duomo

Siena
cathedral

of SIENA, in which we find Italian Gothic fully developed. It is not known exactly when it was begun, but its construction was in progress during the first half of the 13th century, and it was consecrated in 1267. The west front, by Giovanni Pisano, dates from 1284, and was finished within the century. He is supposed to have carried out a design of his father Niccola, who died in 1278, and according to Vasari had been concerned with the building of the cathedral. The church is planned on a magnificent scale, and shows all the peculiarities which distinguish the Gothic of Italy from that of the North (Fig. 194). The plan, which on paper seems fairly simple, is

[1] Illustrated in M. Enlart's *Origines Françaises de l'Architecture Gothique en Italie.*

[2] Tranne il convento di S. Galgano, opera di artisti stranieri, l'architettura gotica non aveva dato in Siena gran saggio di se, prima della costruzione del Duomo. *Italia Artistica. Siena.*

extremely intricate and difficult to understand in the Siena
cathedral
building, being complicated by the irregularity of the
transept and its adjuncts, the unusual form of the

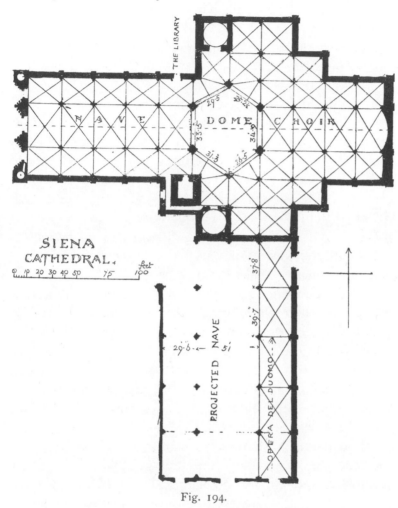

Fig. 194.

hexagonal dome, and the intrusion of the campanile into
the body of the building. The wide spacing of the National
in style
columns and great span of the arches, the absence of

buttresses and triforium, and the flatness of the roofs all belong to the Southern School, as well as the small windows, which would have been wholly insufficient in the North. Inside and out the walls are faced with white marble banded with black. The columns, which are also of black and white marble, are clustered, and have capitals *à crochet* with two tiers of leaves, and the hollow Corinthian abacus surmounted by a shallow square one with little dentils. Above them is a pedestal or stilt, from which the arches spring (Plate CL). In the choir the arches have a suspicion of a point, and the extrados seems slightly to widen as it rises, but of this I cannot feel quite sure. In the nave the arches seem semi-circular. The vaults are quadripartite, the transverse rib of a plain flat section is round-arched, the wall rib is pointed and very slight, with dentils; the diagonal is a pointed roll in section. All the windows are pointed and have tracery (*v.* Fig. 197, p. 207).

At the east end the ground falls precipitously, so that under the choir there is a lower church, dedicated to S. Giovanni Battista, and serving as a baptistery, which is entered on the level from a street behind the cathedral. It contains the famous font with sculptures by Jacopo della Quercia, Donatello, Ghiberti, and Turini, with its picturesque centre piece, a favourite subject for artists. There is a cast of it at South Kensington.

The dome is an irregular hexagon (Plate CLI), all the sides being unequal, and it is gradually brought by tromps to a circle for the lantern. At each angle the inner shaft of the clustered pier runs up into the tromp like that at Vercelli, but here it carries a statue. A colonnade, as at Vercelli, surrounds the dome below the springing.

Plate CL

T. G. J.   SIENA CATHEDRAL—The Choir

Plate CLI

SIENA CATHEDRAL

The plan of the dome area is very successful, and gives a greater sense of expansion and spaciousness than the octagon at Ely, which never seems quite to realize its promise, though Ely is the larger of the two[1].

The famous white marble façade (Plate CLII), the work of Giovanni, son of Niccola Pisano, abounds in magnificent detail, but it is too full of ornament and the sculpture is overcrowded. The rose window, without which no Italian Gothic front would be considered complete, has some extremely beautiful painted glass, but it is too large for external effect, and causes the middle compartment of the upper stage in the façade to be wider than that below. Consequently one misses the vertical division of the composition into three parts corresponding to nave and aisles, there being no line from top to bottom to mark them. This is a serious defect, which is avoided in the similar front at Orvieto. It is interesting to compare the carving on the shafts of the great portals (Plate CLIII) with the earlier scroll-work on those of the baptistery door at Pisa, which is more Classic[2]. But though the Siena example is more Gothic than the other, it still retains something of the Roman touch, and the smaller members have real arabesques quite in the Renaissance manner.

The fronts of the two churches of Siena and Orvieto are perhaps the most splendid achievements of Italian Gothic, and show most completely the merits and defects of the style. The two are much alike ; the lower stage is divided into three square compartments containing the

---

[1] In the western angles of the dome may still be seen the two standards of the Florentine Carroccio, captured by the Sienese at the battle of Montaperti in 1260.

[2] v. my *Byzantine and Romanesque Architecture*, vol. I. Plate LXXIV.

three pedimented doorways of nave and aisles. Above these runs at ORVIETO (Plate CLIV) a band of arcading, and at Siena an enriched cornice. In the upper storey a square panel in the centre contains the great western rose window of the nave, and each of the three divisions is finished with a gable. Turrets crowned with spirelets flank the façade, and two smaller piers with pinnacles divide the three compartments and run up beside the central square. At Siena the doors are round-arched ; at Orvieto the aisle doors are pointed and the pediments are much steeper. Such are these famous fronts, enriched with precious sculpture and inlays of coloured marble and mosaic, exhausting all the resources of contemporary art. Their beauty is incontestible, but it is strongest when most distinctively national, and weakest when it challenges comparison with Gothic on its native ground.

Both of them have portals recessed, order within order, under gabled pediments, as are those of Paris, Amiens, or Reims ; but beyond this bare fact they have little enough in common with them. The recessing is much shallower, the effect much flatter, the whole treatment more superficial, and this is consistent with their different artistic motive. The ideal of the Italian was colour ; that of the Frenchman light and shade. The sentiment

was wholly different ; on the one hand there was the mystery, the romance, the seriousness and gloom of the North, on the other the clear, positive directness of the Italian mind, its freedom from illusion, its sensuous enjoyment of beauty and gaiety. Portal for portal we may give the palm to Reims or Chartres rather than to Siena ; but there is no need to compare them ; least of all is it reasonable to try them by the standard of Northern Gothic as most modern critics have done, from

Plate CLII

SIENA—West front

Plate CLIII

Column white marble
c . 1.6" diam

Red Marble — white marble
7"   5½"   7½"   6"

T. G. J.   SIENA CATHEDRAL—Scroll on Column of West door

Fergusson downwards. Each must be regarded from the national point of view: each in its own way expresses the temper of the people who made it what it is, and therefore each in its own way is right. To the Italian, French Gothic is unsympathetic. One Italian writer says of Siena that "although the general plan, the profile, and some details show us the French style, in everything else Italian art in interpreting it has enlivened and transformed the cold and austere style of France." Another critic says it is the "most admirable flower of Gothic art, but it is a new Gothic, blooming in a better clime, among cultured minds, more serene, more beautiful, religious and yet sane, and compared with French cathedrals it is like the poems of Dante and Petrarch compared to the sonnets of the Troubadours." Whether we agree or disagree with this estimate is nothing to the purpose; it does not touch the point of the suitability of each form of art to local circumstance.

In one respect it must be admitted that these two fronts sin against the canon that design should follow construction, for the three gables of the façades have no correspondence with the roofs behind them, the aisles being covered with lean-to roofs at a much lower level, while the nave has a flat roof behind the steep gable.

The patriotic ambition of the Senesi was not content with their cathedral, however magnificent, and it was no sooner finished than they wanted to double its size. The present cathedral was to serve as the transept to a much vaster fane. Lando di Pietro, a Sienese architect, was summoned from Naples, and an enormous nave was actually begun on the south side, of which the side and end walls and one aisle were actually built (Fig. 194, p. 197). Then came the black death of 1348, and

constant wars with neighbouring states, and there seem also to have been some structural difficulties, for the pillars of the only arcade that was erected are out of the
upright, and so the scheme was abandoned. The proportions of the projected nave are immense, the span of the arches being nearly 40 feet and the width of the nave 50 feet. The plan must have involved the destruction of the dome and the transept, for the pillars carrying them would have been in the middle of the proposed nave, and even had they been left they would have had no abutment. That this destruction was intended seems certain, for the new nave is so planned as to get the area of the dome central with it, and this is perhaps the explanation of the advice given by some Florentine architects who had been consulted, to pull down a great part of what had been done and to begin again[1].

The cathedral of ORVIETO commemorates the miracle of Bolsena, which is said to have occurred in 1260. The building was begun in 1290, and consecrated in 1309, the architect being Lorenzo Maitani of Siena, who lived to see it completely finished in 1330. Under his superintendence were employed no fewer than forty architects, sculptors, and painters from Florence and Siena, who settled at Orvieto and were formed into a corporate body with a separate head for each craft[2]. It shows a curious reversion to the basilican plan of long colonnades, not divided into bays, with wooden roofs over both nave and aisles instead of vaulting (Plate CLV). There is a shallow transept not extending beyond the aisles, and at

---

[1] Three bays of the aisle of this intended nave are now enclosed and floored at several levels for the Museum or Opera del Duomo. The opposite wall has buildings against its outer side.

[2] Perkins, *Tuscan Sculptors*, vol. I. p. 89.

Plate CLIV

ORVIETO CATHEDRAL

Plate CLV

ORVIETO CATHEDRAL

each end of the transept, which is as high as the nave, is Orvieto cathedral a lower chapel. That on the south contains the famous frescoes by Luca Signorelli and Fra Angelico, with their portraits, and the marvellously foreshortened figures by which Luca astonished his contemporaries. That on the north contains the reliquary of the Bolsena miracle. The choir ends square, with a single long window of four lights, and there are quadripartite vaults over choir and central crossing. The columns and walls, both within and without, are of white and black stone in bands, marble being reserved for the façade. The nave arches are semi-circular, but those across the aisles are pointed. The outside walls being of stone and not of marble, have attracted lichens, which give them a delightful texture. Altogether this is an extremely beautiful building, both inside and outside.

The aisles have two-light windows with marble The alabaster glazing tracery, the upper part glazed and the lower half filled with thin slabs of alabaster instead of glass, through which the brilliant Italian sunshine passes with admirable effect, so that from a distant point of view the windows seem painted in brown monochrome. Some windows are entirely glazed with alabaster, and seen from outside they have the disagreeable appearance of being walled up.

Between the aisle windows the wall is, as it were, buttressed by narrow semi-circular apses, probably intended for small chapels, with handsome arcaded cornices (Plate CLVI).

The façade is better than that at Siena. The three The façade bays are divided logically from top to bottom by pilasters, an arrangement in which Siena is defective, and the general proportion of the doorways is happier. The

Orvieto
cathedral

jamb shafts are inlaid with mosaic, and mosaic pictures fill the tympana and spandrils. But alas! the original mosaics are gone, one of those from the tympana is now in the museum at South Kensington, and the modern pictures are only worthy of a *Caffè Ristorante*.

The false
gables

The three gables, it must be confessed, are a fraud and a sham here, as they are at Siena, but much may be forgiven to so lovely a composition.

The
sculpture

The piers between the portals, and beyond them, are covered with sculpture of a most interesting kind. The resurrection and last judgement and other sacred subjects are represented by groups of small figures, tier above tier, divided by sprays of delicate foliage branching right and left from an upright growth of interlacing stems. It is uncertain to what artist these admirable sculptures must be attributed. Vasari says they are by Niccola Pisano, but it is now believed that they were carved between 1325 and 1331, and Niccola died in 1278 and his son Giovanni in 1320.

Italian
window
tracery

The window tracery of Italy differs in many ways from that of Northern Gothic, and it can nowhere be studied to better advantage than at Siena and Orvieto. In a former chapter the development of the Gothic window was shown to be a gradual and logical growth, from distinct and unrelated openings divided by piers to grouped lights under an including arch, then to plate-tracery, and finally to the perfection of bar-tracery. But this was not its history in Italy. Tracery did not grow up there, but was taken ready-made from the northern styles and adopted as a beautiful architectural feature.

Windows
less im-
portant in
Italian
architec-
ture

It does not play so important a part in Italian architecture as with us or in France and Germany, for the climate of Italy forbids large window openings, and the

Plate CLVI

Alabaster

Orvieto.
oct 1915
T. G. J.

10'.10"

T. G. J.   ORVIETO CATHEDRAL

Plate CLVII

LUCCA CATHEDRAL—The Triforium

great clerestories of Amiens or Beauvais and the vast Italian window tracery
east windows of York or Gloucester would have been
intolerable south of the Alps. The Italian windows,
even in the largest churches, are often only of two-lights,
and the rose window, which came to be an indispensable
feature of the façade, never attains the proportions of

Fig. 195.

those at Laon and Chartres or Westminster and Lincoln.
In pure Italian Gothic, setting aside buildings where
Trans-Alpine influence enters, the tracery does not follow
the logical construction of the northern window. The
tracery bar does not always ramify and coalesce; the
cusping remains soffit-cusping to the last, and the idea of
plate-tracery was never quite thrown aside. In domestic

work, where several lights were grouped under an including arch, the shield was often left unpierced, as in
the Palazzo del Comune at Siena (Plate CLXIII, p. 234),
where it bears the arms of the Republic.   In the window of
the Palazzo Saraceni (Fig. 195) the shield has three sunk
circles and a scutcheon.   In the brickwork window from
the Palazzo Comunale at Fano (Fig. 196) the lights are

Fig. 196.

trefoiled and the shield is pierced with a traceried circle[1].
This, with few exceptions, notably at Venice, is as far as
tracery went in domestic work, and is the type of window
in all the brick palaces at Pavia, Piacenza, and other

---

[1] In all these windows the colonnettes dividing the lights are not
mullions : the glass is not set in the stone work, but in wooden frames
behind it. And this is the method employed generally in the Domestic
Gothic windows of Italy.

North Italian towns. The limitations of the material Italian
interfered with anything more elaborate. In the churches, window
where stone and marble were more freely used, we get tracery

SIENA
CATHEDRAL.

Black
Marble

White Marble
Brescia

Black
Marble

|<-. 18⅜". .->|<--. 20½". -->|

Fig. 197.

more complete tracery, but the figures do not always
come together as in northern work, but are juxta-posed
rather than united. The two examples from the cathedral

Italian
window
tracery
at Siena

of Siena (Fig. 197) have a delicate beauty of their own which is quite original, but are like nothing in Northern Gothic. A curious feature is the stilt, or pedestal, above the proper capital, which occurs also in the main arcades of the interior and in the arches of the portals at Orvieto. It seems to be a faint echo of the Classic entablature.

At Orvieto

The tracery of the side windows at Orvieto (Plate CLV) is more like Northern Gothic than those at Siena; the arches are stilted but without the stilting pedestal, and the fillet of the circle coalesces regularly with that of the lights. The cusping, however, is all of the soffit type.

At Lucca

The triforium of the cathedral at LUCCA (Plate CLVII) is contained within a round arch, and shows the characteristics of Italian tracery very well. It has the stilted feature of the windows at Siena, though it is less conspicuous here, and the design is a compound of plate-tracery with very delicate pierced work. In fact, not only these windows, but those of Siena, and many others, have more the effect of being pierced through a slab, in the manner of plate-tracery, than of being constructed in the northern manner. This is still more evident in the

In cloister,
Viterbo

cloister windows of S. Maria della Verità at VITERBO, where there is no idea of constructive form whatever (Plate CLVIII).

Campo
Santo,
Pisa

The traceried arcades of the Campo Santo at Pisa are of the same character as those of Lucca. At Venice there is a more structural character in the Gothic window, but even there the cusps are of the plate-tracery kind. To this, however, we shall return in a later chapter.

Plate CLVIII

VITERBO—Cloister of S. Maria della Verità

Plate CLIX

T. G. J. Mens. et Del.

Scale

PISA—Pulpit in Baptistery

CHAPTER XXVI

CENTRAL ITALY, *continued*

THE SCHOOL OF NICCOLA PISANO. ARNOLFO AND GIOTTO—LUCCA AND MILAN

THE history of Niccola Pisano, architect and sculptor, Niccola Pisano affords a notable instance of what we observed in a former chapter: that in Italy, unlike what happened in other countries, we can often trace the influence of a single artist in giving a new direction to the art of his day. Niccola was perhaps the first of the eclectics, His eclecticism working in the Gothic style then current, but engrafting upon it fresh motives borrowed from the antique, and in so doing he paved the way for Donatello and Brunelleschi and the Classic Renaissance.

He was born in 1205 or 1207, the son of a notary, and he died in 1278. He was so early proficient in architecture that Frederick II, passing through Pisa when Niccola was only fifteen years old, carried him away to Naples and employed him there to finish the Castel dell' Ovo. It is doubted whether he designed the fantastic church of S. Antonio at Padua, with its S. Antonio, Padua domes in imitation of S. Mark's at Venice and its eastern-looking minarets, which is attributed to him by Vasari and others, or that of the Frari at Venice, which is more likely by one of his scholars. The lunette over a door in the cathedral of Lucca, of the deposition of Christ from the cross, sculptured by him, according to

Niccola
Pisano

Vasari, in 1237, shows more careful study of composition than is usual in works of that time; but it is doubtful whether he was really the author of it. The churches he built during the next ten years at Florence, Arezzo, Volterra, and Cortona have all been remodelled, but his

The pulpit
at Pisa

famous pulpit in the baptistery at PISA survives unaltered as a monument of his skill both in architecture and sculpture (Plate CLIX). It bears an inscription with the date 1260:

> Anno milleno bis centum bisque triceno
> Hoc opus insigne sculpsit Niccola Pisano
> Laudetur digne tam bene docta manus.

Its
eclecticism

Though designed in the Gothic style, it is frankly eclectic in execution. The Classic egg and dart ornament appears amid trefoiled arches and Gothic mouldings; and the sculptured panels, representing biblical scenes, are adapted from the reliefs on an antique sarcophagus in the Campo Santo. The subjects are the nativity, the visit of the Magi, the circumcision, the crucifixion[1], and the last judgement. A Juno-like Madonna sits like a Roman empress to receive the adoration of the wise men, and reclines like another Agrippina in the scene of the nativity, with little resemblance to her portraiture in the stiff Byzantine manner of preceding artists. The pulpit is hexagonal, probably a novel form, for the earlier pulpits, of which there are several examples at Pistoia, were rectangular. Of the six supporting columns, the alternate three rest on the backs of lions in the traditional manner[2]; the centre is supported by another column

---

[1] The panel of the crucifixion happens to be the one I drew, and is shown in the plate, but it is really in the next panel to the left.

[2] The lion, according to the Bestiaries, typifies the Resurrection: for the lion cub is born dead; the mother keeps it three days, when it is raised to life by the father's breath and voice.

with a group of a griffin, a lion, and a dog alternating with three human figures round its pedestal, and its abacus has the classic ovolo moulding. The section of the bases of the various parts is very refined (Fig. 198), resembling to an unusual extent the quasi-Attic base of northern Gothic at Paris and Amiens (Fig. 22, vol. I. p. 63), and at Chichester and elsewhere in early English buildings. All the mouldings throughout are exquisitely delicate.

Niccola Pisano. The pulpit at Pisa

Five years later, in 1265, Niccola was employed to make a similar pulpit in the Duomo of Siena. It is octagonal, and not, to my taste, so beautiful as the hexagonal pulpit at Pisa[1]. The hexagonal form is much more elegant than the octagonal. I noticed the same thing in comparing the hexagonal pulpit at Spalato in Dalmatia with the octagonal one at Traü[2]. A handsome but rather incongruous staircase of Renaissance work was added to it in the 15th century by Il Marrina, a Sienese sculptor.

Pulpit at Siena

The new motive introduced into Italian art by Niccola Pisano will be apparent if his sculpture is compared with that of his predecessors in Italy, and with the contemporary work in France and England. It turns away from mediaeval tradition, and looks back to the art of Pagan Rome. His figures are squat and often clumsy, but they are based on Classic models, and the composition of the groups is more studied and artificial than was the practice before him. Hitherto sculpture, nurtured in the Church, had been bound by conventional rule. It followed certain formulas established by tradition and consecrated by authority as proper for each subject.

The new classic manner

---

[1] He was assisted by his pupils, Arnolfo, Lapo, and Donato, and his son Giovanni ; the pulpit was finished in 1268. *Italia Artistica. Siena*, p. 52.

[2] The Spalato pulpit is illustrated in my *Dalmatia, the Quarnero and Istria*, vol. II. pp. 44, 45.

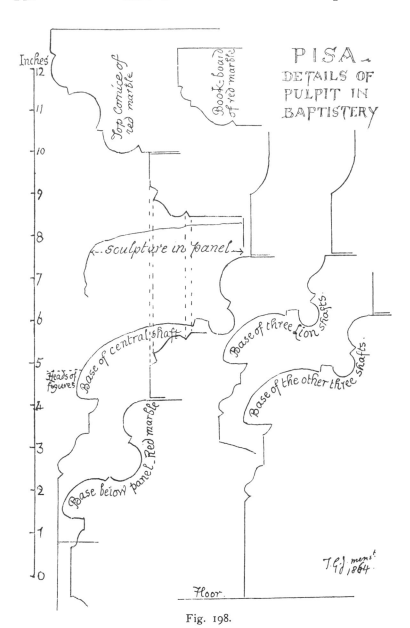

Inches

PISA.
DETAILS OF
PULPIT IN
BAPTISTERY

Top Cornice of red marble

Book-board of red marble

←..sculpture in panel..→

Base of central shaft

Base of three lion shafts.

Base of the other three shafts.

Heads of figures

Base below panel. Red marble

T.G.J. mens.t 1864

Floor.

Fig. 198.

The art of Niccola broke with the hieratic tradition, and, in returning to Classic example, returned in fact to greater naturalism.   Niccola Pisano

The Classic strain introduced into Italian sculpture by Niccola Pisano produced at first no impression on the architecture : though in the fine pulpit by his pupil, Fra Guglielmo d'Agnello, made in 1270 for the church of S. Giovanni Fuorcivitas at Pistoia, there is less of the Gothic character than in the work of his master.   But the work of Giovanni Pisano, son to Niccola, shows Italian Gothic in its fullest development, and his sculpture, though more forcible, has less Classic repose than the designs of his father.   In 1278 he began the Campo Santo, or cemetery of Pisa, in which was laid the sacred earth brought by Archbishop Federigo from the Holy Land when the Christians had finally been expelled from it.   His great pulpit for the Duomo, begun in 1302, in which he made figures take the place of some of the columns, exists in fragments which are put together in the museum[1].   To him is attributed the lion and lectern on the stairs leading to his father's pulpit in the baptistery (Plate CLIX).   His hexagonal pulpit in the church of S. Andrea at Pistoia has ugly sprawling pointed trefoils in the place of the graceful cusping of Niccola's baptistery pulpit, and the figures in the sculptured panels have more of the violent movement of earlier Gothic sculpture.

Fra Guglielmo

Giovanni Pisano

The little chapel DELLA SPINA on the quay of the Arno at PISA has generally been attributed to Giovanni Pisano, or at least its decoration, for the building we now see is remodelled on an older foundation.   Vasari says " Giovanni, with the aid of some of his young men, applied many ornaments to that oratory, and brought it

Pisa. Capella della Spina

[1] There is a cast of it at S. Kensington.

Pisa.
Capella
della
Spina
to that perfection which we see to-day." Further researches, however, show that the enlargement and adornment of the building dates from 1323, three years after Giovanni's death. The building, which has lately been restored and raised some feet, is of marble, and consists of two aisles. The side windows are simple, but are surmounted by a series of arcades containing statues and rich with tabernacle work, gablets, and pinnacles (Plate CLX). In spite of many beautiful details, the design has in excess the redundancy of ornament into which Italian Gothic fell, and to a northern eye it seems fussy and overdone.

Pisan
arcading
Gothicised
Some of the churches in Pisa show a curious conversion of the traditional arcaded front of Pisan Romanesque into Gothic. The church of S. Michele in Borgo[1], attributed to Fra Guglielmo, has three tiers of arcading, but the arches that spring from the colonnettes are pointed and have trefoil cusping. Otherwise the general design, with a high central part corresponding to the nave, and triangular sloping wings at a lower level corresponding to the aisle, is precisely that of the Duomo and of S. Pietro a ripa d'Arno on a reduced scale. The façade of the church of S. Caterina[2] has arcading Gothicised in the same way.

Arnolfo
del
Cambio
A fresh impulse was given to Italian Gothic by Arnolfo del Cambio, who was born in 1232 and died in 1310, "to whose talent," says Vasari, "architecture was as much indebted for improvement as painting to that of Cimabue." Arnolfo was the son of Cambio and his wife Perfetta, and a pupil of Niccola Pisano at the same time as Giovanni, who was his junior by eight years. He distinguished himself first as a sculptor, and the fine

[1] Illustrated in *Italia Artistica*. *Pisa*, p. 56.   [2] *Ibid*. p. 55.

Plate CLX

PISA—Capella della Spina

monument of Cardinal Braye in S. Domenico at Orvieto
is attributed to him [1].　He is supposed to be the Arnolfus
who designed the tabernacle in S. Paolo fuori le mura
at Rome, which bears the inscription—

Hoc opus fecit Arnolfus cum suo socio Petro.

In 1294 he began the great Franciscan church of
S. CROCE, the Westminster Abbey of FLORENCE.　Like
most of the churches of the preaching orders, it is planned
with an enormous open nave for congregational use
between narrow aisles, and with a wooden roof.　At the
east end is a transept, from which project five chapels on
each side of an apsidal chancel, which is reduced to a
convenient span by bringing the next chapel on each
side within the width of the nave.

In 1298 Arnolfo refaced the Baptistery of Florence
with marble, and began the DUOMO, charged by the
Signoria to make it such that the industry and wit of
man could conceive or execute nothing more magnificent.
Vasari records the extraordinary care he bestowed on
the foundations, which were so massive that Brunelleschi
did not fear to build on them his mighty cupola, which
Vasari says was much heavier than anything Arnolfo had
contemplated.　We have, however, little to tell us what
Arnolfo did contemplate, for he died when the church
had reached the point at which the problem of covering
the central space presented itself.

In the Duomo of Florence, and the churches built by
Niccola Pisano and his scholars and followers we see
what Gothic became in purely Italian hands.　The
churches of the Frari, and SS. GIOVANNI E PAOLO
(Fig. 199) at VENICE, if not designed by Niccola himself,

Marginal notes:

Arnolfo del Cambio

S. Croce, Florence

S. Maria dei Fiori, Florence

The Frari and SS. Giov. e Paolo, Venice

---

[1] Illustrated by Perkins, *Tuscan Sculptors.*

were at all events the outcome of his school.   They are
all on a grand scale, but of the simplest architectural construction.   The Franciscan church of the Frari was begun
in 1250 and finished in 1338, and the Dominican church of

Venice.
SS. Gio-
vanni e
Paolo

SS. Giovanni e Paolo, which imitated it, was not finished
till 1385.   SS. GIOVANNI E PAOLO is prepared for a
marble porch or loggia which never arrived, but otherwise it is of the plainest brickwork outside, as is also the
church of the Frari, adorned only by cornices of intersecting brick arches.   Inside they are simple to the verge
of insipidity.   Plain cylindrical columns with poorly
sculptured capitals of meagre foliage support pointed
arches of a single order with wide soffit, and a mere roll
moulding on the edges (Fig. 199).   The vaulting shaft in
these and similar churches is generally a shallow pilaster,
flat and wide, rising from the capital, which has a very
poor effect: and a similar pilaster carries the aisle vault.
A northern eye, at all events, finds the wide spacing of

Narrow
spacing of
piers in
Northern
Gothic

the bays unsatisfactory.   In French and English Gothic
the aisle bays are generally square, and this gives the
articulation of the building, or in other words the distance between pier and pier and the length of the bay.
Consequently the bay of the nave is oblong in a transverse
direction, whence arose all the difficulties of cross-vaulting
it, which were met and overcome by the adoption of the
pointed arch and rib-and-panel construction[1].   But the

Wide
spacing in
Italian
Gothic

Italian reversed this plan, and made the nave bays square
and the aisle bays oblong, and oblong, of course, lengthways of the church, and not transversely.   This caused
the length of the bay and the spacing of the piers to be
double what they would have been on the other plan,

---

[1] *v. supra*, Chapters II. and III.

Triforium
& Abacus

Nave
Arcade

Vaulting rib
in aisles

D° in Nave

SS Giovanni & Paolo
Venice. Nov 8. 1864

Fig. 199.

and diminished the number of piers by a half.   There is
no doubt an audacity in this that appeals to the imagination.   All the parts in a design of this kind are large,
the floor is open and unencumbered, and the area of the
voids is extraordinarily great in proportion to the solids.

In the vast church of S. Petronio at Bologna the solid
supports are said to be only one-twelfth of the voids, a
proportion which, says Fergusson, "would have been
a merit in a railway station, but something more is
wanted in a monumental building."

When the whole design consists of but a few parts,
each of them of gigantic proportions, it is obvious that
the effect of size will be lost unless there are some
features by which to scale it, and some details to bring it
into relation with the human standard.   But in many of
these great Italian interiors there is hardly any architectural detail at all.   The wall arcadings, delicate
traceries, string-courses, shafted columns, capitals either
richly carved or deeply moulded, and other decorative
features which often make our great churches look larger
than they are, have no counterpart in these Italian buildings.   Especially do we miss in most of them the tripartite

division of arcade triforium and clerestory, for at the
Frari there is no triforium, and at SS. Giovanni e Paolo
it is only represented by a diminutive window in each

bay (Fig. 199), while in nearly every case the clerestory,
which plays so large a part in northern churches, is
reduced to very small openings; at Florence and many
other churches to mere round holes.

It is true that we must not judge these buildings
from the standpoint of northern architecture.   The light
needful in our latitude would be intolerable in Italy:
even here it is inconvenient in our late Gothic churches

except when the windows are filled with the painted
glass for which they were intended.   Painted glass, Italian use of stained glass
though Italy has some splendid examples of it, was not
the normal mode of decorating these interiors.   It was
unsuited to the small windows of Italian churches, and
where it was employed as at Florence and in the lower
church at Assisi it wraps the interior in an oppressive
gloom.   There is no doubt that the vast plain wall-spaces
left by these small windows were meant to be painted,
and where the interior has been so treated the necessary Painted decoration essential
amount of detail is supplied, the eye is satisfied, and the
building recovers that effect of scale and proportion
which is painfully wanting where such decoration is
absent.

A good instance of successful treatment in this way S. Anastasia, Verona
is the interior of the church of S. ANASTASIA at VERONA.
It has the wide bays of Italian Gothic, square in the
nave, oblong longitudinally in the aisles, cylindrical
columns with rather better capitals than usual, and
simple quadripartite vaulting.   No string-course marks
the division of arcade triforium and clerestory, the triforium being represented by a mere round hole, and a
rather larger cusped circle serving for the clerestory.
Nothing could well be simpler and less interesting
architecturally, and yet the interior is one of the most
beautiful in Italy.   For it is decorated throughout with
painting, and though that on the walls is sadly decayed,
that of the vaulting remains.   It consists chiefly of
coloured borders on a white ground, with sometimes a
medallion containing a figure, and sometimes a foliated
device in each panel of the groining, not unlike those in
the choir ceiling at S. Alban's.   With such a decorative
treatment as this it is obvious that so long as the fabric

Architec-
tural detail
superseded
by paint-
ing

is solid and well proportioned purely architectural ornament may be dispensed with. The effect depends on
colour rather than on form. There is a church a little
way from Cremona, dedicated to S. Sigismondo, where

S. Sigis-
mondo,
Cremona

the interior is entirely covered by fresco paintings, still
in good preservation when I saw them in 1873, which,
so far as I can remember, has no architectural features
in the interior but the mere arches, and does very well
without any.

Assisi

In the interior of the churches at Assisi where the
walls are covered with frescoes by Cimabue and Giotto
and other early Tuscan masters, enclosed in borders of
arabesques and geometrical patterns, architecture is not
absent, but it certainly takes the second place in the
design.

Siena and
Orvieto

At Siena and Orvieto, on the other hand, the desired
effect of colour is obtained by other and more durable
means than painting, and fuller play is given to the
architectural ornament, leaving little room for painted
decoration in the interior of nave and choir, and con-
signing it to spaces specially prepared for it in the library
at one place and the transeptal chapels at the other.
This seems to place the three sister arts of architecture,
painting, and sculpture in a truer relation to one another
than that which they bear in buildings where the decorative
arts predominate over the great master art to which they
ought to be subsidiary.

The
Duomo of
Florence

The interior of the DUOMO at FLORENCE affords a
typical instance of the want of something to give the
true effect of scale (Fig. 200). Inspired by his instruc-
tions, which demanded a design of unrivalled splendour,
such as the wit of man could not surpass, Arnolfo not
only planned his building of a gigantic size, but also

gave a colossal proportion to each member. The nave of Norwich cathedral in a length of rather less than 250 feet has fourteen arches; in Arnolfo's nave, which is rather longer, four immense arches suffice to stride from end to end of it. The span of the nave is 55 feet in the clear, the arches, which are pointed, are nearly 90 feet high, and the vault is nearly 150 feet to the apex, about equal to Beauvais or Cologne, and higher than Amiens.

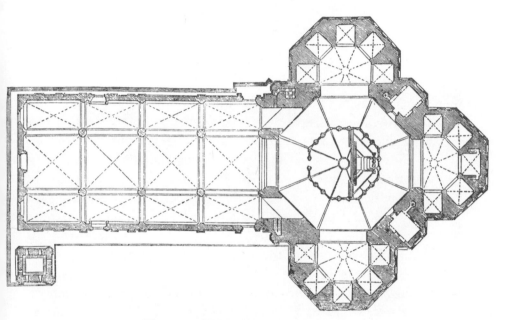

Fig. 200.   (*From* Fergusson.)

Eastwards of the nave the plan expands into an enormous octagon, from which to east, north, and south radiate the choir and transepts, each a semi-octagon covered with a semi-dome.

The general conception is magnificent, and appeals strongly to the imagination, and yet there is no building so utterly disappointing when you cross the threshold.

Cathedral
of
Florence.
The dis-
appointing
interior
Had the interior been decorated, as no doubt it should have been, for the Italians never could have contemplated leaving it in its present state of bare walls, and had the lower part been lined with marble, the floor paved with *opus Alexandrinum,* and the upper part covered with fine fresco painting or mosaic[1], the magnificent dimensions would have asserted themselves, and Florence might have had the most superb church in Christendom. As it is, the interior looks less than half its size, and as the windows are filled with coloured glass, which, though beautiful in itself, makes the church very dark, the whole effect is gloomy and uninteresting.

Arnolfo's
plan for
the centre
Arnolfo died in 1310, when the critical moment had arrived for covering his great central octagon, which has a diameter of 138 feet 6 inches. It is doubtful how he meant to do it. That something important, requiring unusual support, was in his mind is clear, from the massive substructure he had prepared; but Vasari says his model had been lost by the carelessness of the authorities. According to him Arnolfo's plan was to spring his vault from the lower cornice on which Brunelleschi raised the drum with the round windows, from which his dome starts. Probably Arnolfo's central tower would have been something of the same kind as that at Chiaravalle (Fig. 191, p. 186), but I doubt whether a structure of that kind could have been managed safely on so vast a scale.

The
marble
facing
Arnolfo's walls are faced outside with red, white, and very dark green marbles in regular panelled work, like that with which he veneered the baptistery and like the

---

[1] Brunelleschi intended mosaic for the inside of his dome. Vasari, *Vita de Filippo Brunelleschi.*

churches of S. Miniato and the Badia at Fiesole. The doors and windows are gracefully surmounted by steep pediments between pinnacles like those at Siena, and both aisle and nave are crowned with a bold projecting trefoiled cornice on corbels.

The same system of decoration, though more agreeably designed, is applied to the famous campanile—Ruskin's "Shepherd's tower,"—which stands alone near the south-west corner of the church (Plate CLXI). GIOTTO'S TOWER was begun in 1334, only two years before his death, so that he could have seen only the lower part of his building, where are the sculptured panels of the creation and the arts and sciences of civilized life which, on the authority of Ghiberti, we are told were designed by Giotto, and some of them carved by his hand. The tower, for which, says Vasari, Giotto made the model "in the German manner then in fashion," was finished after his death by his pupil, Taddeo Gaddi. It is square, with octagonal buttresses at the angles. At the base it is about 24 feet wide inside, and the walls are 10 feet 3 inches thick. Externally it has five storeys, the two lowest nearly solid, the next two with a pair of two-light windows in each face, the highest with a fine three-light traceried window under a pediment. It is crowned with a great cornice projecting 2 feet 7 inches. Inside it is divided into three by a quadripartite vault level with the top of the second storey and another at the top of the fourth. Level with the top of the third storey a gallery on corbels runs round the inside. The ascent is by a ramping stair 3 feet 3 inches wide in the thickness of the wall, sloping from corner to corner round the building. The total height is 269 feet, and Giotto's model included a spire of 90 feet more, which the later

Florence.
Giotto's
tower

architects omitted, as being a German affair and old-fashioned[1].

Criticisms of Giotto's tower Various have been the opinions about this campanile. "The tower of Giotto," says Ruskin, "is the loveliest of those raised on earth under Christian influence. Of living Christian work there is none so perfect as the tower of Giotto." "The series of bas-reliefs which stud the base of this tower must be held certainly the chief in Europe[2]." Fergusson, more coldly, allows its beauty, but thinks it overrated. On the other hand, I have heard the northern Goth condemn it as only "painter's architecture." It is the misfortune of Italian Gothic never to be judged fairly on its merits. While the glamour of Italy hurries one critic into a fit of passionate enthusiasm, another can only see that many of those characteristics are wanting which he has learned to associate with Gothic architecture. If we bring ourselves to consider Giotto's tower without Scheme of its composition prejudice either way we can hardly fail to see that it has all the elements of a fine composition. The lower part is solid, as it should be in so lofty a building, and is agreeably subdivided and decorated with sculpture and inlay. From this basement the structure rises with gradually increasing splendour, storey by storey, to the magnificent window in the topmost stage. Each division is firmly marked by the strong horizontal line of cornice and inlaid band which is needed to give an air of stability to so slender a construction, and a peculiar charm is imparted by the lovely colour with which the whole is invested. It may be doubted whether a spire would have improved it: the Italians were not very happy in their spires, an architectural feature in which we of the North certainly

[1] per essere cosa Tedesca, e di maniera vecchia. Vasari, *Vita di Giotto*.
[2] *Mornings in Florence*.

Plate CLXI

T. G. J.   GIOTTO'S TOWER—FLORENCE

Plate CLXII

LUCCA CATHEDRAL

excelled them. As it stands the tower is a triumphant work of lovely architecture, though the artist of the Cinquecento slighted it as old-fashioned, and the neo-Goth condemns it as not being according to his formulas.

In the piers of his Duomo, Arnolfo abandoned the round columns of the school of Niccola Pisano, the vast scale of his church needing something stronger. His supports are composed of flat pilasters grouped round a square pier, and the fashion for such piers became common afterwards. They occur in S. Petronio at Bologna and in the nave of the Duomo at Lucca (Plate CLXII), which was rebuilt at the end of the 14th century. It is hard to contrive an agreeable capital to such a pier, and it must be confessed that the way the Italians did it is not successful. In other respects the nave of Lucca is one of the most beautiful in Italian Gothic. Instead of round holes or diminutive windows for the triforium as at Verona and Venice, we have fine large openings with delicate tracery (Plate CLVII, p. 205), and these, together with the main arcades, are carried without interruption as a screen across the transept arch.

The Italian clustered pier

It is curious to find the round arch retained both for the arcade and the triforium. But Romanesque tradition was strong at Lucca: the façade by Guidetto in 1204 is purely Romanesque; so is the interior of the portico, which dates from 1233; while the new tribune and apse at the east end, built in 1308 and continued, after an interruption, in 1320, might have been built two hundred years earlier but for some trifling details in the sculpture[1].

Strong Romanesque tradition at Lucca

In Milan Cathedral we find introduced, once more,

Milan cathedral

---

[1] Illustrated in my *Byzantine and Romanesque Architecture*, vol. I. Plates LXIX and LXX.

Milan
cathedral a direct foreign influence (Fig. 201). It was founded in
1387 by Gian Galeazzo Visconti, who invited architects

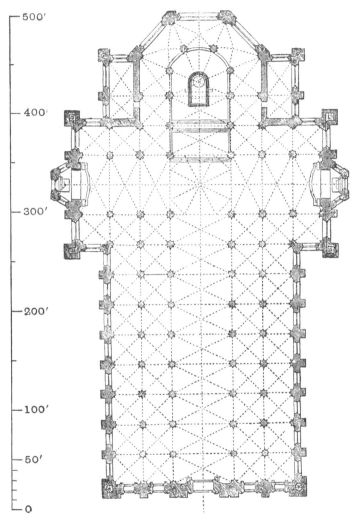

Fig. 201. (*From* Fergusson.)

The
German from Germany. Heinrich Ahrler of Gmunden, or, as
architect the Italians call him, Henrico di Gamodia, seems to have

been the principal architect, though others from beyond Milan cathedral
the Alps are mentioned with him, as well as Italians.
Jealousy between natives and foreigners seems to have
retarded the work, which progressed slowly, and it was
not till between 1490 and 1522 that the central cupola
was vaulted by Omodei and Francesco di Giorgio of
Siena, nor was the western part continued by Pellegrini
till the middle of the 16th century. It was left for
Napoleon to finish it.

In spite, however, of the fact that German architects The German element limited
were employed,—for even as late as 1486 Gian Galeazzo
Sforza wrote for the master-mason of Strassburg to come
and advise about the central tower,—there is very little
in the building resembling anything beyond the Alps.
The exterior, with its pinnacles and imagery and its
extravagant cresting of pierced pediments, is like nothing
in northern Gothic[1], and the central tower, resembling
those at Chiaravalle and the Certosa at Pavia, is a purely
Italian feature (Plate CXLV, p. 179).　Nor do I understand how Fergusson can call the details of the interior
thoroughly German.

After S. Peter's at Rome and the cathedral of Seville,
Milan cathedral is said to be the largest church in the
world, and being built entirely of white marble, it may
claim to be the most splendid (Fig. 201).　It is cruciform The plan
in plan, with double aisles ; and it is perhaps due to the
transalpine architect that the bay is square in the aisles
and oblong transversely in the nave, as it would be in a
French or English building.　Consequently the piers
are spaced at half the distance apart at which they would
be on the plan of Arnolfo at Florence.　The nave vault is

---

[1] There are a few pierced pediments as cresting however at the east end
of York Minster.

Milan
cathedral quadripartite and level at the longitudinal ridge, but
the cross-vault rises very much to the centre from the
wall-rib, which springs at the same level as the transverse
instead of being stilted as in northern work, the side arch
being consequently much lower than the others. By way
of capital, the piers, which are clustered, have a group
of niches with statues, a very original and so far as
I know unique feature, which does much to give character
to the interior.   Above the pointed arch of the arcade is
a small clerestory window : there is no triforium nor
anything to mark the stages, and a short vaulting shaft
rises from the cluster of niches to carry the ribs (Fig. 202).
The panels of the vault are painted with tracery.   The
inner aisle has a clerestory of its own above the roof of
the outer aisle, in that arrangement resembling the section
of Bourges, or the choirs of Le Mans, and Coutances.

The apse　　　The only other feature that may have a transalpine
origin is the apsidal end with an ambulatory round the
choir, but that is managed differently from any French
plan and carried out in an original way with only three
cants and three enormous windows in the aisle.

German
element
modified
by Italian　　　It is clear, therefore, that whatever part of the design
may be due to the German it was modified by passing
through Italian hands.   An Italian, Marco da Campione,
is said to have been associated with Heinrich von
Gmunden, and the assistant artists and the workmen
would naturally have been Italians also.

　　　Whatever we may think of the rather fantastic outside, no one can fail to be impressed with the splendid
interior, which is one of the most solemn and majestic in
Christendom.

Milan
cathedral

Fig. 202. (Drawing by G. Horsley.)

CHAPTER XXVII

CIVIL AND DOMESTIC GOTHIC IN ITALY

Civil
architec-
ture in
Italy is
urban

THE secular buildings, which form so much larger a proportion of mediaeval architecture in Italy than in other countries, are almost entirely urban. In England and France remains of the castles of feudal nobles are dotted about all over the country, savage fortalices at first, but gradually increasing in refinement and comfort as society became less barbarous, and life and goods more secure, and many are still inhabited. But in Italy the feudal castle could not long coexist with the powerful Commune. Early in the 12th century the great cities

Destruc-
tion of the
rural
castles

set to work to destroy, one by one, the neighbouring castles of "those gentlemen who would not be obedient to the city." These gentlemen held their fiefs from the Emperor, and in 1113 the Imperial Vicar tried to defend the Cadolingi, whose castle had been taken and destroyed by the Florentines, but he was himself defeated and slain. The lords of Monte Boni, robber chiefs like the rest who took toll of passengers, were also dispossessed by the Florentines, and they themselves were forced to come into the city, where, as Buoni del Monte, Buon-delmonti, and Buonaparti, they afterwards figured in history, one section of the latter branch settling in Corsica[1] where they have since been heard of. The

---

[1] Trollope, *Hist. of Florence*, vol. I.

castle of the Guidi at Monte Croce was thought, says
Villani, to be much too near the city, and accordingly
after one failure it was taken and destroyed by the
burghers.   The same policy was pursued elsewhere, and Settlement of the nobles within the walls
the un-housed nobles were made to come within the walls
as citizens, where, being wealthy, for their lands were
not as a rule taken from them, they became powerful and
built themselves palaces.   Into their new home they
imported the feuds that had divided them when outside.
Each noble raised one or more towers to his palace, from Their towers
which he could defend himself or annoy his neighbour.
Each family grouped the palaces of its members together,
so that in case of need they could be enclosed by a
common barricade, and reached by galleries from one to
another.   The cities became, in fact, filled with these
interior fortalices, held by noble families who, like the
Montagues and Capulets, were in a constant state of
private warfare among themselves, until things became
so intolerable that the burghers were driven to suppress
them.   Every old picture of an Italian city shows it
bristling with these tall towers.   In an old print of
Siena we count twenty-five or more still standing in the
17th century.   The little town of S. Gimignano has
thirteen, one of which is 175 feet high.   Bologna has,
besides others, the leaning towers of La Garisenda,
familiar to lovers of Dante, and degli Asinelli, which is
296 feet high without the lantern.   There are several
at LUCCA, one of them belonging to the PALACE of the
GUINIGI, once lords of that city (Fig. 203).   The tower
of the Tosinghi at Florence, destroyed in 1248 by the
Ghibellines when they expelled the Guelphs, was
130 *braccia* high, circular and arcaded like the Campanile at Pisa, "so beautiful that it would have sufficed

Lucca.
Casa
Guinigi

Fig. 203.

for the residence of an emperor[1]." To destroy the Destruction of towers and palaces of opposite factions towers and palaces of the rival faction was the first care of a triumphant party. The tower of the Adimari, called the Guardamorto, was doomed by the Ghibellines in 1248, and ordered to be thrown down so as to fall on the Baptistery of S. Giovanni, the old cathedral of Florence, because that church had been the meeting place of the Guelphs. It was so massive that Niccola Pisano was called in to contrive its destruction. He cut away the foundation and propped the tower on wood, then setting fire to the props, but the tower luckily fell clear of S. Giovanni, saved intentionally, we may hope, by the contrivance of Niccola. Two years later, in 1250, as the result of a popular movement against the nobles, all the towers of private houses in Florence that were above 50 *braccia*, that is about 90 feet in height, were demolished. In 1258 the palace of the great Ghibelline family of the Uberti was stormed and destroyed, and a decree was passed that no building should thenceforth stand on the accursed spot. Consequently the plan of the Palazzo Vecchio is distorted, for, as Vasari tells us, " the houses of the Uberti, rebels against the people, and Ghibellines, having been thrown down and a piazza formed, the silly obstinacy of some people so far prevailed that Arnolfo could not carry his point and set the palace square, because the Government would on no account allow the foundations to be placed on the ground of the rebellious Uberti[2]."

Arnolfo's public palace, the well-known Palazzo Palazzo Vecchio, Florence Vecchio, was built in 1298. Its slender bell-tower, boldly set forward on a projecting cornice, rises to the

[1] Coppo Stefani, cited Trollope's *Hist. of Florence*, vol. I. p. 127.
[2] *Vita di Arnolfo.*

height of 308 feet. Every Italian town, from Venice, Florence, and Siena down to the humblest municipality, had its town house and bell-tower to proclaim its corporate existence and civic freedom. The great bell of the town in its campanile on the public palace was the tongue of an Italian Commune. At its sound the burghers hurried to the assembly in the Piazza or to the muster for war, as the clerks of Oxford rushed to the fray at the sound of the great bell of S. Mary's and the towns-men at that of S. Martin's. When Charles VIII in Florence threatened to sound his trumpets if his conditions were refused, Pietro Capponi started up, tore the conditions, and said, "Sound your trumpets and we will ring our bells," and it was enough to silence the Frenchman.

The Palazzo Comunale of SIENA is one of the most interesting. It stands quite dramatically on the chord of a vast hemi-cycle, rising from the centre like a theatre up to a ring of Gothic palaces. The lofty tower was built between 1325 and 1345 : it has a projecting gallery on corbels surmounted by a smaller turret for the bell like Arnolfo's campanile at Florence. The whole palace is of brick with stone dressings. Within are fine halls and a chapel with beautiful paintings by early Sienese masters.

Contemporary with these public buildings are numerous private palaces which line the streets of Florence, Siena, Bologna, and almost every great town in northern and central Italy. Their exterior architecture is generally rather sombre and monotonous : the front is flat and unbroken, and whether of stone or brick has little architectural ornament. The doorway, through which in the larger buildings you pass into a Cortile, has a plain arch pointed or round, with fine rings and hooks of wrought

Plate CLXIII

T. G. J.   SIENA—Cortile of the Palazzo Comunale

iron for fastening horses to. Windows in tier upon tier are ranged above with little variety, and the façade finishes with a deep overhanging cornice and eaves. Siena abounds in examples of this design, some in brick, others in stone like the PALAZZO SARACENI, of which a window is shown by Fig. 195, and the PALAZZO TOLOMEI. Fig. 203 shows the PALAZZO GUINIGI at LUCCA, where the main arches are round, though the window lights are pointed. The same mixture occurs in the cortile of the Palazzo Publico at SIENA, where the main pillars that support the building are made of brick (Plate CLXIII), and there is no stone but in the capitals, the shafts of the windows, the band to which the horse-hooks are fixed, and the scutcheons of the Priors or Gonfalonieri of the Republic.

Palazzo Guinigi, Lucca

Cortile at Siena

The same stern quasi-defensive character runs through the domestic architecture of north and central Italy, and especially at Florence, where it continued even into Renaissance times; for the great palaces of the Strozzi and Riccardi, and Brunelleschi's palace of the Pitti, have somewhat of a sullen prison-like air about them.

Florentine palaces

At VENICE and in the Venetian provinces we find a very different history, and a very different character in the architecture. Here alone in Italy there were no internal troubles, no factious Neri and Bianchi, no internecine struggle between Guelph and Ghibelline. The strong secret government of its close aristocracy was never seriously shaken at Venice; she had no private wars to trouble her within, while her position behind the impassable lagunes and her maritime supremacy in the Adriatic protected her against attack from without, and made artificial fortification needless. At Venice, therefore, there are no fortified houses, no threatening towers,

Venice

no gloomy prison-like walls; all is open, joyous, and gracious; all breathes an air of peace, security, and wealth.

But this is not all the difference. Venice, through the whole of her history, especially while she possessed no Italian territory, stood for the most part aloof, and outside the questions that agitated the rest of Italy. In the 9th and 10th centuries she still considered herself part of the empire of eastern Rome, and defied the Franks. Her commerce in the Levant brought her into constant touch with the East, and her dependencies across the Adriatic, and in Candia, Cyprus, and the

Morea lay outside the sphere of Italian politics. Her different history is well reflected by her architecture, which forms a school apart, and unlike any contemporary form of Gothic on either side of the Alps. The early work at Venice was purely Byzantine; S. Mark's might very well have been built on the shore of the Golden Horn; and the type of Gothic developed at Venice in the 13th and 14th centuries is strongly touched with

Eastern feeling. Not that we shall find in it any such positive Orientalism as we shall have to notice in Sicily; but the whole sentiment of Venetian architecture, with its grace of line, its lovely curves, its sensuous colour, its refined sculpture, the soft and luxuriant foliage of its capitals, all breathe an air more akin to that of Monreale and Palermo than that which inspired the stern palaces of Florence, the scarcely less severe façades of Siena, or the brick and terra-cotta buildings of Lombardy.

The earliest palaces that remain at Venice are Byzantine, with round arches, much stilted, and veneered with marble. The best example of this was the FONDACO DEI TURCHI, as I remember it before its deplorable

Plate CLXIV

VENICE—Fondaco dei Turchi, before renovation

Plate CLXV

T. G. J.   VENICE

restoration (Plate CLXIV). It has since been altered out of all knowledge, and is now hideous[1]. The arches were lined on the soffit with a thin casing of white marble which projected enough to support the plaques with which the wall was faced. This projecting edge had the double dentil which is a Venetian characteristic, and was derived from Constantinople (Fig. 204). S. Mark's is full of similar arches. The Fondaco dei Turchi seems to

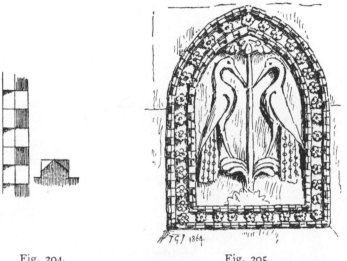

Fig. 204.   Fig. 205.

have had an open arcaded centre on both floors, flanked at each end by a solid compartment with four blank arches.

Another Byzantine palace remains not far off, on the other side of the Rialto (Plate CLXV). Here are the same stilted arches and the same panels surrounded by

[1] This palace was built in the 12th or 13th century for the Pesari: afterwards it was acquired by the Republic and given to Niccola d' Este, Marquis of Ferrara. It was not made the Turkish Exchange till 1621. Molmenti, *Italia Artistica.*

Byzantine palaces

dentil borders, in which sculptures are framed, some of them with the peacocks familiar in Byzantine ornaments (Fig. 205). To the same class as this building belong the palaces Loredan and Farsetti, now the Municipio of Venice.

It will be noticed that in this case (Plate CLXV) the label or hood-moulding over the round arches points upwards with an ogee curve : this gives it a distinctly Oriental look, and this feature once adopted runs through all succeeding domestic work at Venice and forms one of its principal characteristics[1].

The Ducal palace

The rebuilding of the PALACE OF THE DOGE or Duke of Venice was begun about the middle of the 14th century. The oldest part is the front to the sea, which was finished, together with the first few arches of the return front towards the Piazzetta, during the 14th century. There is no reason to believe that Filippo Calendario, who used to be supposed the architect of the earlier part of the palace, and who was hanged for participation in the conspiracy of Marino Faliero in 1355, had anything to do with it. He appears to have been

The architects

a seaman, and not an architect. From documentary evidence we learn that the front to the lagune was built between 1340 and 1404 by Pietro Baseggio[2], who in the softened Venetian dialect is called the *Prototaiapiera*, and by Maestro Enrico, *Proto del Comune.* The rest of the Piazzetta front was continued in 1424, when Francesco Foscari was Doge, by Giovanni Bon and his son Bartolommeo, who also built the Porta della Carta at its north

---

[1] Selvatico gives an illustration of another "Arabo-Byzantine" palace near S. Moïsè, which he says had lately been demolished. *Guida di Venezia*, 1852, p. 75.

[2] Selvatico calls him Pietro Basejo, the softened form of Baseggio, and says he was a relation of Calendario.

Plate CLXVI

VENICE—The Ducal Palace. Front to Piazzetta

end in 1440–1443. The documents also mention one Andrea di Milano (Plate CLXVI).

The building is too well known to need a detailed description, and has been admired by some and condemned by others as heartily as Giotto's campanile. The pillars of the lower storey have sunk more than a foot in the ground, and have no bases, nor, as it appears, did they ever have any, but stood simply on a continuous stylobate. The corridor behind them is cross-groined. The upper storey has an arcade with two bays to each bay below it, and the corridor behind has a wooden ceiling forming the floor of the great halls above. On this arcade rests the vast wall of the main storeys of the building faced with chequers of rose marble and white. This solid block, which is not much less in height than the two lower storeys put together, places an enormous load on a comparatively light structure, and has naturally provoked criticism. The arcades of the lower storeys run out to the ends of the building, and the last arch has consequently no abutment, but depends on the iron ties with which all the arches are provided. It is not surprising, therefore, that ruptures occurred, that the condition of the building created alarm, that the angles of the loggia were forced dangerously outwards and were only prevented from falling by being shored up, and that the structure has lately been undergoing serious repair. Yet in spite of its hazardous construction the palace has stood for more than five centuries, and survived many rude shocks of earthquake and other disasters. In 1577 it was gutted by a fire, and the Senate proposed to pull it down and remove it to another site. Thirteen architects were asked to report upon it, nearly all of whom condemned it, hoping, as Selvatico maliciously

The
Ducal
palace.
Opinion
of Paolo
da Ponte suggests, to get the rebuilding. Paolo da Ponte points out the fault of placing a solid storey over a voided lower one, and says "the man who built it evidently doubted its standing, and therefore tied it together with iron."

of Palladio Palladio finds the same fault: he says that the upper wall, 2½ feet thick, rests on columns of 1¼ feet, that it has a false bearing, that the capitals of both storeys, to the number of thirty-two, so far as has yet been discovered, are broken, that the beams, where not burned, are rotten, the iron rusted away, and that the building could not safely be left standing. Two only of the number seem

of Sanso-
vino to have taken a more hopeful view. Jacopo Sansovino says "the public palace of Venice is the strongest and firmest fabric I have ever seen in any part of Italy." He praises the superior support given by pointed arches, and reminds the Senate that the building has survived great earthquakes, explosions in the arsenal, and salvoes of artillery for two hundred and thirty-four years without

of Antonio injury[1]. Antonio da Ponte wrote in the same strain, and
da Ponte said he thought the building could very well be repaired. He was entrusted with the task of doing it, and to him we owe its preservation to this day.

Restora-
tion of
1889 Palladio does not seem to have over-stated the damage, for at the restoration which was completed in 1889 every capital in the upper row was found to be split, and that at the south-west corner of the lower storey, below the group of Adam and Eve, was broken into thirty or forty pieces. The worst part was the south-east corner, where the foundation was defective. The report issued at the end of the repairs states that the whole of this angle has

[1] "La fabbrica fatta già 234 anni non s' era smossa ne risentita in qualsiasi parte per la sua maravigliosa composizione e struttura." This throws the date back to 1343. Magrini, *Vita de Palladio*, p. 203.

Plate CLXVII

VENICE—Angle of the Ducal Palace, with the Judgment of Solomon

Plate CLXVIII

A

B   VENICE—Capitals in Ducal Palace

been rebuilt, mostly with new material, that the broken The Ducal
palace capitals throughout have been repaired, or where they were past repair faithful copies have been substituted, and that the iron sockets are replaced by bronze let into the springer of the arch instead of the capital, to which the iron ties are screwed. It would seem that the restoration was only just in time to prevent a catastrophe, but it is a misfortune that so much new work was needed.

Though built at different times, the design of the Continuity
of design later part built by the Bons follows that of their predecessor. This is probably the intention of the decree of the Maggior Consiglio in 1422 : *Palatium nostrum fabricetur et fiat in forma decora et convenienti, quod respondeat solemnissimo principio palatii nostri novi, et sit pro honore nostri dominii.* The Porta della Carta, where the Bons were left to themselves, is in a much later and more florid style of Italian Gothic. The two fronts of the main building, towards the Molo and the Piazzetta, retain something of the chaste severity of an earlier style.

The extreme beauty of the two arcaded storeys needs The
arcades
and tracery no commendation : their simplicity befits their infinite repetition, which would otherwise have been tedious, and no more lovely work was ever done in Gothic architecture. The curvilinear tracery of the upper order is well moulded, and the roll moulding of the circles mitres and coalesces regularly with that of the lights. The quatrefoils are pierced as plate tracery, and finish with a ball on the points of the cusps. The cusping of the arches also is unmoulded and works out of the soffit.

At the corners of the lower storey are the famous The
sculpture groups of sculpture, the drunkenness of Noah with the vine tree, Adam and Eve with the fig-tree, and next the Porta della Carta the Judgement of Solomon (Plate CLXVII).

In the sculptured ornament we are introduced to a new style peculiarly Venetian. It seems to have sprung to life suddenly, late in the 14th century, with the Delle Massegne who worked at S. Mark's, and the family of Buono or Bon. Till then Venetian sculpture had been backward, and Tuscans or Lombards had to be employed. The sculptors Buono, and after them the Lombardi, not only raised Venetian sculpture to an extraordinary degree of beauty, but endowed it with a distinct national character. The capitals of the Ducal palace are superb (Plate CLXVIII). They are compact and solid in outline, as befits their function under so great a load. The foliage is in two tiers; the lower very delicately relieved from the surface, which is not cut into so as to diminish its strength: the upper projects, and is carved with greater depth and freedom, and figure-subjects are charmingly introduced amid the leafage. Under the group of the Judgement of Solomon at the corner next the Porta della Carta are the lawgivers, Aristotle, Solon, Isidore, Numa, Moses, and Trajan with the widow (Plate CLXVIII A). Others have figures of virtues and their opposite vices, the seven deadly sins, the sages of antiquity, Solomon, Priscian, Aristotle, Cicero, Pythagoras, Archimedes, Orpheus, and Ptolemy, and elsewhere are representatives of arts and professions, of various nations, and symbols of the months. The foliage is broad and soft in treatment, the ends of the leaves curled up; the modelling and the raffling of the edges have little affinity with any other Gothic type, nor with the Classic acanthus, and it is difficult to say from what plant the type is

conventionalized. The same leaf runs through all Venetian Venetian
sculpture
Gothic, and is adapted for the riotous crocketting of the
gables in S. Mark's and the doorways of S. Stefano and
the campo of S. Zaccaria[1] (Fig. 206). If Giovanni and

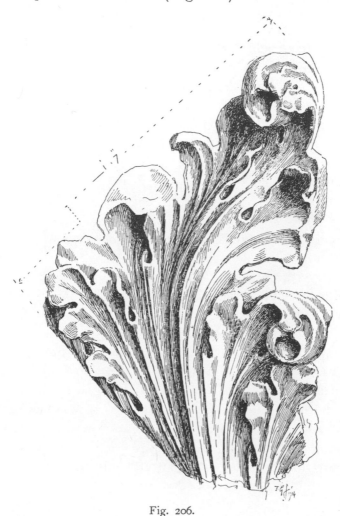

Fig. 206.

[1] The crocket shown in Fig. 206 is drawn from a broken one belonging to
Mr William Brindley, who found it thrown aside among builders' rubbish. The

Bartolommeo Bon were not the inventors of this type of foliage, they at all events developed it and made it an integral part of the Venetian school of architecture.

The
Venetian
palace
The palaces and houses of the better class are modelled more or less on one type. They have one door to the canal and another to the street or campo behind, the water-front being always the more important. The general plan is to have one large room on the principal floor from front to back with a fine window to the canal, right and left of which are small rooms and staircases. Sometimes in the larger houses there are two storeys of rooms at the sides in the height of the one in the middle. The great front window is enclosed in a square frame, within which all is marble, and all outside except in a few cases, is of brick plastered. The door or doors to the canal have steps to the water, where are painted posts for mooring the gondolas, and the arch is pointed and the label or hood mould is generally ogeed. The main feature is always the great window of the *piano nobile*, which is richly shafted and generally has graceful traceries. The other windows, when not surmounted by tracery, are always ogee-arched and almost always have trefoil soffit cusping, as at the Ducal palace. Sometimes, however, the head itself is trifoliated instead of being cusped. One of
Palazzo
Sagredo
the earlier palaces, the PALAZZO SAGREDO (Plate CLXIX) affords an instance of this. The great window of the *piano nobile* is enclosed in a decorated frame, and above its four trifoliated lights, but not connected with them, is a row of four circles with quatrefoil cusping. The single lights right and left have ogee heads with trefoil cusping, and the row of windows below has ogee arches but no

material is Istrian stone : it is carved superficially, a great lump of rough stone being left on the back.

Plate CLXIX

T. G. J.

VENICE—Palazzo Sagredo

Plate CLXX

Palazzo Cicogna
All Arcangelo Raffaelle
Nov. 19/76 —

following the story may be incustable below ?

cusping.　There is another instance of trifoliated ogee lights in a small house on the Rio S. Pantaleone, which has a horse-shoe arch to the doorway.

The fine palace FACANON ALLA FAVA has the great window filled with arcading and curvilinear tracery of quatrefoiled circles exactly like the Ducal palace.　Below and above are trefoil-cusped ogee windows, and there are two doors to the canal.

Palazzo Facanon alla Fava

The PALAZZO CICOGNA[1] (Plate CLXX), which perhaps dates from the 13th century, is unlike any other, and of remarkable beauty.　The lower storey, unluckily, has been altered in Renaissance times, but the singular window of the upper floor remains perfect.　A row of six pointed arches with trefoil soffit-cusps carries a beautiful composition of interlacing circles enclosing quatrefoils, which are not moulded, but cut square into the wall.　The lower part of the lights is filled with marble panels, diapered and charged with heraldry.

Palazzo Cicogna

In the PALAZZO CAVALLI (Plate CLXXI), of the 15th century, and the Palazzo Giovanelli, which is very like it, we have another type.　In the Cavalli palace the central composition is carried up into the second storey, the windows of both floors being united.　In the lower and principal window the lights have intersecting round arches over them, carrying a row of circles which unite with them as true tracery.　The circles have quatrefoil cusps and the lights trefoil cusping, all of the plate tracery order.　The upper window has interlacing tracery of a different kind.　The PISANI palace is one of the finest examples of this class.

Palazzo Cavalli

It should be observed that in all these windows the

---

[1] I used to know it by this name, and it is so named by Selvatico, but it is called Palazzo Ariani by Molmenti, *Italia Artistica.*

The
windows glass is not set in the stonework, but in wooden frames behind, which could be taken away when desired ; that is to say, the marble shafts are not mullions, but stand alone as a colonnade in front of the window frame.

In the Palazzo Boelan (?) in the Rio S. Marina is another instance of the windows in two storeys being combined in one great central composition.

The Ca'
d' Oro The most sumptuous palace in Venice is the famous CA' D' ORO, which was built in 1430 for Messer Marino Contarini, the architects being, as appears from documents that have been found in the archives, Giovanni— in Venetian Zuane—Bon and his son, who made the Porta della Carta at the Ducal palace[1]. In the contract for that work they call themselves "*Io Zuane Bon tajapiera de la contrada de San Marzilian e mio fio Bortolamio.*"

In the Ca' d' Oro (Plate CLXXII) the usual Venetian plan is complicated by an additional wing on the right, and by an open loggia on the ground floor leading to the canal. The whole front is gorgeous with marble facing, enriched bands, and splendid traceries. The blank space above the topmost ornamental border originally contained a coved cornice of trefoiled arcading, of which traces were The
cornice
and
cresting discovered when the building was restored some twenty years ago, and on this rested the pierced cresting or battlementing of pinnacles cut out of slabs of stone and furnished with balls on the points like those on the cusps of the Ducal palace (Fig. 207). The pinnacles are highest in the middle and at the ends of the front, and lower between these points.

This cresting, like that on the Ducal palace, is akin to

[1] Giacomo Boni, *La Ca' d' Oro e le sue decorazioni policrome.* Venezia, 1887.

Plate CLXXI

Palazzo Cavalli sul Canale Grande
(ora del duca di Bordeaux.) No. 25/67.

T. G J.   VENICE—Palazzo Cavalli

Plate CLXXII

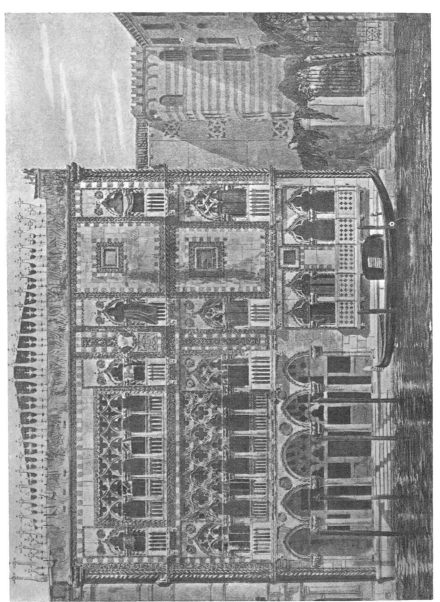

From the "Builder"

VENICE—Ca' d' oro

similar battlementing on buildings in Sicily, where it is The Ca'
d' Oro distinctly derived from Saracen sources, and its presence at Venice is another instance of the Oriental touch already alluded to.

The Ca' d' Oro was originally decorated with colour and gold, whence no doubt it got its name. The contract Decora-
tion in
colour and
gold

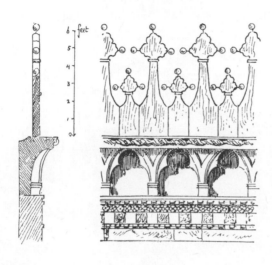

Venice
Parapet of the Ca d'oro
from G Boni.

Fig. 207.

with Maestro Giovanni di Francia has been preserved. It is dated 1431, and gives in full detail the scheme of decoration. The balls on the pinnacles were to be gilt, as well as the torus moulding below the arcaded cornice, also the leaves of the capitals, the lions at the angles, and the heraldry, the ground being painted with ultramarine. The rosettes,—ducats he calls them,—of the cornice are

The Ca'
d' Oro
to be gilt, and the red marble to be oiled and varnished[1].
Also, what is rather surprising, the sculptured ornament
of the various borders or bands was to be painted white in
oils, and the ground painted black. The decorator binds
himself to use ultramarine of the value of 18 ducats of gold
for the pound, which Commendatore Boni estimates to be
worth 216½ *lire* of modern money, or about £8. 12s. 6d.

Colouring
on Ducal
palace
He tells us also that he found traces of similar treatment on the chequer work of Istrian stone and Veronese
brocatello outside the Ducal palace; the stone had been
whitened and the marble reddened. Very likely other
palaces in Venice were decorated to some extent, though
perhaps not so gorgeously as the Ca' d' Oro. We know
that the Porta della Carta was painted with blue, and
gilt. An old Tuscan proverb says, *Azzuro e oro non
guastan lavoro*[2].

Persistence
of Vene-
tian type
The foregoing are only a few typical examples of the
domestic architecture of Venice. Among the numerous
palaces that line the canals in all parts of the city a
certain variety will be found, but they conform on the
whole to the general arrangement that has been described.
The Gothic type of façade, with the large window of the
principal floor as its chief feature, survived the Gothic
period. Many of the Neo-classic palaces of the Renaissance follow it. In the Palazzo Manzoni the arrangement
of the fenestration is identical with that of the Palazzo
Cavalli, though all the details are Classic. It survives
also in the Palazzo Contarini delle Figure, and in the

---

[1] Apresso vuol che tute le piere rosse che se in la dita fazada e tute le
dentade rosse sia onte di oio e de vernixe con color che le para rosse.
Apresso vuol che tute le ruosse e vide che se entro la dita fazada sia tute
dade de biacha a oio e penzer i campi de negro a oio per muodo chel stia
ben. Boni, *op. cit.*

[2] Boni, *op. cit.*

16th century Palazzo Tiepolo, though the details are still further removed from Gothic. The same idea is retained in the Palazzo Corner Spinelli, by Pietro Lombardo, which indeed is more Gothic than Classic, with its colonnated windows and traceries. In the similar Palazzo Vendramin-Calergi, by the same architect, the arrangement is nearly lost, but may be faintly traced. In the Grimani palace by Sammichieli and the Rezzonico by Longhena it has disappeared.

The little palace CONTARINI-FASAN, on the Grand Canal, is peculiar, and makes up for its smallness by the beauty of its detail. The windows have no columns or tracery, but are plain openings under an ogee arch, enriched with carving. The balconies with their pierced tracery, resting on fine sculptured consoles, form the chief ornament of the façade (Plate CLXXIII). *Palazzo Contarini-Fasan*

In the Venetian balconies, indeed, we have one of the principal charms of the city. No house is without them, and they must have played a considerable part in domestic enjoyment. Life in this strange city, with water for the main streets, seldom room for a patch of garden, and only alleys to walk in on dry land, except for a piazza here and there, was cramped and confined, and the balconies afforded almost the only resting-place in the open air. They are treated with great attention, enclosed with marble balustrades, with carved capitals to the shafts and finials to the newels; and the consoles that carry them are beautifully sculptured. Below them passed all the busy life of the city on its watery highways. Those on the Grand Canal commanded the best view of the State processions and festal pageants for which Venice was famous. But the houses in the narrow side streets were equally well provided with their balconies, which *The Venetian balcony* indeed seem a necessary part of Venetian architecture and are general in the poorer houses as well as in the princely palace.

Like ancient Rome, Venice carried her arts with her wherever she carried her rule. Her style of building is to be found high up in Titian's mountain home at Pieve di Cadore. Ceneda and Serravalle in Friuli are full of Venetian windows and balconies, and there is a pretty town hall with a campanile, and the judicial Loggia which is universal throughout the dominion of S. Mark. At Udine is a public palace with two columns in front to remind one of the Piazzetta in the mother-city. All the towns in Istria and on the coast and islands of Dalmatia are full of Venetian architecture; the walls bear inscriptions with the names of Venetian counts, and are studded with their heraldic escutcheons, invaluable for fixing the date of the structure. The treasuries of the churches are stored with beautiful silversmith's work and fine embroideries, produced under Venetian rule, if not actually wrought at Venice itself. From every town-gate, bastion, and campanile the lion of S. Mark looks down, and in every Loggia presides over the judicial bench. The soft Venetian dialect is heard in the streets of every town on mainland and island from Zara to Cattaro, and Italian is still the language most useful to travellers who do not speak Slav, even up to Cettigne in Montenegro.

The rule of Venice over her provinces was not perfect; it was coloured by jealousy and suspicion, and her subjects had much of which to complain. But there is something admirable in the way in which she impressed her stamp on all her ancient dominions, to an extent perhaps beyond any power save Rome itself.

Plate CLXXIII

T. G. J.

VENICE—Palazzo Contarini Fasan

CHAPTER XXVIII

SICILY

THE NORMAN LINE

Tancred of Hauteville a Norman knight

William Bras de Fer Count of Apulia 1043	Drogo and others	Robert Guiscard Duke of Apulia and Calabria 1059, d. 1085	Roger I the Great Count conquered Sicily with his brother Robert 1061–1071, d. 1101

ROGER II united Sicily
and S. Italy.   Crowned
king 1130, d. 1154

HOHENSTAUFEN LINE

Roger Duke of Apulia d. 1149	WILLIAM I the Bad 1154–1166	CONSTANCE = Henry VI Emperor d. 1198　conquered Sicily 1194, d. at Messina 1197

ᴀNCRED of Lecce.
ᴇgitimate. Crowned
1190, d. 1193

WILLIAM II
the Good
1166–1189

FREDERICK II Emperor
1198–1250

ᵍer d.
ᵉfore
father

WILLIAM III
conquered and
deposed by
Henry VI 1194

CONRAD
1250–1254

CONRADIN
conquered and
put to death
by Charles of
Anjou 1268

MANFRED.
Illegitimate.
1254–1266

Constance = PETER OF
ARRAGON.
Sicilian
vespers
1282

SICILIAN GOTHIC

SICILIAN architecture is peculiar and needs a chapter Varied
to itself. No other country has been the scene of so history
many revolutions, and of such various conflicts of race
and creed : and probably nowhere is there a population
into which more different constituents enter. The Sicani

and Siculi, who seem to have been Latin, were succeeded
by the Greek colonists, who came at first fearing to find
the man-eating Cyclopes and Laestrygones of the Odyssey.
For nearly two centuries the island was held by the
Carthaginians. They were expelled by the Romans
who made Sicily a Roman province in 210 B.C. It was
ravaged by Vandals, ruled by Goths, and recovered by
the Empire of Eastern Rome. For two hundred years
it was a Saracen kingdom, till conquered by Robert
Guiscard and Roger the Great Count between 1061 and
1071, who founded the Norman dynasty, to be followed
in turn by the Hohenstaufens, Angevins, Aragonese,
and Bourbons.

Most of the various races who have occupied the
island have left their mark on its art, even though of
some among them there are no actual buildings now
standing. Of Punic work, indeed, we know next to
nothing: probably it was not very distinctive: the Semitic
races never excelled in the plastic arts. The Museum at
Palermo has some Carthaginian sarcophagi, and that at
Syracuse some Punic coins with Phœnician legends, but
the head they bear is that of Arethusa with two dolphins
which we know on the Greek coinage. Greek art in
Sicily is represented by the temples of Syracuse, Selinus,
Segesta and Agrigentum, and by the most beautiful
coinage the world has ever seen. Of Roman and Byzantine
work little has survived the desolating conquests of the
Arabs. There is the rock-cut chapel of S. Marcian at
Syracuse, and there are a few small buildings popularly
known as Saracen mosques, but once no doubt Byzantine
churches. Mr Freshfield[1] has described and illustrated
a small basilica at Priolo near Syracuse, with an eastern

---

[1] *Cellae Trichorae*, by E. H. Freshfield.

apse, a nave and aisles divided by square piers with Byzantine
remains
round arches, and originally barrel vaulted. Also two
early chapels near Camarina ; and a square church with
apses to the E., N. and S., and a central dome, at
Malvagna on the slope of Etna. There is another like
it at Maccari ; and one at S. Teresa, south of Syracuse,
known like that at Malvagna by the Arabic name of
La Cuba[1].

　　The art of Eastern Rome however affected all that Byzantine
influence
on Arab
art
followed. It was the parent of that of the Arabs in
Sicily as it had been in Africa whence they came. For
the Arabs brought no art with them out of their desert :
the holy house at Mecca was and is a plain square tower
of no architectural character. But wherever they went,—
in Egypt, in Persia, in India,—they adopted and as-
similated the arts of the conquered race, and employed
native architects to build for them. In Egypt they found
Roman buildings which supplied them with columns and
capitals for their mosques, and Byzantine churches whence
they borrowed the idea of the dome, grafting it on the
simple colonnades of their original houses of prayer.
Saracen architecture of the 8th and 9th centuries in
Egypt is in fact a version of the Byzantine style, just as
the great mosques built at Stamboul after the conquest
are versions of S. Sophia. For the Arabs were not The Arabs
not
creative
inventive ; they wanted imagination. The immortal tales
of the thousand and one nights come from the Aryans of
Persia and India, not from Arabia. A recent writer
says " after their conquests they translated and com-
mented on the writings of the ancients ; they enriched
certain branches of science by their patient, accurate and

---

[1] Cuba is the Arabic قُبَّة, *Kubbah*, meaning a dome. We have from the
same source the word " alcove."

Arab
learning

minute observations, but they made no capital discoveries, and we are not indebted to them for a single great and fruitful idea[1]." It was the same with their architecture, for which they had to employ the native workmen, mostly Greek, who speedily learned to adapt their own Byzantine style to the use of their new masters. And

Norman
influence

when the Normans came, a handful of rough soldiers, they naturally employed the native school of artists, who were ready to their hand. They of course worked in the style they were familiar with, and consequently Byzantine influence, filtered through an Oriental medium, runs through all the work of King Roger and his successors, affecting the structure of the buildings, as well as their decoration by mosaic, for which Greek artists were largely, and at first probably solely employed.

Nothing now remains of actual Moslem work either in Sicily or Calabria. There is no trace of the 300 mosques at Palermo seen by the traveller Ibn Haukal in

Oriental
influence

962. But we can trace Oriental influence in all that succeeded the conquest down to the 13th century and even later. We see it in the patterns of the interlacing pavements; in the pierced window-slabs of *gesso*; in the stilted and pointed arches, which are so unlike those of Northern Gothic; in the domed churches; in the embattled parapets; in the rough mosaic of stone and basalt on the outside of the buildings; in the square frames within which the pointed windows are set, and in the wide and shallow orders that surround the openings. Standing in the garden of the Eremiti, or in the alcove of La Ziza at Palermo with its stalactite vaults, one may imagine oneself *in pieno oriente*.

---

[1] *Spanish Islam*, R. Dozy, transl. by S. G. Stokes. There is an admirable review of Saracenic learning in Giannone's *Storia di Napoli*.

All these elements of design, half Greek and half Norman element in Sicilian Gothic Arabian, were adopted by the Normans after their conquest; but they too set their own stamp on the architecture, and the zigzag, so familiar to English eyes, was used quite down to the 14th century, together with the undercut mouldings of Northern Gothic.

For Gothic traceries the Sicilians seem to have had a great liking :—they were somewhat akin to oriental taste ;—and one is often surprised to find regular Flamboyant windows that would not have been out of place at Rouen or Abbeville. Mixed with later details such as Mixture of styles these, are scrolls of an early character, almost Romanesque, springing perhaps from a base that speaks of the Renaissance. This curious mixture of style often makes it very hard to date the buildings, which at one time seem much later, and at others much earlier than they are. Their irregularity will no doubt offend the Purist, for though a certain consistency runs through them, there is no regular conformity to any one of the forms of mediaeval art with which we are familiar.

But for a few Roman ruins,—chiefly at Syracuse and Taormina,—and the unimportant remains of Byzantine work already mentioned, the history of architecture in Sicily is a blank for nearly sixteen hundred years; and we go at one bound from the Greek temples at Girgenti to the buildings of the Norman Roger, who was crowned The Norman buildings king of Sicily and Southern Italy in 1130[1]. The churches built under the Norman dynasty from that date down to the coming of the Hohenstaufens are of two kinds, the one basilican, and other domical. The basilican type

---

[1] He is often called Roger II. But Roger I, "the Great Count," was never king. The assumption of the Royal title without leave of either Pope or Emperor, both of whom claimed that a new kingdom could not be created without them, embroiled Roger for a time with both powers.

The
basilican
type

however is sometimes combined with a dome over the crossing, and in all cases has a semi-dome over the apse. To this class belong the Capella Palatina at Palermo, the cathedrals of Cefalù, Monreale, and that of Messina, now unhappily almost destroyed, and it included originally the Duomo of Palermo which has now been modernized inside, and altered out of all knowledge.　Examples of

The
domical
type

the other type are the churches of the Eremiti, La Martorana, and S. Cataldo at Palermo, and the desolate church of S. Pietro in Agro near Taormina.

The
pointed
arch

Throughout all these buildings we find the arches pointed, both in the main arcades, in the semi-dome of the apse, and in the intersecting blank arcading which forms so interesting a feature in their decoration[1].　At the time when this pointed architecture was fully developed in Sicily it will be remembered that the pointed arch had hardly begun to make way in the rest of Europe, and was only employed tentatively for some time afterwards. The Sicilian pointed arch, with its high stilt, and rather obtuse curve, is oriental, and has nothing to do with that of Northern Gothic, but comes from the Saracen school in Egypt, where it had already been known and used for many centuries[2].

In the second or domical type a strong likeness will

---

[1] The cathedral founded by King Roger in 1130, and the church of the Annunziata dei Catalani at Messina, both ruined by the recent earthquake, were exceptions, and had round arches.　The cathedral had ancient pillars of various heights surmounted by abaci or blockings of different thickness to bring the spring of the arches to a level.　It had a magnificent painted roof, illustrated in a fine monograph by M. Moret.　Some of the patterns are based on the Kufic or old Arabic character.

[2] In the mosque built by the Sultan Ibn Touloun at Cairo in 878 all the arches are stilted and pointed.　The architect was a Copt.　v. *Art of the Saracens in Egypt*, Stanley Lane Poole, and *Architecture East and West*, R. Phéné Spiers.

Plate CLXXIV

PALERMO—Capella Palatina

be observed to the plan of several Byzantine churches in
Constantinople and elsewhere within the limits of the
Empire of Eastern Rome. This is especially remarkable
in La Martorana and S. Cataldo at Palermo, as will be
pointed out when we come to describe those buildings.

The palace at Palermo of Robert Guiscard and his
nephew Roger, the first Norman king of Sicily and
South Italy, has been much altered and added to in later
times, but is said to contain part at all events of that
of their Saracen predecessor. The chapel, the famous
CAPELLA PALATINA, was begun by King Roger in 1132
and finished in 1143. The plan is basilican with a nave
and side aisles five bays long, divided by antique pillars
of marble, alternately smooth and fluted, that next the
ambo spirally (Plate CLXXIV). The capitals seem to be
of late Roman work, some misfitting the column, being
too small. The arcade is much stilted, and more sharply
pointed than usual. The construction of wall and arch is
no doubt of brick, as may be seen in the arches of the
vestibule where the material is exposed, but no stone or
brick is shown within the chapel, the whole being lined
with marble or mosaic. The side walls, up to the cills
of the small pointed windows are covered with marble,
divided by bands of mosaic into large panels, inlaid with
discs or slabs of porphyry on a white ground. Below
the windows this dado finishes with a frieze of mosaic
and marble of a very oriental character (Fig. 208). The
upper part of the walls is covered with mosaic, which is
carried round the arris of the arches and all other features
in the usual Byzantine fashion, no masonry, as I have
said already, being visible.

The nave roof is of wood gorgeously decorated, with
pendants of a kind of stalactite formation, of which

Palermo.
Capella
Palatina

a model may be seen in the Museo Nazionale. The aisles have a lean-to roof of wood.

Above the nave arcade is a clerestory of small pointed windows like those in the aisle, very high up, and lost in the thickness of the wall except when viewed from the aisle. The chapel is very dark, and except on a bright day, and early in the morning it is difficult to see the detail.

The
transept

East of the nave is a transept of the same height, not projecting beyond the aisle wall, and over the

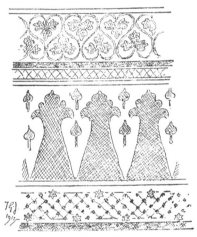

Fig. 208.

The dome

crossing is a circular dome carried on squinch arches of the same kind as those to be described presently at S. Cataldo. Round the base of the dome are eight little windows of clear glass which rather prevent the mosaic

The
mosaic

from being well seen. A half-length figure of Christ occupies the centre of the dome, and on the circle round Him we read,

✝ OOYPANOCMOIΘPONOCHΔEΓHYΠOΠOΔION
TWNΠOΔWNMOYΛEΓEIKYPOCΠANTOKPATWP

Below, round the dome, are angels with white draperies
and prismatic coloured wings, and with their names in Greek letters.

The arches of the dome are supported on the west by doubling the last pillars of the arcades : on the other sides by the walls of transept and sanctuary.

The apse has in mosaic a seated figure of the Virgin, said to be of later date; and round the facing arch of the pointed vault is an inscription in Latin.

The mosaics of the nave are rather later, and were finished by William I in 1160 after the death of his father. The inscriptions in this part are in Latin, and it is probable that while the mosaics of the eastern part were done by Byzantine Greeks, those of the nave are by Sicilians, their pupils[1].

At the west end is a grand mosaic, covering the whole wall above a lofty dais prepared for the royal throne with side screens of marble. At the eastern part of the south nave aisle is a fine ambo, inlaid with Cosmatesque mosaic, and close by is the famous marble candelabrum, enriched with semi-Romanesque sculpture. The mosaic inlays in dados, and such furniture as the ambo, or choir screens in Sicily are largely made with porphyry and serpentino and not like the Cosmatesque work entirely of glass. The figure work of the upper walls no doubt is all of glass like Byzantine work elsewhere.

The pavements throughout the Capella Palatina are
of *opus Alexandrinum*, but the interlacing patterns are very different from those of Rome, or Lucca, and their straight angular twists have a distinct resemblance to oriental arabesques. This characteristic runs through all the pavements I saw in Sicily (Fig. 218, p. 276).

---

[1] *v.* Diehl, *Manuel, etc.* p. 522. Dalton, *Byzantine Art*, p. 407.

The choir has lately been fitted with stalls of walnut, made in Palermo, which are excellently designed and executed.

The Norman palace is partly disguised by a Neo-Classic building in front, but the old work remains behind and is exposed at both ends.   There is however only a small part of the date of King Roger.   It contains on the upper floor a room lined like the chapel with a dado of marble and mosaic ; and above it in the vaults and

on the walls are mosaics of various ornamental patterns, and figures of men shooting at deer, doubly interesting because secular subjects are so rare.   This lovely room is, I think, finer than anything else here.

Nearly coeval with the palace of Palermo is the cathedral of CEFALÙ, which was founded by King Roger in fulfilment of a vow after his escape from shipwreck in 1129.   Cefalù, the ancient Cephaloedium, is a poor unfrequented town, with only rough accommodation for visitors, about 40 miles east of Palermo on the north coast.   The views on the way are enchanting, and the historical associations, here as everywhere in Sicily, are of surpassing interest.   You pass the vacant site of

Himera, where in 480 B.C. the Greeks destroyed the Carthaginian army, when Hamilcar, after in vain sacrificing human victims to Baal and Ashtaroth, at last in despair threw himself on the sacrificial fire.

Cefalù stands picturesquely at the foot and creeps up the side of a stupendous rock crowned with a Norman castle and the remains of a Greek temple.   The plan of the cathedral, which seems to have been finished between 1145 and 1148 is basilican ; it has a nave seven bays long with side aisles, a transept projecting a little beyond the aisles, and a choir and aisles of two bays ending in

Plate CLXXV

CEFALÙ

B. H. J.

Plate CLXXVI

T. G. J.   CEFALÙ—The Cloister court

three apses (Plate CLXXV). The nave and transepts Cefalù
cathedral have wooden roofs, the choir is vaulted, and the apse has a pointed semi-dome set within an arch. The building is rather dilapidated and has been a good deal spoiled by later alterations. The nave is now very bare, the arches and wall being plastered and whitened. The columns are of granite all of one height, raised on pedestals, and with good classic bases. Many of the capitals seem of late Roman work, the rest are based on Corinthian, but some have animals and figures mixed with acanthus leaves. They all have the Byzantine pulvino of moulded marble, with the hollow Corinthian abacus below. Many are much damaged, and in some the horns are gone and only the bell remains. The arches have a shallow outer order, higher and more acute than the inner.

The two bays of the choir are cross-vaulted; the first The
mosaics is ruined by rococo work, but the second together with the great apse has retained its mosaics which are perhaps the finest in the island. In the centre is a large half-length figure of Christ, dominating the church magnificently. The head seems to have been a good deal restored, but has preserved a singularly dignified and impressive aspect. The right hand is extended in benediction, the thumb touching the third and fourth finger-tips, the first and second fingers extended and bent. In the left hand is a book with this text in Greek and Latin from S. John viii. 12 :

```
ΕΓѠΕΙΜΙΤΟΦѠC        EGOSV̅LVXMV̅DIQVI
ΤΟΥΚΟCΜΟΥΟΑ         SEQVITVRMENONAM
ΚΟΛΟΥΘѠΝΕΜΟΙ        BVLATINTENEBRIS
ΟΥΜΗΠΕΡΙΠΑΤΗC       SETABEBITLV̅ME
ΗΕΝΤΗCΚΟΤΙΑΑΛ       V    I    T    E    ✠
ΛἘCΕΙΤΟΦѠCΤΗCΖѠΗC
```

In the drum of the apse are three tiers of mosaic, the two lower being interrupted by the only window. The uppermost has in the centre a figure of the Virgin with hands extended as an *orans*, in the attitude of prayer, between two angels on either hand. The two lower tiers contain figures of the Apostles with their names in Greek. The quadripartite vault has four seraphs, CEPAΦHM, radiating from the centre, with six wings as in the pendentives of S. Sophia, and eight cherubs, XEPδBIM, emerging from a nebulous space in the pointed base of the cell. These M. Diehl believes to be later work.

The columns at the starting of the apse are in two heights, the upper half seems of porphyry, but on closer inspection proves to be covered with porphyry-coloured mosaic. The half-way capital is not carved but has a pattern of leaves worked in mosaic. The lower shaft is made up of two lengths of old marble columns.

On a band at the base of the mosaics, above the cornice surmounting the ground storey, is the following inscription in rhyming hexameters, giving the date 1148 A.D.:

✠ ROGERIVS REX EGREGIVS PLENVS PIETATIS
ḣOC STATVIT TEMPLVM MOTVS ZELO DEITATIS
ḣOC OPIBVS δITAT VARIIS VARIOQ; DECORE
ORNAT MAGNIFICAT IN SALVATORIS HONORE
ERGO STRVCTORI TANTO SALVATOR ADESTO
VT SIBI SVBMISSOS CONSERVET CORδE MODESTO
ANNO AB INCARNACIONE D̄N̄I MILLESIMO
CENTESIMO XLVIII INDICTIONE XI ANNO V̊
REGNI EIVS XVIII ḣOC OPVS MVSEI FACTVM EST

There is another inscription round the face of the arch within which the apse is set, as follows:

FACTVS hOMO FACTOR hOMINIS FACTIQ; REDEMPTOR
IVDICO CORPOREVS CORPORA CORDA DEVS

It would be difficult to praise these splendid mosaics too highly. They preserve the decorative quality of the earlier Byzantine school of Ravenna, with less stiffness than those of the 6th century, and escape the slight tendency to grotesqueness which shows itself in the later work at Monreale.

The west front is retired to the back of two great flanking towers, and the space between them is filled by a loggia or vaulted porch of three pointed arches in a later style. It was once adorned with mosaics of King Roger and his successors, of which no trace now remains. Above and behind this loggia the upper part of the front shows itself with two tiers of pointed arcading, the lower interlacing, and interrupted by the only western window.

North of the nave is a sadly dilapidated cloister with stilted pointed arches and coupled colonnettes (Plate CLXXVI). Many of the shafts are gone and are replaced by rough piers of masonry, and one side of the cloister has been rebuilt plainly in comparatively modern times. Some of the capitals have Byzantine foliage (Fig. 209), others have animals (Fig. 210) and one is an amusing composition of an acrobat with his head between his legs at each corner representing no doubt some jester who had amused the court of King Roger, and caught the sculptor's fancy (Fig. 211). The north transept rises finely from the cloister, and is backed up by the great mountain behind the town.

The cathedral has an interesting font of a material resembling our Frosterley marble, consisting of a bowl 4' 6" in diameter with four lions in relief, resting on two spirally fluted stones.

Cefalù
cathedral
cloister

Fig. 209.

Fig. 210.

Fig. 211.

At the entrance of the choir is on each side a short screen of marble and mosaic to mark the *Sedes Regia*, and the *Sedes Episcopalis*, and two picturesque organs stand on lofty platforms just outside the choir, borne each by four granite columns, of which some have antique Corinthian capitals.

In the middle of Palermo is another church of King Roger's reign, LA MARTORANA, founded in 1143 by George Antiochenos his high admiral[1]. This is a building of the domical type, following the Byzantine plan of a square surrounding a central dome, and with three apses at the east end (Fig. 212). It was originally preceded by a portico or narthex and an atrium. The central apse was destroyed in 1685 by the excrescence of a rococo choir, and the original plan of the nave is obliterated by an extension westwards made in 1588 on the site of the atrium. Originally the church stood four-square, with a central dome on four columns, supported on each side by a short barrel vault reaching the outer wall, the four square bays in the corners being covered with cross-vaults at a lower level. It conforms therefore to what has been called the "four-column plan" of domed churches, of which S. Theodore the Tiro, the Pantocrator, and S. Saviour Pantepoptes at Constantinople are examples[2]. The dome with the four barrel-vaults to north, south, east, and west forms a Greek cross, and the square bays between the arms of the cross fill the plan out to a square. Here however all the arches

Side notes: Cefalù cathedral. Palermo. La Martorana. The original "four-column" plan

[1] S. Maria dell' Ammiraglio was renamed La Martorana in 1433 when granted to a nunnery founded by Eloisa Martorana in an adjoining building.

[2] See Van Millingen's *Churches of Constantinople*, pp. 9, 200, 217, 249, and my *Byzantine and Romanesque Architecture*, vol. I. ch. IX. Mr Freshfield describes and illustrates a very perfect church of this type, S. Trinità di Delia, near Castelvetrano.

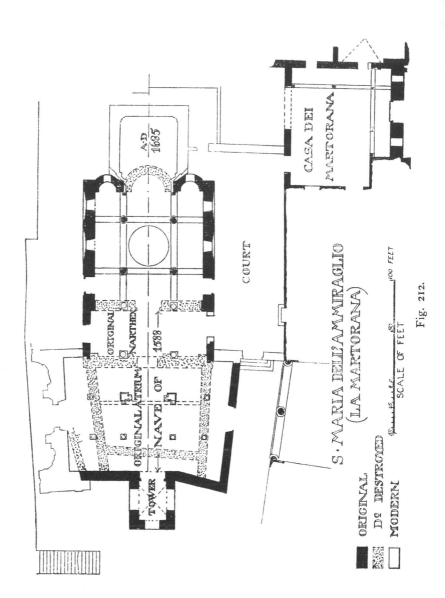

S . MARIA DELL'AMMIRAGLIO
(LA MARTORANA)

SCALE OF FEET

100 FEET

Fig. 212.

ORIGINAL
D⁰ DESTROYED
MODERN

Plate CLXXVII

PALERMO—La Martorana

Plate CLXXVIII

PALERMO—La Martorana. King Roger crowned by Christ

and vaults are pointed, and stilted; at Constantinople
they are round (Plate CLXXVII).

The marble capitals and columns of the main order
are antique, of late Roman work, some of them misfits.
But at the jambs whence the apse starts are small nook-
shafts with foliage of a Byzantine character. These
nook-shafts at the opening of the apse are a Sicilian
feature : they occur at the recesses of La Ziza, at
Monreale, and though the shafts are gone their nooks
remain at S. Cataldo and the church of the Eremiti.

As at the Capella Palatina the walls were lined with
a dado, now mostly destroyed, of white marble panelled
and inlaid with plaques of porphyry and surmounted by
a mosaic frieze. The arches and vaults are covered
with extremely fine mosaics of a purely Byzantine type.
In the two side apses are S. Joachim and S. Anna with
their names in Greek. The small cross-vaults in the
angles of the original square plan have gold stars on
a blue ground, and on the soffits of the arches are
patterns in colour on gold. In the western barrel-vault
is a Nativity on one side with the word ΓΕΝΝΗCIC,
and on the other the death of the Virgin. Christ
receives the soul and delivers it to two angels who float
above ready to take it in their arms, which are draped
with napkins like those of the two Saxon angels at
Bradford-on-Avon. Four more similarly draped fly
round the dome, the centre of which has a full-length
figure of Christ seated on a throne, within a circle, round
which is the text ΕΓω ΕΙΜΙ ΤΟ ΦωC, etc., which we have
seen at Cefalù.

The original west end of the nave was destroyed for
the extension mentioned already, but two of its mosaics
have been preserved ; one represents the founder *Georgios*

Antiochenos at the Virgin's feet[1], the other shows King Roger being crowned by our Lord. The figures are named ΙC̅—X̅ and ΡΟΓΕΡΙΟC ΡΗΞ (Plate CLXXVIII).

These mosaics with those of Cefalù, and of the eastern part of the Capella Palatina, are splendid both in colour and design, and are certainly the finest in the island. The figure of Christ, last mentioned, has a grave dignity that is very remarkable.

West of the church stands the Campanile (Plate CLXXIX), of two dates, the two lower storeys probably coeval with the church, the upper part being of the following century. It is now joined to the church by the later nave, but was divided from it originally by an atrium open to the sky, much in the same way as that at Parenzo in Istria, though here without the intervention of a baptistery. In the lowest storey are arches on all four sides. The first storey above has large pointed two-light windows, the outer order made with pulvinated courses and voussoirs like the windows of the church of the Holy Sepulchre at Jerusalem. They are enclosed by an incised border of ornament, and the whole is set in a square panel with a border of inlaid work, and a
bounding moulding. The effect of this is thoroughly oriental, and reminds one of the panelling in majolica tiles that enclose the Mihrab of a mosque. A broad band of similar inlay runs round the tower below the windows. The patterns are sunk in the solid and filled in with black basaltic stone, of which a good deal has fallen out.

The two later storeys above are in the same style, with pulvinated voussoirs and inlaid patterns, and they

---

[1] This mosaic and that of the dome and others are illustrated by Dalton, *Byzantine Art*, pp. 408–409, 665, and Diehl, *Manuel, etc.* p. 517.

Plate CLXXIX

T G. J.   PALERMO—Tower of La Martorana

have octagonal turrets at the corners. The tower no Palermo. La Martorana
doubt once finished with a dome, which has disappeared.
The whole design for one fresh to Sicilian architecture is
novel and most instructive.

The church and convent of S. Giovanni Evangelista, Gli Eremiti
or as it is generally called S. GIOVANNI DEGLI EREMITI
is another of King Roger's foundations, founded and
built between 1132 and 1148. This is a domical church,
but it is not planned on the Byzantine model as a square

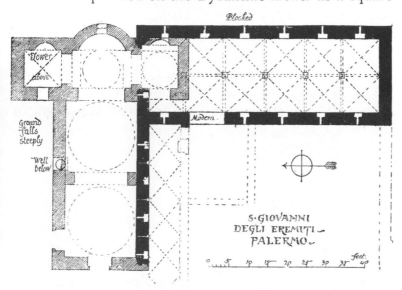

Fig. 213.

round a central dome (Fig. 213). It has a nave and
choir covered with three domes in a line, an eastern
transept with a dome over the southern arm, and over the
other is a tower, crowned with a dome, the lower storey
being cross-vaulted. In the belfry stage are windows
surrounded by wide shallow concentric orders, enclosed
within a square border in Arab fashion, like those at La
Martorana. There are three apses at the east end, of

which only the central one projects on the outside. The cross arches on which the domes rest are pointed, and the domes are carried by squinches of a kind to be more fully described when we come to S. Cataldo. The light comes from windows in the domes and in the end walls, and there are openings in the cross walls from dome to dome ranging with the windows. The ground falls rapidly eastwards, so that the elevation of the apse from the Via dei Benedettini is considerable, and on the north side, below the level of the floor, is a recess containing a well. The building is now disused, and is quite bare and devoid of any ornamentation.

This church is built into an older building on the south side consisting of a long chamber once vaulted with six bays of pointed arches, in two spans, with a row of five piers dividing it down the middle. The vaults had transverse ribs, developed as they rose, but dying into the vaulting surface at the springing : the groins were plain without diagonal ribs. These vaults and piers have disappeared, and the walls have been raised and covered with a single-span vault of the 17th or 18th century. The hall is now lit by windows in this more modern work, but originally it had only very narrow slits in the wall, widened out on the inside with a pointed arch. It was approached by a cloister, of which the wall ribs remain in the south wall of the church, where also may be seen the inside of small windows like those in the main chamber (Fig. 214). As the outside of these windows is in the nave, it proves that the wall belongs to the older building. The groining of this cloister was like that of the chamber, but had no transverse ribs.

What this older structure was is a mystery. The local story is that it was a mosque, which I think very unlikely. It is not orientated for Mecca, nor is there any suggestion of a place for the Mihrab. Nor does the

Fig. 214. (Basil H. Jackson.)

architecture, which is more Gothic even than the church that was built into it, seem possible in a Saracenic building. There can be very little difference in date between the two, and indeed but for the obvious intrusion of the south transept, which obliterates one bay of the older hall, and the position of the windows just referred to, one would imagine the church to be the older building. I fancy that this hall and its cloister must be part of King Roger's foundation, possibly a refectory or chapter house opening from the court of which there are traces on the south side of the church; and that the position of the church is due to some change of plan very soon afterwards.

After being incorporated with the church this hall seems to have been used as a chapel; traces remain on the east wall of early fresco paintings in which one can recognize the figures of the Madonna and attendant saints.

A few steps farther westward of this court is the charming little cloister which is the delight of every artist who visits Palermo (Plate CLXXX). It is very roughly worked, and evidently later than the other buildings. The arches are pointed and segmental, but the shallow order and the label that surmounts them are round. Many of the marble colonnettes have perished and been replaced by rude piers of masonry. The surviving capitals are delicately carved, but in a stone too rough to do the work justice. In the middle of the court is a well: clustering roses climb over it, the garden around is full of palms and semi-tropical vegetation, and above rises the church with its five pink domes, and its Saracenic windows; the whole picture is so completely oriental that one almost forgets that this is still Europe.

The little church of S. CATALDO adjoining La Martorana,

Plate CLXXX

T. G. J.   PALERMO—S. GIOVANNI DEGLI EREMITI—The Cloister

Plate CLXXXI

T. G. J.   PALERMO—S. Cataldo

built in 1161 during the reign of William I, *il Malo*, has
an almost more Saracenic look than any other building
in Palermo (Fig. 215). It is a simple rectangle of a nave
and aisles, ending eastwards in three apses of which only
the central one shows outside (Fig. 216). The nave is
divided by cross arches into three bays, covered by three
domes in a row, and the aisles have transverse ribs and
cross-groining. It is lit by simple windows high in the
side walls, and by lights in the domes (Plate CLXXXI).

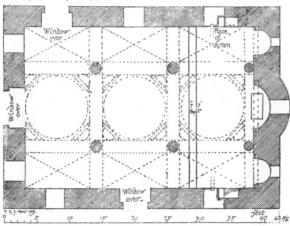

Fig. 215.

The domes are carried by a curious sort of squinch across
the angles of the square, half a squinch and half a niche,
a feature which occurs also at La Martorana, and at the
Capella Palatina, and is the typical mode in Sicily of
bringing the square into an octagon, and so into a circle.
In the cross walls, between the squinches and ranging
with the windows, are openings from dome to dome, and
between the heads of the eight arches a small pendentive
brings the octagon to a circle. The squinch consists of

two orders, the inner one forming a semi-circular niche, with pointed head. At the foot these orders stand out and show a flat soffit below, an awkward finish which would not have satisfied a northern Gothic architect, who would have made the arches die into the side walls.

Fig. 216.

At S. Cataldo, whence all mosaic decoration has disappeared, if it ever had any, the effect of this unsupported overhang is disagreeable, and looks as if the architect had not known how to finish it off. At the Capella Palatina where the mosaic is carried over it, smoothing

off the awkward angles, the effect is not very noticeable, but even there it has somewhat the look of a
bungle.

At the sides of the apses were nook-shafts, of which
the nooks only remain. The main columns are of marble,
probably antique, with good classic bases, but the principal
capitals are original, and curious. They have the hollow

Fig. 217.

Corinthian abacus but no pulvino, and with the volute
and caulicolus is combined the angular twist of the
Saracen (Fig. 217).

The pavement of *opus Alexandrinum*, of which part
is shown in Fig. 218, also displays a mixture of East and
West, for though the general idea is reminiscent of pavements like those in S. Maria Maggiore, the Ara Celi, and
numerous other churches in Rome, Lucca, and elsewhere

Palermo.
S. Cataldo

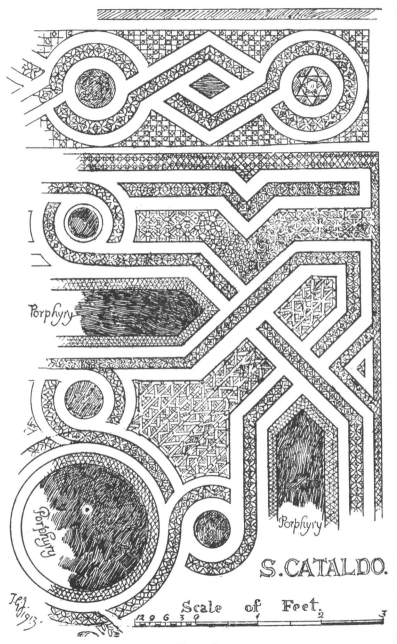

Porphyry

Porphyry

Porphyry

S. CATALDO.

Scale of Feet.

Fig. 218.

in Italy, the straight angular form of the interlacing bands that break away from the easy curves of the centre are distinctly Saracenic.

In the triapsal termination of this chapel, and that of La Martorana, the Capella Palatina, and other churches in Palermo we see the influence of Byzantine tradition, for the two side apses required in the Greek church for the prothesis and diaconicon, were not needed by the Latin rite. In the central apse at S. Cataldo still remains a small altar of white marble, such as the Greek use

Fig. 219.

required, incised with a cross between the four beasts of the Apocalypse, and bearing in the centre the Lamb and flag.

The windows outside are enclosed in a sort of outer order, which, however, is not recessed in the wall, but the whole wall above the window-cill is brought forward to form it—a very singular device (v. Fig. 216 and Plate CLXXIX). Similar arches enclose the windows of La Martorana, but they are managed in the substance of the wall in the usual way.

Palermo.
S. Cataldo
The
parapet
Externally the walls are crowned by battlementing or cresting of a very oriental form, inlaid with patterns and pierced. It is now mostly new, but enough of the old remains to justify the design (Fig. 219). It was discovered behind a coat of plaster and exposed by Professor Salinas.

La Ziza
Outside the town, beyond the Piazza d'Ossuna, stands the palace of LA ZIZA, built by William I, where he indulged in the soft indolent ease of a true oriental. The king was like his architecture, compounded of northern vigour and eastern luxury. When roused to action he showed himself a warrior and a leader of men, but at other times he shut himself up in his palaces and lived the slothful idle life of an eastern sultan. He surrounded himself with Saracen courtiers and eunuchs, and was accused of being half a Mussulman himself. Finally he forbad anyone to trouble him with the affairs of state, and left his kingdom to the mercy of unworthy ministers, who ruined and oppressed his subjects, whence, says the historian, he acquired the name of *Guglielmo il Malo*[1].

La Ziza now forms a cubical block of building, with windows of the same type as those we have been describing. It is inhabited as a private house, but there is a central hall, which can be visited, preceded by an arched vestibule, now opening on the public street, where once were beautiful gardens. This hall, or alcove,

[1] Dopo questo si diede si fattamente all' ozio, ed alla quiete, che vietò espressamente a' suoi famigliari che non gli significassero cos' alcuna che noja e travaglio recar gli potesse ; onde da questo suo non volere udir nulla degli affari del Regno si cagionò che Gaito Pietro, e gli altri Eunuchi del Palagio, con molti lor partigiani afflissero con rapine, e con straziargli nelle persone grandemente i Siciliani, &c. Giannoni, *Storia di Napoli*, Lib. XII. cap. 4.

is thoroughly oriental (Fig. 220). It is a square chamber Palermo.
La Ziza with square recesses on three sides, the fourth being open to the vestibule. These recesses are vaulted with Saracenic stalactites, to bring them out to the central

Fig. 220.

square, which is cross-vaulted. The walls were lined with marble, divided into panels by upright bands of mosaic between bead-mouldings of white marble, and over this dado was a high band of glass mosaic. Much of this mural decoration has been defaced, or carried off, we are told, by the French; but there are considerable remains of the mosaic, especially in the central recess, where, within lovely borders of colour on gold, are three circles with trees and birds, and archers shooting at them. Here again, as in King Roger's room in the palace, one

escapes for the moment from the saints of church mosaic and welcomes the rare opportunity of seeing what the secular work of the 12th century was like. Such as this must have been the splendid decorations of palaces and churches by Theophilus and the Iconoclastic emperors at Constantinople. At the corners of the recesses are the characteristic nook-shafts referred to above, and their capitals are the most European feature in the building (Fig. 221). All the rest might very well be in the Alhambra or on the other shore of the Mediterranean. In the back wall from a niche, decorated probably by Frederick II with an imperial eagle in mosaic, gushes out a

Fig. 221.

stream of water, which pours down an inclined plane of marble, wrinkled with zigzags to break the stream into sparkling wavelets; and thence through a channel between marble sides adorned with mosaic it falls into square pools sunk in the floor. A more delicious retreat from the sun of a Sicilian summer, where, lulled by the tinkling murmur of water, one looked out on shady groves through arches of marble and mosaic, could not be desired by the most indolent and luxurious oriental. Now the groves are gone, and the interior is exposed to every passer-by on the dusty high-road : the marble Palermo. is mostly stripped from the walls, and the mosaic picked out, but much of the old oriental charm still hangs about what is left.

The palace of LA CUBA, outside the Porta Nuova, La Cuba which was built by William II in 1185, as is recorded by an Arabic inscription on the frieze, has some Saracenic details; and the pavilion called LA CUBOLA, once belonging to it, has all the characteristics of a Mahometan Turbeh[1].

[1] Boccaccio makes La Cuba the scene of the adventure of Gian di Procida and Restituta. *Decam.* v. 6.

CHAPTER XXIX

SICILIAN GOTHIC, *continued*

WITH the reign of William II, *il Buono*, we seem to open a new chapter in the history of Sicilian architecture. Between four and five miles from Palermo, on a terrace some thousand feet above the sea, on the lower slopes of Monte Caputo, King Roger had formed a royal park and built a hunting lodge, whence the place took the name of Mons Regalis, or MONREALE. Hither, says the chronicler Romualdo di Salerno, in the year 1153 the King led a limpid stream of water; possibly the same which now fills a great cistern in the cloister, of which the courses of supply and overflow are equally unknown. In this delicious spot, overlooking Palermo and the rich plain of the Conca d'Oro, girdled with mountains, carpeted with groves of oranges and lemons, and intersected by the road that leads straight as an arrow to the city and through the Porta Nuova to the sea, William II reared the great church and convent which were the crowning wonder of Sicilian architecture.

The story goes that he was warned in a dream by the Virgin Mary to build a church in her honour on this spot, with a treasure which he should find there. Gravina[1] suggests that he discovered a hoard hidden by

Monreale cathedral

Legendary foundation

---

[1] *Il Duomo di Monreale*, by Don. Benedetto Gravina, 1859.

Plate CLXXXII

MONREALE CATHEDRAL

his avaricious father. The work was begun in 1172, Monreale cathedral
and in 1176, though the church was still unfinished, the
first monks and the Abbot Theobald from the Benedictine abbey of La Cava were installed in the new
convent.

The church is a basilica (Fig. 222), transeptal, and The plan
ending in three apses, but there is no dome at the
crossing. There are two western towers, standing, like
those at Cefalù, in advance of the nave, with an open

MONREALE CATHEDRAL

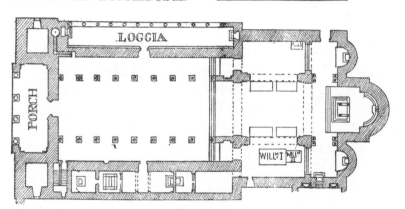

Fig. 222.

loggia filling the space between them, above and behind
which appears the west wall of the nave, ornamented
with interlacing arcading and with a large window. The
south-west tower is finished with a rather later storey,
and the other was never finished at all, but is semi-
ruinous. The present loggia is of Renaissance work,
replacing the original structure of pointed arches adorned
with mosaic. The western doorway is rather magnifi- The west doorway
cent with Norman zigzag and 12th century scroll-work,
but the treatment is much flatter than it would be with

us, the orders being very slightly retired within one
another, and a border of mosaic is introduced among
them. The bronze doors of Bonanno of Pisa, which
were made in 1185, are extremely interesting. Borders
of scrolls and rosettes divide them into panels. Four
ramping lions occupy the foot, one of them misplaced,
and the forty-six small panels above have figures of prophets and biblical groups, with their titles in Lombardic
lettering. Another doorway on the north side, surrounded
by mosaic, under a loggia erected by Cardinal Alessandro
Farnese in the 16th century, contains bronze doors by
Barisano of Trani, which are later and less interesting
than those by Bonanno.

　　　The interior is magnificent; the great span of the
nave gives an air of spaciousness, and the treatment of
the east end is superb (Plate CLXXXII). In the apse
is a huge figure of Christ in mosaic, which dominates
everything; marble lines the lower walls, and mosaic
the rest. The wooden roofs are modern, replacing those
that were burnt not long ago, of which I assume they
are a copy. They are rich in gold and colour, and the
effect is splendid. The part over the crossing has large
beams with stalactite coffering between them. The nave
ceiling is equally rich,—a tiebeam roof with the timbering
exposed.

　　　The great half-length figure of Christ in the pointed
semi-dome of the apse resembles that at Cefalù, with
the right hand in the same act of benediction, and a book
in the left, inscribed with the same text in Latin and
Greek[1]. There are only two zones of figures here in the
drum of the apse, of which the upper one has a seated
Madonna with the child Jesus in her lap, between two

---

[1] There are mis-spellings in the Greek.

angels, beyond whom are figures of saints. The line of figures in the lower tier is interrupted by a large window.

The nave is eight bays long, with nine columns on a side, of which one to the right on entry is of cipollino and the rest are of granite. Some of the capitals are evidently Roman antiques misfitting the columns ; but half of the number are rather puzzling. They consist of cornucopias forming volutes above acanthus leaves, and between the cornucopias is a disc with a classical female head. They are admirably carved, and yet so perfect and free from any sign of age or any mutilation that one can at first sight hardly accept them as antique. And yet it is impossible they can be works of the Renaissance, which is the only alternative, for such an introduction of new capitals would not have escaped the historian. One can only suppose that the columns were taken from some Roman building, and as the capitals fit them perfectly, they probably belonged to one another and were brought here together. This seems to be the opinion of the local archaeologists.

All the arches are pointed and stilted, and spring from a pulvino, which is encased in mosaic like the rest of the superstructure. No string-course or cornice of any kind breaks the smooth surface of the wall above, which is only divided by the bands of the mosaic patterns. There is a clerestory window over each arch, and the aisles are well lit by similar openings.

The interior of Monreale, with its blaze of colour and gold, its rich marbles, its delicate sculpture, and its ample and spacious dimensions, has no rival ; and being well lit, it is much better seen and enjoyed than the Capella Palatina. But this effect which now delights us was not the intention of the original architects. The Sicilian

Monreale
cathedral

The
original
leaden
windows

churches, says Professor Salinas[1], were originally lighted
dimly by windows filled either with sheets of lead pierced
with small openings, or with traceries of plaster, at first
unglazed, and afterwards glazed with coloured glass.
This lead-work was employed in the cathedrals of Monreale and Palermo, so that the scarcity of light might
"strike a sacred horror." An account of Monreale in
1595, says: "This church has little light, because the
windows for the most part are not splayed inside, and
instead of glass, have plates of lead pierced with certain
patterns." It was not till 1659 that the lead was taken
away and glass substituted. Cefalù seems to have had
lead-work windows of this kind, for in the time of
Frederick II the Bishop Arduin was accused of selling
the lead which was wanted at the church *ut fierent inde
fenestre.* These lead fillings were not the only means
of intercepting and reducing light. The museum at
Palermo contains a window-filling of *gesso* from the
church of the Eremiti, and a model of it in wood is now
placed in the opening from which it was taken. At
Grado, in the Adriatic, there still remains a fine window
of *gesso* or concrete, though not in its original place[2].
There are examples of pierced stone fillings at S. Lorenzo
in Pasenatico in Istria, and at Barnack in Northamptonshire[3].

Splendid as is their general effect in the interior, the
mosaics at Monreale, when carefully examined, will be
found inferior in design to those we have described in

[1] *Trafori e vetrate nelle finestre delle chiese medioevali di Sicilia,* by Prof.
Ant. Salinas, 1910. He gives an illustration of a leaden window still existing
in a little church at Taormina. There is another in the cathedral of Troja in
Apulia. See Hamilton Jackson's *Italian shores of the Adriatic,* p. 150.

[2] Illustrated in my *Dalmatia, the Quarnero, and Istria,* vol. III. p. 420.

[3] Illustrated in my *Byzantine and Romanesque Architecture,* vol. II. p. 192.

Plate CLXXXIII

MONREALE CATHEDRAL—The West wall

Plate CLXXXIV

MONREALE CATHEDRAL—East end

the choir of the Palatine Chapel, at Cefalù, and at La Monreale
cathedral Martorana (Plate CLXXXIII).   It is suggested that they were not the work of Greek artists, but of Sicilians who had learned from them.   Most of the inscriptions are in Latin.   Mr Dalton[1] thinks that the work was hurried, the whole building being finished in eight years between 1174 and 1182, and that this accounts for the conventional and inferior character of much of the decoration.   But Gravina says the church was not paved nor the lining of the walls finished at William's death in 1189, so there seems to have been delay rather than hurry.   However this may be, no one, I think, can fail to see the superiority of the Christ at Cefalù to that at Monreale, which was obviously copied from it, and though a fine work, has not the expressive dignity of the original.

Among the mosaics appears the figure of the King, Mosaic of
William II REX GVLIELMVS SC̃DS, offering his church to a seated Madonna, M̃P - O̅D̅.   Two angels with outstretched arms float above, and the divine hand is extended in benediction.   The regal costume is the same as that borne by Roger at La Martorana, where he receives his crown from Christ (v. Plate CLXXVIII, p. 267).   But here also in mosaic is a coronation of William II by Christ, who is enthroned with a book in his left hand, inscribed EGO SVM LVX MVNDI QVI SEQVITVR ME, and by his right hand, which is placing the crown on the King's head, is written, MANVS EN̅I MEA AVXILIA-BITVR EI[2].

The only part of the exterior which shows much The
exterior attention to design is the east end, which is covered

[1] *Byzantine Art and Archaelogy*, p. 410.
[2] Psalm lxxxviii Vulg. (lxxxix A.V.), v. 22.

with an extraordinary, and perhaps extravagant, display of polychrome masonry and interlacing arcades of pointed arches (Plate CLXXXIV).

On the south side of the nave is the great cloister, which is singularly well preserved. The arcades are pointed and stilted, and rest on coupled columns of marble, except at the corners of the square, where is a pier composed of four columns grouped together. These angle groups have the shafts richly sculptured with arabesques : the other colonnettes are alternately plain and decorated with mosaic inlay. They are tapered and have good Attic bases, with toes at the angles. In the south-west corner of the cloister a square enclosure is formed by breaking out three arches each way to

enclose a small court in which is a beautiful fountain, discharging little streams into a basin from small lions' heads. This gives a distinctly oriental touch to the whole (Plate CLXXXV).

There is a perplexing inequality in the work of this cloister. The arches are stilted and pointed, and on the outside are inlaid with intarsia of basalt, and surmounted by a band of the same work under the eaves (Plate CLXXXVI). The outer order has a fillet and a hollow, and the inner is a rather heavy semi-circular roll. The work is like that of the campanile of La Martorana, which was built in 1143, and is roughly executed in a rather coarse stone like that used in the cloister of the Eremiti. But the abacus of the coupled colonnettes does not take the inner order, which hangs in air unsupported, and would fall were it not worked in the solid of the outer order.

The colonnettes and their capitals, unlike the arches they carry, are of the finest 12th century work, exquisitely wrought in marble ; the alternate shafts are inlaid with

Plate CLXXXV

Γ. G. J. MONREALE—The Cloister

Plate CLXXXVI

Monreale.
Cloisters.

B. H. J. MONREALE CATHEDRAL—The Cloister

glass mosaic, like those at the Lateran and S. Paolo
in Rome, and the capitals are magnificently finished,
some with foliage, others with figure subjects (Plate
CLXXXVII). The unsupported roll moulding has a hole
for a dowel in the soffit, suggesting that it once had a supporting shaft, but that would have been inconsistent with
the present coupled colonnettes, their abacus not being
prepared for anything of the kind. Gravina suggests that
originally there was a pier corresponding with the outer
order, inlaid like it, with an attached shaft on each side,
and he gives a drawing of it so composed. His design is
not convincing, nor is the roll moulding big enough for
any shaft but one so slender as to be altogether out of the
question. His theory is that all the columns and capitals
are later insertions, but it is difficult to believe in the
insertion of 216 pairs of colonnettes without disturbance
of the superstructure so soon after the original building.
For among the subjects in the capitals is one of King
William II offering his church to the infant Christ seated
on the lap of the Virgin Mary, which fixes their date in
his reign[1]. Nor would this explain the omission of
support to the roll moulding, for which provision would
naturally have been made when ordering the new capitals[2].
The only explanation I can offer is that the arches were

Monreale
cathedral.
Cloister

[1] On the abacus is inscribed

　　　REX Q CVN̄TA REGIS SICVLI DATA SVSCIPE REGIS. ·

On another capital the sculptor has put his name, perhaps ungrammati-
cally

　　　EGO ROMANVS FILIVS CONSTANTINVS MARMORARIVS.

The subjects are partly taken from the Bible, partly secular. On one
are figures of Norman knights with drawn swords, and kite-shaped shields.

[2] Gravina's theory is that the coarse upper work is part of an older
building, preceding the Arab conquest in the 9th century, when it was ruined
and deserted till restored by William II. It is hardly necessary to say the
architecture is quite inconsistent with this theory.

Monreale cathedral. Cloister

prepared by native Sicilians, the same who built the Duomo itself, which is inlaid in the same way, and that the capitals and colonnettes were imported from Italy and worked away from the building without sufficient communication with the local men. The sculpture is superior to anything else of the kind that I saw in Sicily. The men who carved the west doorway would have been incapable of carving these splendid capitals, which are equal to the finest examples of 12th or early 13th century work I have ever seen (Plate CLXXXVII)[1]. The dwarf wall on which the colonnade stands is of rough masonry, no doubt by the same masons as the arches.

Suspension of building

William II who married the Princess Joan of England, daughter of Henry II, did not live to see his church finished: he died in 1189, at the age of 43. In the troublous times which followed the work was interrupted, and the dedication did not take place till 1267. The nave ceiling was probably renewed in 1398, and that of the presbytery in 1440. Both, as I have said, were burnt, and have been restored. An extensive repair of the mosaics took place between 1811 and 1847, of which Gravina gives full particulars[2].

Palermo. The Duomo

The cathedral of PALERMO stands on the site of an older church which the Arabs had used as a mosque. It was built in 1185 by an English archbishop of Palermo, Gualterio Offamilio,—Walter of the Mill,—who, as archdeacon of Cefalù, had been tutor to William II during the regency of his mother. During the two centuries of Arab rule most of the churches had no doubt been turned into mosques; though it appears that the Christians were allowed to continue their worship according to the Greek

---

[1] This capital illustrates the story of Joseph and his brethren.
[2] *op. cit.* p. 21.

Plate CLXXXVII

B. H. J.   MONREALE—Capital in Cloister

rite, for when the Normans came they found a Christian community here under a bishop named Nicodemus, whom, however, they replaced by one of their own followers.

Not much except the east end remains of the English prelate's church, which has been repeatedly altered, the whole interior being converted into a modern classic building with a cupola, by a Florentine architect, Fuga, in the 17th century, in spite of the remonstrances of the Sicilians. The east end, however, retains its apses, inlaid with polychrome interlacing arches, like Monreale, and flanked by two towers. The chief interest of the interior is centred in the monuments of the Emperor Henry VI, his wife Constance, daughter of King Roger, and, above all, that of their son Frederick II. These monuments, however, have been removed from their original places. The south porch, dating from the 15th century, has a column inscribed with texts from the Koran. Under this porch is the principal entrance to the church, with scroll-work in the jambs and arch of a Romanesque character. The west front, also of the 15th century, has a fine marble doorway, and separated from it by a street is what seems the real west end, a strange pile of turrets and pinnacles surmounting an earlier structure, and united to the main building by two fine arches across the street (Fig. 223).

Interlaced arcading in polychrome masonry of white stone and basalt is very characteristic of Sicilian architecture, especially in the later buildings. Interlacing arches are a common feature in Norman buildings of France and England: we have plenty of them at Canterbury, at Christchurch, at Castle Rising and Castle Acre, and elsewhere. But in the North the arches are round : here in Sicily they are always pointed, and the mixture

of colour is also unlike northern work.   These intersecting arches do not occur in the earliest buildings, at
La Martorana, S. Cataldo, or the Eremiti.   At Cefalù

Fig. 223.

we find them (*v.* Plate CLXXV), but they are not parti-
coloured.   At Monreale and the Duomo of Palermo we
have polychrome interlaced arcading in full force, and the

Plate CLXXXVIII

S. Pietro del Agro
Near Taormina.

B. H. J.   S. PIETRO IN AGRO

Plate CLXXXIX

B. H. J.   TAORMINA—La Badia Vecchia

interesting little church of S. Pietro in Agro, near S. Pietro in Agro
Taormina is covered entirely with it (Fig. 224).

This church (Fig. 225) has the peculiarity of a square
apse (Plate CLXXXVIII) flanked by two shallow round
ones. The walls are entirely of brick arranged in zigzag
and other patterns, something like the churches of the
Apostles and S. Elias at Salonica, but white and black
stones are introduced to give character to the intersecting
arches. There are two domes carried on antique columns
with rude capitals, the larger one over the nave on
squinches, the lesser over the sanctuary on stalactites.
The rest of the nave roof is of wood. At the west end
are two staircases in what seem to have been a pair of
towers, now destroyed. The inside of the building has
been much injured by rococo vulgarity.

Taormina has two interesting buildings with poly- Taormina Badia
chrome masonry, the Palazzo S. Stefano and the ruined
Badia, which has windows of good geometrical tracery
(Plate CLXXXIX).

Most of the towns have specimens of domestic Domestic Gothic
Gothic, in doorways and windows. Illustrations of
many at Randazzo and at Nicosia will be found in the
pages of *Italia Artistica*. Syracuse has one fine old Syracuse
house, the Palazzo Montalto, hidden away in a court
not easy to be found. But the interest of Syracuse is
classical and historical, and beyond the cathedral, which,
passing from Paganism to Christianity, has never ceased
to be a temple, there are no other monuments of interest
within the present city[1].

---

[1] The present city is confined to the island of Ortygia, and all the
ancient remains are on the hill beyond, except the cathedral. This is a
Greek temple of a massive Doric type, converted into a church by walling
up the intercolumniations of the peristyle, and cutting arches through the
walls of the cella to form a nave and aisles.

S. Pietro
in Agro

Fig. 224.

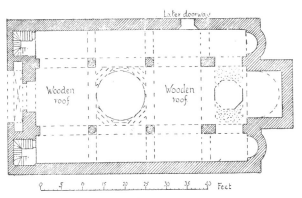

Fig. 225.

In the streets of Palermo are numerous fragments Palermo of old work that invite a sketch. The doorway of the suppressed convent of the Annunziata (Fig. 226) has the Norman zigzag surviving amid natural foliage of the 14th century. The ARCIVESCOVADO, opposite the west Arcives-
covado end of the Duomo, has an interesting doorway dating from the middle of the 15th century, but surrounded by scroll-work of an almost Romanesque character (Fig. 227).

Fig. 226.   Fig. 227.

The PALAZZO CHIARAMONTE has a splendid window of Palazzo
Chiara-
monte three lights in which Norman zigzags are combined with spiral colonnettes, and Saracenic traceries in circles decorated with dog-teeth (Plate CXC). East and west seem here to meet with a vengeance.

TAORMINA in particular abounds in doorways and Taormina windows of Gothic work. Here basalt is used freely and with excellent effect (Fig. 228). Traceries of rather

Flam-
boyant
tracery
a flamboyant type occur, especially in round windows,
of which there is a very rich example at the church of
S. Giovanni dei Catacombi at Syracuse, and a still finer
one at S. Agostino, Palermo.   The Palazzo Corvaja at

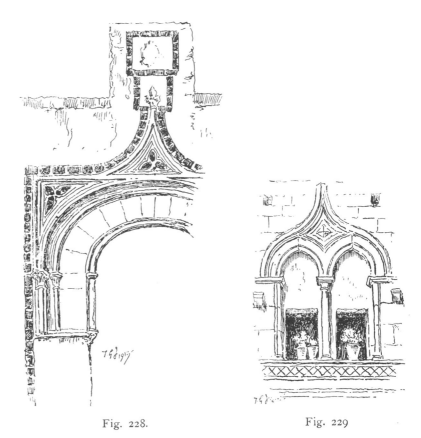

Fig. 228.   Fig. 229

Taormina   Taormina has a curious doorway to the court, where is
a fine exterior staircase (Plate CXCI) with a balcony or
landing at the top, on which are sculptures of the creation
of Eve, the fall, and the expulsion from Paradise, which
however seem to have been misplaced.   The windows

Plate CXC

PALERMO—Palazzo Chiaramonte

Plate CXCI

TAORMINA—Palazzo Corvaja

facing the piazza at the foot of the ascent to the Greek
theatre are also characteristic (Fig. 229). The palace is
dated 1372.

It is remarkable how the Gothic style lingered Tenacity
in Sicily and overlapped the early beginnings of the of Gothic
in Sicily
Classic Renaissance. Professor Salinas showed me in
his museum at Palermo a piece of perfectly pure Gothic
work of the 16th century, which might have been
wrought in the 14th; and *vis-à-vis* with it was a contemporary niche in the fully developed Renaissance style
containing a neo-Classic figure.

CHAPTER XXX

SOUTHERN ITALY

Oriental-
ism in
S. Italy

THOUGH Sicily was united with Southern Italy into one kingdom under the Norman dynasty and the Hohenstaufens, the influence of Sicilian art in Italy and the orientalism which formed part of it was principally felt in the district round the Gulf of Salerno. There are however discs with oriental arabesque on the bronze gates of the tomb of Bohemond at Canosa[1], and in the spandrils of the exterior arcading at Troja are inlays of the same character. Arabo-Sicilian artists were invited to Amalfi early in the 13th century, and others again to Salerno in 1260. Oriental feeling shows itself in the architectural decoration of these places and in that of the cathedral of Sessa near Capua. But beyond Campania it is less noticeable.

Domed
architec-
ture in
S. Italy

Nor did domed architecture make much way in *Il Regno*. The 12th century cathedral of Canosa in Apulia has five domes set like those on the church of the Eremiti at Palermo (*v.* Fig. 213, p. 269). Trani has two domed churches: S. Andrea[2] is grouped squarely round a central dome like the Gul Djami at Constantinople[3], and the church at Delia in Sicily

[1] Illustrated by Schultz, *Denkmäler der Kunst des Mittelalters in Unter-Italien.* Plates X, XLI.

[2] Bertaux, *L'Art dans l'Italie méridionale.*

[3] *v.* my *Byzantine and Romanesque Architecture*, vol. I. p. 122.

illustrated by Mr Freshfield[1]; and the church of Ogni Domed archi-
Santi has three domes in a row like S. Cataldo at tecture in
Palermo, but they are covered with pyramidal roofs. S. Italy
Both these churches are small. The cathedral at
Molfetta has an apse with semi-dome, and three domes
in a row, octagonal outside and covered with pyramidal
roofs[2]. The Cattolica at Stilo in Calabria[3] has five domes
like the Souk-Su Djami, or church of the Twelve
Apostles at Salonica[4], and is decorated on the outside
with chequer-work like S. Pietro in Agro or the Badia
Vecchia at Taormina (*v.* Plates CLXXXVIII, p. 292
and CLXXXIX, p. 293). S. Cataldo at Lecce has a
central drum-tower containing a dome, surrounded by
exterior arcading which has a very Byzantine look[5], and
so has the curious little church at S. Severina in Calabria,
with a small cupola on a lofty drum decorated with
exterior arcading, which is illustrated in a monograph
by Professor Orsi of Syracuse. But the domed church
would seem to be exceptional in Southern Italy[6].

Nor is there very much in the architecture of that Northern influence
part to remind one of the Norman style north of the
Alps. One feature however the Normans seem to have
loved and taken with them wherever they went, namely
the interlacing arcades with which we are familiar at Inter-
Canterbury, S. Cross, and Christchurch in Hampshire. lacing arcades
We have already noticed them in Sicily at Cefalù and
Palermo, and it was probably thence that they passed

[1] *Cellae Trichorae*, p. 36.

[2] Schultz, Plates XI, XII. Hamilton Jackson, *Italian Shores of the Adriatic*, pp. 97, 101.

[3] Freshfield, *op. cit.* p. 95. Schultz, Plate LXXXIV. Bertaux, *op. cit.*

[4] My *Byzantine and Romanesque Architecture*, vol. I. p. 138.

[5] Schultz, *op. cit.*

[6] Bertaux says the Apulians call a cupola *trullo*. This is the τροῦλλος of Theophanes, Cedrenus, and the Byzantine historians.

Interlaced
arcading

into Italy, for they abound especially in Campania where Arabo-Sicilian influence was most felt. At Caserta Vecchia[1] is an enormous central tower of 1153, containing a cupola, and covered with interlacing arches. There are others in the towers of Amalfi and Gaieta[2], dating from the last quarter of the 13th century, which are pointed like those at Monreale (Plate CLXXXIV, p. 287) and S. Pietro in Agro (Fig. 224, p. 294), whereas those at Caserta are round-arched. Round interlacing arches occur also at the east end of the cathedral of Molfetta on the Adriatic, which is flanked by two towers[3]. The loggia at Amalfi, built probably in 1208, and the cloister of 1266–1268 have interlacing arches, and there are others like them at S. Pietro Toczolo, and at S. Domenico in Salerno[4]. These, says M. Bertaux, are the only cloisters in South Italy with interlacing arches. This kind of ornament is distinctively Norman, and is not found in Central or Northern Italy, nor in Central or Southern France.

Northern
ground
plan

Occasionally we find churches with a regular northern plan. The cathedral of Aversa, a Norman foundation, has a *chevet* with three radiating chapels attached to the ambulatory of a semi-circular apse. The ambulatory is cross-vaulted like that at Langres (*v.* Fig. 17, vol. 1. p. 47), the diagonal groin being straight, so that the intersection does not come over the centre of the passage. The plans of the cathedrals at Acerenza[5] and Venosa[6] are very similar : they are cruciform with apsidal chapels on the east side of the transepts, and have a prolonged choir with a round apse, ambulatory aisle, and three

[1] Schultz, Plate LXXII.
[2] Illustrations, Bertaux, p. 622.
[3] *Ibid.* Plates XI, XII.
[4] Schultz, Plate LXXXIV.
[5] *Ibid.* Plate XXXI.
[6] *Ibid.* Plate XLIII.

attached apsidal and radiating chapels. These plans have a very French look, and remind one of Clermont-Ferrand, Issoire, and S. Nectaire.

There are traces of northern influence at Bari. The church of S. Niccola has a triforium of three round arches under a semi-circular including arch, which recalls S. Donnino in Lombardy, and the same feature occurs at Trani above a round arched arcade which has a Lombard character[1]. M. Bertaux observes that the Lombards naturalized in Apulia introduced the monsters and grotesques of the North. The cathedral at Bitonto, built in 1200, is round-arched with Romanesque detail, much like Norman work, but the orders are much shallower than in our northern style, and this is a southern characteristic as I have observed in a former chapter. *Lombard details*

Another feature, essentially Italian and inconsistent with northern practice, is the projection of an outer order over the doorways beyond the wall-face instead of recessing it in the wall. These outer orders are carried on colonnettes that rest upon lions as in Lombardy, and sometimes there are more lions at the spring of the arch, a feature that occurs also in Dalmatia across the Adriatic. *The projected order*

A different influence shows itself at Troja. Both there and at Siponto the aisle walls are surrounded on the outside by lofty blank arcadings like those at Pisa, with the very same discs and diamond-shaped figures in the head of the arches. The cathedral at Bari has also tall arcades on the aisle walls. *Pisan influence*

The Collegiata at Barletta has an arcade in place of a triforium open to the aisle, as at S. Lorenzo in Genoa, the Cathedral of Rouen, and the nave of Rochester. *The false triforium*

[1] Schultz, Plate XVIII.

Roman-
esque
persistency

French
influence
under
Frede-
rick II

Italian
difference

Saracen
workmen

French
influence

Architecture in the "Kingdom" under the Normans seems to have lingered in the Romanesque stage, and there is little that can be classed as Gothic till the time of Frederick II, when a strong French influence shows itself. The Castel-del-Monte, his great country palace, is an octagonal building surrounding an octagonal court, and with an octagonal turret at each corner[1]. The rooms are vaulted in the French fashion, and the shafts have capitals à crochet, though they look as if cut by an Italian imitating a French model. But after all the plan, which anticipates Vignola's Caprarola, is more Italian than French, and the great entrance doorway is very unlike northern Gothic. It has a blunt pointed arch, flanked by fluted pilasters carrying a quasi-classic cornice and surmounted by a very classic-looking low-pitched pediment, a feature quite foreign to Gothic beyond the Alps. French feeling appears again in that part of the Castello Maniace at Syracuse, which was built by Frederick II on the point of the island of Ortygia, where there are capitals à crochet ; and according to M. Bertaux the same feeling is noticeable in other buildings of his in the territory of Bari, and at Castro-Giovanni in Sicily. For the mosaic decorations at Castel-del-Monte Frederick probably employed the Saracens whom he had established as a colony at Lucera in Campania[2].

The grotto church of Monte S. Angelo, said to have been rebuilt by Charles of Anjou, has pointed blank

---

[1] Schultz, Plates XXIX, XXX.

[2] ...magistris Saracenis tarisiatoribus, carpentariis, magistris facientibus arma, custodibus camelorum, et ceteris magistris, qui tam de ferro quam de arcubus et aliis operibus laborant ad opus nostrum in Melfia, Canusio, et Luceria, etc. etc.
    Ordinance of Frederick II, Feb. 21, 1240. Cited Bertaux, p. 738.

arcading in the walls above the naked rock between triple clustered wall-shafts with *round* abaci that carry pointed vaults of regular rib and panel construction. The bishop's throne in this chapel has arabesque ornament of an oriental character[1].

The architecture of South Italy—*Il Regno,*—reflects by its mixed details the mixed character of the population. On a basis of Greek and Roman antiquity were grafted varieties of race almost as many as in Sicily. The country has been a Byzantine theme, a Lombard duchy, and a kingdom successively Norman, Hohenstaufen, and Angevin. Each revolution has left its mark on the art of Southern Italy. We find there the Byzantine dome, the Lombard arcade, the Norman interlacing arches, the Semi-French Gothic vault and capital, while through the whole runs a thread of orientalism derived from the Arabo-Saracenic art of Sicily.

Mixed population

Reflected in mixed styles of art

If the architecture of this part of the peninsula does not reach the level of that in the centre and north, where national life was stronger and more free, it forms none the less a very interesting chapter in the history of art.

[1] Schultz, Plates XL, XLI.

CHAPTER XXXI

CONCLUSION

To the practical artist the study of bygone art will not be a mere archaeological exercise. However fascinating that may be, if he really loves his art, he will feel that for him the matter does not end there. All art being based on what has been done already, he has to consider how the art he is studying bears on his own practice, and to that end he must not only admire, but make sure he understands it.

This intelligence is scarcely less necessary in those who employ him, for after all it rests with the public to make or mar the art of their day. No genius however great can effect much in the face of an unintelligent society.

By the account, therefore, necessarily brief, for which there is room between the covers of two moderately sized volumes, it has been attempted to explain the nature of the art which we call Gothic by tracing a reason for the successive phases through which it passed. In those countries which gave it birth it followed naturally upon the Romanesque style, out of which it grew so insensibly that there is no actual line of division between them. In the same way it passed in those countries insensibly through change after change down to the 16th century. In Germany it was not so : there it was adopted ready-made from France, and its place in the history of Art is comparatively unimportant. But in France and England there was an uninterrupted course of development, an unbroken history of progress from the Gallo-Roman work at Poitiers and Beauvais to the wildest Flamboyant vagaries, and from the transepts of Winchester and the nave of Durham to the Royal chapels at Windsor and Westminster.

The history of the art reflected that of civilization : as society in the Middle Ages progressed the art constantly took new forms to accommodate itself to it. A living style must have a meaning and must represent its age ; and accommodation to circumstance is the clue to the history of every true and living style. It is only when this is recognized that it becomes intelligible.

Art in the earlier Middle Ages was essentially religious, and it was in the churches that architecture had its new birth. To the unlettered vulgar they were the visible embodiment of all that was holy; the Palladium to save them from all that is evil. The very stones of the walls had a sanctity we can hardly realize. To be buried as close to them as possible, even sometimes under them, or, as I have seen, partly under the pillars so as to imperil the structure, was to be protected from the evil one. When just before the first millennium the church of S. Peter at Rome caught fire the people cried upon the chief of the Apostles with curses, threatening that if he did not protect his own many would depart from the faith. When Canterbury cathedral was burned in 1174 the people beat their heads and hands against the walls, blaspheming God and His saints for the disaster. At the building of S. Denis (1132–1144) Suger describes how noble and gentle, freeman and serf, men and women of all ranks, harnessed themselves to the cart and drew the stones to the building, while officials, leaving their proper duties, cleared the way[1]. The same thing happened at Chartres in 1145. In Normandy, where this frenzy reached its height, Haymo, the abbot of S. Pierre sur Dives, tells with exultation how "Tyrants, Lay Potentates full of honours and riches, Nobles both men and women, bent their proud and swelling necks to the traces of waggons laden with wine, corn, oil, lime, stone, timber and other things useful for victuals or for construction of churches, and drew them to the shrine of Christ like brute beasts." A thousand men and women marched in silence. At each halt prayer and confession was made. Anyone cherishing malice against another had his offering cast out of the cart and was himself rejected. Sick persons placed on the waggons recovered, the dumb spake, devils were cast out, roads became miraculously easy, and way was made, as for the Hebrews of old, through rivers and even through the waters of the sea. Children drew waggons "not with bent backs like their elders, but erect as if feeling no weight and outstripping the others[2]." Should the miracles come too slowly, all, both men and women, stripped themselves down to their loins, lay on the ground, and implored the priests to flog their naked bodies, crying, "Strike, strike, and spare not."

[1] Suger, *De Consecratione Eccl. S. Dionysi*, cap. II.

[2] Haymo, *Relatio de miraculis B. Mariae*; Delisle, Ser. V. tom. I. p. 120. There is a translation of the whole letter of Abbot Haymo or Haimon to his dependent cell at Tutbury in Coulton's *Mediaeval Garner*, p. 100. Bouquet, *Recueil des Historiens des Gaules et de la France*, XIV. pp. 318–9. Suger, *De Consecratione S. Dionysi*, cap. III., says eye-witnesses told him they had seen children draw a load from the quarry which generally required a hundred men. Mr Porter, to whose *Mediaeval Architecture* I am indebted for reference to many of these authorities, says the "Cart-cult" flourished especially in Normandy, and except at S. Denis and Chartres is not mentioned in the Ile de France.

This high-pitched enthusiasm did not last, and Robert du Mont, writing about 1184, speaks of it as a tradition[1]. But there was no lack of miracles to help the builders ; they were detected in every accident. A scaffold threatened to give way, but "the Saint seeing this from afar, ran up quickly, and making the sign of the cross set his shoulders to the load, whereby he supplied such virtue that the scaffold was confirmed in the twinkling of an eye[2]." Suger, short of timber, goes to the wood and finds exactly the twelve trees that would give him what he wanted, and no more. For his columns he thought of importing by way of the English Channel and the Seine some that he had seen in the Baths of Diocletian at Rome, but by Divine mercy he is enabled to discover a quarry at Pontoise nearer home. An awful storm arises and throws down houses and towers : the vaulting ribs of his church, not yet steadied by the filling in of the panels, trembled miserably : but the Bishop of Chartres saved them by extending his hand in the attitude of benediction towards the fury of the elements, and opposing the arm of S. Simeon[3]. Just so does the Abbate Fortis describe the priests in stormy weather on the islands of the Adriatic, whom he saw standing in their sacerdotal dress with holy water, running into the waves "with crosses, aspersions and conjurations, while the islanders discharge their pieces towards the place

[1] Robert du Mont, *Mon. Germ. Hist. Scriptores*, vol. VI. p. 496 "quae qui non vidit, jam similia non videbit."

[2] *Life of S. Stephen of Obazine* (c. 1148). Translated by Coulton, *Mediaeval Garner*, p. 88.

[3] Saepe manum benedictionis in ea parte extendebat, et brachium Sancti Senis Simeonis signando instanter opponebat ; at manifeste nulla sua constantia, sed sola Dei pietate et sanctorum merito ruinam evadere apparebat. Suger, *op. cit.* cap. V. Zara however can show an entire body of S. Simeon.

pointed out, as if to kill the Vukodlak or witches who raise the storm "[1].

For the same reason relics used to be put on the top of spires by way of lightning conductors. A box with a bit of some textile material was found at the top of Salisbury spire in 1762. A new cross was set with great ceremony on the spire of old S. Paul's in 1315 which contained relics, "in order that the omnipotent God, and the glorious merits of his saints whose relics are contained within the pommel of the cross, might deign to protect it from danger of storms[2]." So at the Euphrasian basilica at Parenzo we read in the mosaic of the apse that the roof was saved by the relics—*merita*—which no doubt were placed there[3].

In this superstitious regard for the mere fabric, making it almost a fetish, we see only the material side of the popular reverence. But there was also a better and a spiritual side. The carvings and paintings which adorned the churches, however rude at first, were the People's Bible. Biscop in the 7th century hung round his walls at Monkwearmouth pictures he had brought from Rome, probably the work of Byzantine artists, with representations of the Virgin and the Apostles, of the gospel story and the Apocalypse, "in order," as Bede tells us, "that all who entered the church, even if ignorant of letters, whichever way they turned should either contemplate the ever lovely aspect of Christ and his saints, though only in a picture; or should with more watchful mind revere the grace of our

---

[1] Fortis, *Viaggio in Dalmazia*, 1774; *v.* my *Dalmatia the Quarnero and Istria*, vol. I. p. 176.

[2] *v.* F. Bond, *Engl. Church Architecture*, vol. II. p. 942.

[3] *v. sup.* p. 71.

Lord's incarnation; or else having as it were the trial of the Last Judgment before their eyes, they might remember to examine themselves more strictly[1]." Theophilus the artist-monk writes: "if the faithful soul chance to behold the effigy of our Lord's passion then he is pricked to the heart: if again he see how great tortures the saints endured in their mortal bodies, and how precious a prize of eternal life they won, then doth he receive encouragement to a better life[2]." Down to much later times the painting on glass and stone, the sculpture in niche and pinnacle, Ruskin's "Bible of Amiens," the ranks of apostles, prophets, and saints at Arles, Chartres, and Reims, and those at Lincoln, Wells, and Westminster, kept the sacred story alive among common and illiterate people.

"The Middle Ages," says M. Mâle, "had a passion for order; Art was organized no less than dogma, human knowledge, and Society[3]." From the first, religious art, both in sculpture and painting, had to submit to convention. A sort of shorthand had to be invented for the artist: a tower with a door represented a town; if an angel is looking over the battlements it was the Heavenly Jerusalem, as at S. Prassede in Rome. For those who could not read it was necessary that each figure should have something to show whom it represented. So each apostle bore the instrument of his martyrdom. A saint was known by his nimbus, but a nimbus with a cross was sacred to the Trinity. God, Jesus, and angels were to be known by their bare feet: to represent the Virgin or the saints unshod would have

---

[1] Bede, *Hist. Eccl.*, Lib. IV. cap. XVIII.
[2] Theophilus, *Prologue to Book III.*
[3] Emile Mâle, *L'Art religieux du XIIIᵉ siècle en France.*

bordered on heresy. Convention naturally led to symbolism, and art was involved in the mystic system of type and antitype which ran through all Mediaeval Theology. Not only had everything in the Old Testament its antitype in the New, but every text had a double meaning; the book held by God on His throne was written within and without, the one side being the literal and the other the mystic interpretation[1]. Every animal in the bestiaries has its own significance. The four beasts of the Apocalypse typify the four main events in the life of Christ: the man His incarnation, the ox His sacrifice, the lion His resurrection[2], the eagle His ascension. Everything in the New Testament, as S. Augustine says, is the revelation of something in the Old[3]. For this reason pictures from the Old Testament were placed, as Bede tells us, opposite those from the New. It is strange with what, as it seems to us, absurd minuteness the parallel is followed out in some cases. The twelve spies are the unbelieving Jews; the hanging cluster of grapes is Jesus on the cross. According to Honorius of Autun Leviathan is Satan : God throws into the sea a line which is the human generation of Christ : the iron of the hook is His divinity, the bait His humanity. Drawn by the odour of the flesh Leviathan tries to seize it, but the hook tears his jaw. David is Christ; his five stones the five books of Moses; Goliath the devil. David only uses one of his five stones, which is charity, for that

---

[1] Foris quantum ad sensum literalem : intus vero ad sensum mysticum sub littera latentem. Walafridus Strabo (ed. Migne, vol. XXIV.), a monk of Fulda, who died in 849.

[2] *v. sup.* p. 210, note.

[3] Quid enim quod dicitur Testamentum Vetus nisi occultatio Novi? Et quid est aliud quod dicitur Novum nisi Veteris revelatio? Aug. *Civ. Dei* XXVI., cited Mâle, *op. cit.*

fulfils the law. The law contains ten precepts, therefore David sings to a harp of ten strings. The passage in Psalm xc. (Vulg.), "*super aspidem et basiliscum ambulabis: et conculcabis leonem et draconem*," is interpreted thus : the lion is Antichrist, the dragon the devil, the basilisk death, and the asp the sinner, because the asp cannot be charmed, but lays one ear on the ground and puts its tail into the other so that it may not hear[1]. These emblems occur on the pedestal of the "*Beau Dieu d'Amiens*," and the like juxtaposition of type and antitype occurs commonly in other sculptures.

It is clear that the artists could not have devised this elaborate system of symbolism. The subjects were given them by the clergy. Suger tells us he directed the sculptured and other ornament, giving their subjects to the carvers, the glass-painters, the goldsmiths, and supplying the inscriptions[2]. The Council of Nicaea in 787, which closed the Iconoclastic controversy and restored image-worship, decreed that the "making of religious images is not to be left to the initiative of the artists; it springs from the principles laid down by the Church Catholic and religious tradition. The art alone belongs to the Painter, the arrangement and ordering belong to the Fathers[3]." The actual position of the subjects was fixed as a matter of tradition, and the scene of the last judgement was placed at the west end, as we see it at Wells, at Orvieto, and in the tympanum of most of the great portals in France, so as to face the setting sun at the decline of day. The

---

[1] * * sicut aspidis surdae, et obturantis aures suas, quae non exaudiet vocem incantantium, et venefici incantantis sapienter.

Ps. lvii. Vulg. (lviii. A.V.).

[2] Gesta Sugerii Abbatis, cap. XXXII.

[3] Mâle, *op. cit.*

choice of subjects and their treatment was based upon authoritative treatises. M. Mâle mentions particularly the *Speculum majus* of Vincent de Beauvais, the *Speculum Ecclesiae* of Honorius of Autun, the *Legenda aurea* of the lives of the Saints, and the *Glossa ordinaria* of Walafridus Strabo. The cathedral of Chartres, he says, with its 10,000 figures in painting or sculpture, contains the most comprehensive representation of the teaching of the Church. He continues : " By the statues and glass of the churches the mediaeval clergy tried to teach the people the greatest number of truths. They felt the power of Art on souls still childish and dark. For the great illiterate mass of people, for the crowd with neither psalter nor missal, which held only so much of Christianity as it saw, it was necessary to materialize the idea, to clothe it in a form of sense....As Victor Hugo justly said, the cathedral is a book of stone for the ignorant, which the printed book little by little rendered useless. *Le soleil gothique se couche derrière la gigantesque presse de Mayence*[1]."

Or, as Archdeacon Claud says in *Notre-Dame de Paris*, pointing to the book and the edifice, "*ceci tuera cela.*"

Symbolism therefore counted for less and less in Gothic art as time went on. Mysticism seems to have been attended to much more in France than in England, less prolific in sculpture. But even in France, though Chartres cathedral is later than the time of S. Bernard, it would seem that already in his day the power of mysticism had begun to decline and its meaning to be forgotten. He deplores the " curious pictures " which

---

[1] Mâle, *op. cit.* p. 454 *et seq.*

draw the looks of the worshippers to them and hinder true feeling, and seem to him to represent old Jewish rites. "What fruit," he asks, "do we expect of them, the admiration of fools, or the offerings of the simple?" He goes on to ridicule the monsters in the carvings of the cloisters, and concludes, "Good God! if you are not ashamed of such nonsense why not grudge the expense[1]?" Clearly to him these mystic figures conveyed no sacred lesson.

When tracing a symbolic meaning in Gothic art one must not forget the artistic element. How did the sculptor regard his work? He had his subjects given him by the clergy, who attached a mystic meaning to each of them. But within these limits the artist had a free hand in the treatment, and as art improved artistic considerations would tend to push hieratic conventions on one side. A growing art, looking to nature rather than tradition, would chafe against the fetters of symbolism, and try to shake them off. The love of beauty and the desire to teach are two wholly different motives, and interfere with one another. As art progressed symbolism became a clog to the artist and gradually dropped out of his work. The sacred images that appeal to superstition have not been the masterpieces of sculpture, but the multi-mammal Artemis of Ephesus and the black Virgins of the Middle Ages. We ought not therefore in the higher range of Gothic art to look for an under-meaning, as in the earlier stages: a great deal of symbolism has been read into it which never entered the sculptor's mind. It has been attempted to see a significance in every grotesque, an emblem of

---

[1] *Op.* S. Bernardi, ed. Mabillon, vol. I. *Apologia ad Guillelmum S. Theodorici* (S. Thierry) *Abbatem.*

the Trinity in every trefoil, a mystic struggle between good and evil in what the sculptor probably merely meant for a picture, often satirical, of the life of his day, or an historical scene, or perhaps only a sporting subject. "Let us not," as M. Mâle very well puts it, "attempt to know better than S. Bernard." It was only when it had thus attained its liberty that the Gothic style was able to breathe freely and to expand over the whole field of Art. The higher grades of art begin at the point where symbolism leaves off.

It has been the object of these pages, by illustrating its history in countries so different as England, France, and Italy, to convey some idea of what the great Gothic art of the Middle Ages really was. First of all let it be made clear what it was not. It was not a matter of certain forms and details and ornaments; of trefoils and quatrefoils, of pointed arches, pinnacles and flying buttresses: nor can it be confined, as some pretend, to one chapter only of construction, for it no more consists in a peculiar system of vaulting than modern civilization consists in railways and motor-cars. The timber roofs of Westminster Hall, of Christchurch and Hampton Court, or the great barn at Harmondsworth, are as truly Gothic as Westminster Abbey itself. Nor is it an ecclesiastical style, as is proved by the examples just quoted, and by many a manor-house, college, and hospital throughout the land. Gothic was none of these things, because it was all of them: for Gothic art, while it lived, pervaded every field of craftsmanship, and governed the fashioning of every material, whether of stone or brick, timber, glass, or metal.

Gothic art then, properly understood, consisted not in doing certain things, but in doing them in a certain way.　It differs from Classic as freedom differs from convention, progress from stagnation, and the modern or Post-Roman world from the world of the Caesars. In Gothic there are no laws but those of common sense and truth to natural facts.　You must obey the three cardinal rules laid down in our first chapter : build well, build with just economy, and let your work show that you do so.　Beyond that the mediaeval master was tied to nothing.　Hence he was always changing, always advancing, always hitting on some new idea, grasping it firmly, and shaping what he was doing accordingly. The style never stood still, for there was nothing to hold it ; it defies definition, for there is no definition wide enough to cover it all ; its variety seems inexhaustible, for it never exhausted the problems of construction, and the suggestions of natural fact and natural law. Within these limits the artist could do what he pleased, and we have seen the infinitely various result of his labours, from the stern grandeur of Jumièges and Winchester to the west front of Rouen and the great chapel at Cambridge, and from the simplicity of S. Ambrogio and the solemn glories of S. Mark's to the Doge's palace and the beauties of Siena and Orvieto.

To return then to the position with which we began this chapter, how are we of the present day to regard Gothic architecture with reference to our own practice ? Clearly it has no hieratic meaning any longer.　For the symbolic element in its earlier history we have no use : it was indeed played out long ago, and even before architecture became a lay art in the 13th century it had been inspired by artistic rather than by didactic motives. This being so, what influence is the study of mediaeval architecture to have on what we are doing at the present day ? Some influence it is bound to have either for good or for evil. It is impossible to ignore our native art, the only one that has sprung up spontaneously on English soil, amid conditions many of which are still the same ; and therefore the return to Gothic which was attempted when the decline of the Classic Renaissance had set in was natural, and we may almost say inevitable.

It will be admitted even by those who deplore it that the Revival of Gothic was the great artistic event of the 19th century. In painting the Pre-Raffaelites made the stale conventions of the day ridiculous, and revivified the art by bringing back into it sincere conviction, real purpose, and a love for truth. In architecture the neo-Goth broke the chain of Classic tradition, and showed the way to freedom, though at first only dimly, for brought up as he had been in the worship of the five orders, his first idea was that Gothic had its rules and formulas like Classic. An attempt was even made to reduce it to five orders of its own. This was to practise Gothic in the Classic way, and so far as the style has been practised in this manner down to our own time it was foredoomed to fail, and has in fact been a failure.

And yet it is not too much to say that whatever is good in modern art, either in architecture, painting, or sculpture, has been the outcome of the return to our native style so far as we have properly understood it. Even those who would most resent a Gothic attribution work in a very different way from what they would have done had the revival never taken place.

That the Gothic of the past should ever live again exactly in any of its old forms is impossible : no dead art ever did or ever will do so. The very life-blood of Gothic either past or present lies in its adaptability to circumstance; and its merit is to reflect the mind of its own age and no other.   But the whole habit of life now, our knowledge of Nature and our attitude to her are as alien from the mind of the Middle Ages as the cart-cult of S. Denis and Chartres from our modern views of religion, or the lessons of the *Glossa ordinaria* from the higher criticism of modern theology.

It follows, then, that as the Gothic art of the past was the faithful interpreter of the mind of the Middle Ages, it cannot, for that very reason, in its old shape represent the mind of the 20th century.   But that, nevertheless, does not close the matter.   The letter of the old style may not be for us, it is true; and the more slavishly we reproduce the old forms when there is no reason for them, the more shall we merely be performing a masquerade and an interesting feat of archaeology, and the less will our work be a living reality.   Mere imitation will take us no further.   That, as Michel Angelo said long ago, is not the proper use of ancient example[1]. But the old Gothic spirit survives, and that is what is of value to us; that it is which must inspire our modern architecture if it is to be of any good, as it did that of the Middle Ages: for we are the sons of the men who made it, always seeking the new, always striving to be in the van of progress, discontented with our victories as soon as they are won, and ever reaching onward to the next step forward.   To represent the restlessness of the modern world architecture must have the same freedom

[1] Domandato da uno amico suo quel che gli paresse d' uno che haveva contrafatto di marmo figure antiche * * rispose " chi va dietro a altri mai non li passa innanzi ; e chi non sa far bene da se non può servirsi bene delle cose d' altri."

Vasari, *Vita di Michel Agnolo.*

as of old in our forefathers' day. I am convinced that no style will ever have a real life in England which is bound by rigid formula and prescription. To live with us and speak for us it must be free and mobile, ever ready to take advantage of new suggestions, to solve new problems, to accommodate itself to new conditions, just as the old Gothic style, whose changeful history we have been following, did in the olden time. In other words, I believe that our architecture must breathe the old Gothic spirit of liberty, and that only so will it be of any real value. What will be the outcome none can foresee. It will certainly not remain in the Archaeological stage if it is to live : it will not be the Gothic of the Middle Ages.

Let our architects, fully stored with knowledge of the past, but regarding the bygone art as their tutor rather than their model, bend themselves resolutely to the problems of the day, to novel modes of construction, to the use of novel materials, to new habits of life and new social needs, and let them satisfy these demands in the most direct and common-sense way, regardless of precedent and authority, and they will be working in the true Gothic spirit. If a man has the divine fire of Art within him and works on these principles, the details will come of themselves, and it cannot be but that what he does will have all the qualities of good and true Art.

APPENDIX

ON FERRO-CONCRETE BUILDING

IN my concluding chapter I have said that the only hope of Architecture lies in conformity to the conditions of modern life, including novel modes of construction, and the use of modern materials. What suggestions, useful for design, do we find in that of Ferro-concrete construction, of which huge examples are rising all around us?

It is obvious that this new form of construction has next to nothing in common with the old, and therefore that the forms of the old way of building are inappropriate to the new. And yet we have seen hitherto no difference in appearance between a building really carried on an iron framework and one built in the old way. This of course violates our third canon, that the design must express the construction and be suggested by it. If it does not do this it is bad art.

There is this difficulty in applying the canon to ferro-concrete building, that the iron frame, the skeleton which is the real construction, must be hidden. Iron is the strongest and also the weakest of building materials. The least contact with damp, even with damp air, is its ruin. If exposed, its life depends on a coat of paint: if covered up in brickwork or concrete, on the covering being impervious to moisture. If it rusts it expands and bursts all around it. An iron cramp of an inch by half an inch in thickness will by expansion raise a ton of masonry, though when you get it out you may crumble it in your fingers. In ferro-concrete construction therefore the real skeleton of the structure must be hidden : how then is the design to conform to our third canon?

The problem seems almost insoluble ; and yet if we do not attack it we shall only go on building shams, in a dead and worthless pretence of Art, for there is no doubt this way of building is, for the present at all events, come to stay. It is, as I remember my friend Richard Norman Shaw once saying to me, either the beginning or the end of architecture.

A few suggestions occur to me. In the first place this is a trabeated style, and there is no further use for the arch. The skeleton is a mere scaffolding of posts and rails, therefore the rectangle should be the ruling figure, and not the curve. In the next place if we are to have this construction let us take full advantage of its possibilities, and do things in the way of open spans that would be impossible in the old way of building. In this way the iron construction would assert its presence, and the eye growing used to these new feats of building might perhaps learn to take for granted the iron skeleton inside the apparent casing as one takes for granted the skeleton inside the human body. However this may be, let us away with all features proper to the older styles, and for the present be content with plain, bald, undesigned effects arising purely from constructional necessities. Something good may come of it, though the prospect does not seem very hopeful.

There remains, of course, the great question whether these structures are going to last, which is far from certain. I believe all our iron constructions are still on their trial, and that an architect who wishes to build for futurity should keep iron out of his buildings as much as he can. For roof trusses it cannot be avoided on account of the exhaustion of our timber supply; but there it can be protected from the weather, and be exposed so that it may be kept well painted. For fire-proof floors in conjunction with concrete it is safe with proper precautions. For want of such precautions the entire flooring of a great building, not long ago, was to my knowledge entirely ruined, and had to be removed to prevent accident. Fortunately there will always be many buildings, indeed the greatest number of buildings, for which iron construction will not be wanted. There need never be any need for it in private houses or churches, and architecture may survive there till perhaps it comes by its own again elsewhere.

TABLES OF DATES

TABLES OF DATES

FRANCE	ENGLAND	ITALY
	1096-1110. CANTERBURY. Conrad's glorious choir and crypt. *Romanesque.* 1118. PETERBOROUGH. The Eastern part.	1118. GENOA. S. Lorenzo; but *v.* 1307. 1129. CEFALÙ Cath. founded. 1132. PAVIA. S. Pietro in Cielo d' Oro consecrated. 1132-43. PALERMO. Capella Palatina. *Pointed arches and Dome.* 1132-48. PALERMO. S. Giovanni degli Eremiti. *Five Domes, pointed arches.*
1132-44. S. DENIS. Suger's building. *Arches both round and pointed, v.* 1231.		
	1135. MALMESBURY Abbey begun. 1140-50. FOUNTAINS Abbey. *Pointed arcade.* 1141. LINCOLN. Bp Alexander's *Romanesque portals.*	1135. CHIARAVALLE, near Milan, founded. *Round arches, domical vault, v.* 1370. 1143. PALERMO. La Martorana. *Pointed arches and Dome.*
1143-68. SENS. *Pointed arches, Byzantine capitals.* 1143-81. LISIEUX. Nave and transepts, finished before 1218. 1145. CHARTRES. West portals, *pointed arches. Rich formal sculpture.* 1145-70. CHARTRES. The S.W. steeple. *Transitional.* 1150-65. SENLIS. The Eastern part. 1150. NOYON. The choir. Nave later. All except the West end finished in 1190 or 1200. *All pointed arches.* 1152. ARLES. S. Trophime consecrated. *Romanesque with rich figure sculpture.*	1150-80. OXFORD. S. Frideswyde rebuilt by Prior Guimond. *Romanesque.*	1145-48. CEFALÙ Cath. finished. *Basilican, pointed arches.*

1153. PISA. Baptistery by Diotisalvi begun. *Romanesque.*

1161. PALERMO. S. Cataldo. *Pointed arches, three domes.*
1172. MONREALE Cath. *Basilican, pointed arches.*
1173. PISA. Campanile by Bonanno Pisano begun. Top storey added 1350. *Romanesque.*

1175. ZARA. S. Grisogono, apse and S. wall. *Romanesque.*

1155-93. PETERBOROUGH. Transepts and part of nave. *Romanesque.*

1174. ELY. Nave. Finished 1189, with Western tower and W. transept. *Romanesque and pointed.*
1174. CANTERBURY. Choir and E. transept by William of Sens. *Chiefly pointed. Lofty proportion.*
1174-91. WELLS Cath. Eastern part of nave by Bp de Bohun. *Pointed arches. Rich mouldings.*
1175. DURHAM. The Galilee. *Very light Romanesque.*
1175. WORCESTER. Western bays of nave. *Beginning of pointed work.*
1176-98. S. DAVID'S Cath. Nave. *Late Romanesque. Triforium pointed.*
1177-93. PETERBOROUGH. Nave and W. transept. *Romanesque. Archaic.*
1179-84. CANTERBURY. Eastern part by William the Englishman. *Thoroughly developed pointed.*
1180-90. OAKHAM. Castle Hall.

1153. ANGERS. Hôtel-Dieu, founded. *v.* 1184. *Plantagenet style.*
1160. LAON. Rebuilding begun. Nave and choir finished 1205.
1160. VÉZELAY. Narthex. *Pointed.*
c. 1160. POITIERS Cathedral.
1163. PARIS. S. Germain des Prés consecrated. *Arches pointed and round.*
1163-82. PARIS. N. Dame. The choir as far as the transepts. *Transitional, pointed, v.* 1182.

1175-1212. SOISSONS. S. transept. *Thoroughly developed pointed work.*

1182-1196. PARIS. N. Dame. Nave. Except three western bays, *v.* 1218.
1183. CHÂLONS-SUR-MARNE. Notre Dame. Nave and transepts.
1184. ANGERS. Chapel of Hôtel-Dieu, *v.* 1153.
„ S. Serge.

France	England	Italy
1190. S. LEU D'ESSERENT.	1185. TEMPLE CHURCH, LONDON. *Pointed and round arches mixed.*	1183. PEACE OF CONSTANCE.
		1185. PALERMO. Palace of La Cuba. The Cathedral.
1194. CHARTRES. Nave destroyed by fire. Rebuilding begun, finished c. 1212, except the porches, *v.* 1224 and 1250.	1186. GLASTONBURY. Lady chapel. *Round arched with zigzag. Archaic. Pointed arches in crypt.*	„ 1185. MONREALE. Bronze doors by Bonanno of Pisa.
1196. PARIS. N. Dame. Nave finished, except three west bays and front, *v.* 1163 and 1218.	1192. LINCOLN. S. Hugh's choir and apse. Vault later. *Developed Early English.*	1196. PARMA. Baptistery.
1198–1206. VÉZELAY. Choir.	1195–1205. S. ALBAN'S. West portals.	1193–1211. ROME. S. Paolo f. le Mura. Cloister.
1199. POITIERS Cath. High altar dedicated.		„ S. Giov. Laterano cloister.
1200–1240. ROUEN Cath. The nave, *v.* 1280.	1197–1220. ELY. Western porch.	1200. BITONTO. Cathedral. *Round arched and Romanesque.*
		„ ARBE. Dalmatia. The great campanile.
BOURGES Cath. begun.	1200–22. PETERBOROUGH. W. front. *Early English.*	1204. LUCCA. W. front by Guidetto. *Romanesque.*
	c. 1203. RIEVAULX ABBEY. Choir and transepts.	1208. FOSSANOVA. Cistercian convent consecrated. *Pointed arches, lantern over crossing. French influence.*
1208. COUTANCES. Nave begun, finished 1238–40, *v.* 1238.	1204. WINCHESTER. Bp de Lucy's retro-choir. *Early English.*	
1211. REIMS Cath. Rebuilding begun after a fire. Choir occupied 1241. *Beginning of bar tracery.*	c. 1209. LINCOLN. Nave begun, finished c. 1235. Bps Hugh of Wells and Grostête.	1215. COMO. The Broletto. *Pointed and round arches.*
	1213. SOUTHWARK. S. Saviour's choir begun.	1217. CASAMARI. Cistercian convent consecrated.
1218. PARIS. N. Dame. W. front; finished to gallery 1223, the rest in 1235.	1215. SOUTHWELL Cath. Choir.	1218–1300. S. GALGANO. Cistercian Abbey. *French influence.*

1220. AMIENS. The nave begun, finished 1236. Choir and apse finished 1269.
c. 1220. LE MANS. The choir.
1221. ARLES. S. Trophime. East walk of cloister. *Romanesque.*
1224. CHARTRES. The S. porch.
1231–81. S. DENIS. The nave and clerestory, *glazed triforium.*
c. 1235–51. BAYEUX. Choir.
1238–48. COUTANCES. The choir.
1240. S. PÈRE SOUS VÉZELAY. Steeple.

1245–48. PARIS. S. Chapelle.
1247. BEAUVAIS begun. Vaults fell. Additional columns inserted, 1284.
1250. CHARTRES. The N. porch.
c. 1250. REIMS. Nave except west end.
1255–69. AMIENS. Choir.

c. 1260–92. SEEZ Cath. Nave.
1262–76. TROYES. S. Urbain.

1272. NARBONNE Cath. *Plutôt d'un savant que d'artiste.*
1280. ROUEN. Portail des Libraires. *Late geometrical.*

1220. SALISBURY Cath. begun.

1224. WORCESTER. Choir.
1235–51. ELY. East end and presbytery.
1239. WELLS. West front finished except upper part of towers.
1240. LONDON. Temple church choir dedicated.
1241. YORK. S. transept finished.
1243. DURHAM. Chapel of nine altars.
1245–1269. WESTMINSTER Abbey. Henry III's choir and transepts.
1250. YORK. N. transept. *Early English.*
1250–53. WESTMINSTER. Chapter house. *Well developed bar tracery.*
1255–80. LINCOLN. Angel choir.

1262. SALISBURY. Tomb of Bp Bridport.

1270. YORK. S. Mary's Abbey begun.
1270–1307. EXETER. Eastern part, v. 1327.
1280. WESTMINSTER. The Confessor's shrine. *Italian work.*
1281. WESTMINSTER. Henry III's tomb. Effigy finished, 1291.
c. 1280–1300. OXFORD. S. Mary's tower and spire.
1282. THORNTON Abbey.

1219. VERCELLI. S. Andrea founded. *Arches round and pointed. Dome in central tower.*

1228–32. ASSISI. Convent of S. Francis, begun after his death in 1226, v. 1253.
1233. LUCCA. Duomo. Portico. Western *Romanesque.*
1240. TRAÙ. Dalmatia. Western portals by Radovan. *Romanesque.*

1250. VENICE. The Frari, finished 1338.
c. 1250–1385. VENICE. SS. Giovanni e Paolo.
1253. ASSISI the upper Church.
1260. PISA. Baptistery Pulpit, by Niccola Pisano.
1265. SIENA. Pulpit, by Niccola Pisano.
1267. SIENA Cath. consecrated.

1278. PISA. Campo Santo, by Giovanni Pisano.

1284. SIENA. West front, by Giov. Pisano.

FRANCE	ENGLAND	ITALY
1292. SEEZ. The nave finished, begun c. 1260.	1291–1334. YORK Cath. Nave. *Late geometrical decorated.*	1290. ORVIETO Cath. begun, finished 1330.
1296. PARIS. N. Dame. Chapels between the choir buttresses.	1293–1302. WELLS. Chapter house. *Beginning of curvilinear.*	1294. FLORENCE. S. Croce, by Arnolfo.
1302. ROUEN Cath. Lady chapel. *Geometrical.*	1294. SOUTHWELL. Chapter house.	1298. FLORENCE. The Cathedral, by Arnolfo di Cambio.
1308. CAEN. Tower of S. Pierre. *Geometrical.*	1296. LINCOLN. Cloister by Richard of Gainsborough. *Geometrical.*	,, FLORENCE. The Palazzo Vecchio ,, by Arnolfo di Cambio.
1318–39. ROUEN. S. Ouen, E. end. *Late geometrical.*	1306. BRISTOL. Cathedral choir, a "Hall-church." *Curvilinear.*	1302. PISA. Pulpit in Duomo, by Giov. Pisano.
	1318. GLOUCESTER. S. nave aisle. *Late geometrical.*	1307. GENOA. S. Lorenzo remodelled, *v.* 1118.
	c. 1320. WINCHESTER Cath. Feretory screen. *Curvilinear.*	1320. LUCCA. Apse of Cathedral. *Romanesque.*
	1320–27. OXFORD. The old Congregation house and Bishop Cobham's Library.	1323. PISA. Capella della Spina remodelled. *Gothic.*
	1321–49. ELY. Lady chapel. *Curvilinear.*	1325–45. SIENA. Tower of the comune.
	1327–42. ELY. The octagon. *Curvilinear.*	1328–39. MILAN. Tower of S. Gottardo, by Pecorari. *Round arched.*
	1327–35. EXETER. Nave following earlier design, *v.* 1270.	
	1328–47. S. DAVID'S. Bishop Gower's palace screen and tomb.	
	1330–37. GLOUCESTER. Abbot Wygmote's S. transept. *Early perpendicular.*	
	1330–40. SELBY. Presbytery. *Curvilinear.*	
	1331. SALISBURY. Tower and spire begun.	

1346. BATTLE OF CRÉÇY.	1335–40. SOUTHWELL. Choir screen.	1334. FLORENCE. Giotto's campanile. Finished by Taddeo Gaddi.
1348. THE PLAGUE.	1337–50. GLOUCESTER. Remodelling of choir in *Perpendicular* style.	1340–1404. VENICE. Sea front of Ducal palace, by Pietro Baseggio.
	1345. WINCHESTER. Bp Edyngton's west front, *v.* 1366. *Perpendicular.*	1348. THE PLAGUE.
	1348. THE BLACK DEATH.	
1356. BATTLE OF POITIERS.	1350–1420. WESTMINSTER. Seven western bays, following the 13th cent. design.	
	1351–77. GLOUCESTER. E. end and part of cloister, *v.* 1412. *Perpendicular.*	
	c. 1365. BEVERLEY. The Percy tomb. *Curvilinear.*	1370. CHIARAVALLE. Central cupola and tower.
1371–86. COUTANCES. Side chapels of nave. *Geometrical.*		
1375. AMIENS. Side chapels of nave. *Geometrical.*	1378–1410. CANTERBURY. Nave. *Perpendicular.*	1380. ZARA. Silver ark of S. Simeone, by Franciscus de Mediolano.
1379. POITIERS Cath. West front finished.	1385. WELLS. S.W. tower begun by Bp Harewell.	1387. MILAN Cath. begun.
1383. CAHORS. Bridge finished.	1394–c. 1450. WINCHESTER. Nave remodelled by Wm of Wykeham, and his successors. *Perpendicular.*	1390. BOLOGNA. S. Petronio begun.
		1396. CERTOSA OF PAVIA.
	1394–98. WESTMINSTER HALL remodelled with new roof.	1399. VERCELLI. Campanile *Romanesque.*
	1412. GLOUCESTER. Cloister finished.	
1415. BATTLE OF AGINCOURT.		1420. FLORENCE. Brunelleschi's cupola begun. *Coming of the Renaissance.*
1419. NOTRE DAME DE L'EPINE. *Flamboyant.*		
1426. CAUDEBEC. Nave-façade and spire later. *Flamboyant.*	1427–80. OXFORD. Divinity School. Duke Humphrey's library.	1424. VENICE. Ducal palace. The Piazzetta front, by Giov. and Bartolommeo Bon, *following the older design.*
		1430. VENICE. The Ca' d' Oro, by Giov. and Bartol. Bon.
1432–1500. ROUEN. S. Maclou. *Flamboyant. Continuous mouldings in arcade.*	1432–70. YORK. Western towers.	1435. RAGUSA. Palazzo Rettorale, by Onofrio di La Cava.
	1438–96. PETERBOROUGH. Eastern aisle. *Fan vault.*	

France	England	Italy
1443. BOURGES. Jacques Coeur's house. *Flamboyant.*	1447. CAMBRIDGE. King's College Chapel begun, v. 1512.	1440-43. VENICE. Porta della Carta, by Bon.
1456. EXPULSION OF ENGLISH.	1454. GLOUCESTER. Central tower.	1441. SEBENICO. Dalmatia. Cath. remodelled by Giorgio Orsini. *Renaissance style.*
c. 1480-1537. ABBEVILLE. S. Wulfran. *Rich Flamboyant.*	1462. OXFORD. S. Mary. Chancel.	1450. RIMINI. Cath. remodelled by Alberti in semi-classic.
1481-92. ROUEN Cath. Tour de Beurre.		
1484. ROUEN. Screen to N. entrance of the court des Libraires.	1490-1503. OXFORD. S. Mary. The nave.	1481. VENICE. Palazzo Vendramin Calergi, by Pietro Lombardo. *Mixed style of Gothic and Classic.*
1487-1517. S. RIQUIER. W. front.	1492. OXFORD. Magdalen tower.	1485. VENICE. Giant's staircase.
1490. PARIS. Hôtel de Cluny.	1495. CANTERBURY. Central tower.	
" ROUEN. S. Ouen. Nave.	1496-1525. BATH Abbey, rebuilt by Bp King and Prior Bird. Not finished till 1616.	1490. VENICE. Inner court of Ducal palace. *Mixed Gothic and Classic.*
		1490-1522. MILAN Cath. The cupola by Omodei, etc.
1496-1540. LISIEUX. S. Jacques.	1502. WESTMINSTER. Henry VII's Chapel begun.	
1500-48. BEAUVAIS Cath. South transept.	1505. OXFORD. Magdalen tower finished.	1500. ROME. The Cancelleria by Bramante. *Classic.*
" SENLIS. South transept.		
1507-12. CHARTRES. N.W. spire.	1510. CAMBRIDGE. S. John's Coll. gate and front.	1506. ROME. First stone of S. Peter's laid. Bramante architect.
1509-30. ROUEN Cath. West front.	1510. OXFORD Cath. Groining of choir.	
1511-36. BROU EN BRESSE.	1512. CAMBRIDGE. King's College Chapel. Contract with John Wastell for the fan-vault.	1512. ROME. Painting on roof of Sistine Chapel finished.
1512. ALBI Cath. The jubé.		

1515. VENICE. S. Zaccaria, façade. *Gothic.*

1530. ROME. Palazzo Farnese.

1534. PALAZZO Caprarola, by Vignola.
1541. ROME. Completion of painting of Last Judgment in Sistine Chapel.
1546. ROME. S. Peter's. Death of Sangallo, succeeded by Michel Angelo, who saw dome finished and left design for lantern at his death, 1564.
1550. VENICE. Scuola di S. Rocco.
1565. VENICE. S. Giorgio Maggiore by Palladio: finished 1610.
1569. MONREALE. North portico.

1589. VENICE. Façade of prison towards canal, by Antonio da Ponte. The Ponte dei Sospiri probably finished after his death.

1512. WESTMINSTER. Contract with Pietro Torrigiano for Henry VII's tomb.

1525-29. OXFORD. Christ church begun. Hall, kitchen, and part of quadrangle. Hall roof, 1529.
1526. HANS HOLBEIN in England. Employed by Henry VIII.
1530. HAMPTON COURT. The Great Hall by Henry VIII. Timber roof, fan-vaulted oriels.
1532. BOXGROVE. De-la-Warr tomb with *Renaissance details.*

1541. CHRISTCHURCH, Hants. Salisbury chapel. *Gothic design with Renaissance arabesques.*

1567-79. LONGLEAT House. *Mixture of Gothic and Classic.*
1574. CAMBRIDGE. Caius Coll. gate of Honour.
1575. KIRBY HALL, Northants.
1577-85. BURLEIGH House.

1515. BLOIS. Completion of the Flamboyant building.
 ,, CHENONCEAU begun. Plan of a feudal castle but not defensive. *Renaissance details.*
1521. CAEN. S. Pierre. East end. *Gothic in construction. Renaissance details.*
1526. CHAMBORD begun.
1530. IL ROSSO, a Florentine invited to France by François I.
1532. PARIS. S. Eustache begun. *Gothic in construction with Classic details.*
1533. LIMOGES Cathedral. The jubé.

1550. PARIS. Fontaine des Innocens, by Lescot, figures by Jean Goujon.
1564. PARIS. The Tuileries begun.

FRANCE	ENGLAND	ITALY
1601. ORLEANS Cath. begun. *Gothic.*	1592-7. HARDWICK Hall. 1600. CAMBRIDGE. Ceilings by Cobbe at S. John's College. 1603. AUDLEY END. 1610-13. OXFORD. The old Schools and Wadham College. *Mixed Gothic and Classic.* c. 1613. WIMBLEDON. Eagle House. 1618. OXFORD. Trinity College Hall. *Gothic.* 1619-21. LONDON. Whitehall by Inigo Jones. *Pure Classic.* c. 1630. OXFORD. Christchurch, fan vault over staircase. *Gothic.* 1631-6. OXFORD. S. John's Garden court. *Mixed Gothic and Classic.*	1606. ROME. S. Peter's. Extension of front by Carlo Maderno. 1610. VENICE. S. Giorgio Maggiore finished, *v.* 1565. 1631-82. VENICE. S. Maria della Salute, by Longhena.
1670. PARIS. East front of the Louvre by Perrault.		

INDEX

Printed in U.S.A. by
NOBLE OFFSET PRINTERS, INC.
NEW YORK, N.Y. 10003

Date Due

NOV 2 6 1985	MAR 2 4 2004	
6 1986		
98		